A Sailor's Admiral:
A Biography of
William F. Halsey

Books by James M. Merrill

THE REBEL SHORE

QUARTER-DECK AND FO'C'S'LE

UNCOMMON VALOR

TARGET TOKYO: THE
HALSEY-DOOLITTLE RAID

SPURS TO GLORY

BATTLE FLAGS SOUTH

WILLIAM TECUMSEH SHERMAN

THE USA: A SHORT HISTORY
OF THE AMERICAN REPUBLIC

A SAILOR'S ADMIRAL: A BIOGRAPHY
OF WILLIAM F. HALSEY

A Sailor's Admiral:

A BIOGRAPHY OF

WILLIAM F. HALSEY

By James M. Merrill

Thomas Y. Crowell Company
NEW YORK   ESTABLISHED 1834

The maps, drawn by Donald T. Pitcher, are from E. B. Potter's *Illustrated History of the U.S. Navy*.

Manufactured in the United States of America

Library of Congress Cataloging in Publication Data

Merrill, James M
    A sailor's admiral.

    Bibliography: p.
    Includes index.
    1. Halsey, William Frederick, 1882–1959. I. Title.
V63.H34M47   940.54′26′0924 [B]   76-8880
ISBN 0-690-01163-6

10 9 8 7 6 5 4 3 2 1

For Aileen Hillman
In Sincere Appreciation

Preface

WRITTEN FOR THE POPULAR MARKET, *Halsey* is a biography of the most famous and the most colorful admiral of World War II. Many of the battles and strategic moves described in the book have already been recounted, but they have not been incorporated into a biography of the admiral. With the exception of a small paperback, this is the first biography of Halsey. The Halsey Papers at the Naval History Division, Washington Naval Yard, contain vast amounts of material but, unfortunately for the biographer, they are mostly of an official nature, letters written by Halsey to staff members and to his superiors. Personal letters to his family are unavailable. To offset this void I have depended on interviews and letters from his staff and articles or memoirs written by carrier commanders.

I am grateful to Admirals Robert B. Carney, Ralph E. Wilson, and Arleigh A. Burke for their assistance. I am also grateful to Admiral Edwin B. Hooper, Director of Naval History, and to Dr. D. C. Allard and Mrs. Kathy Lloyd of the Operational Archives, Naval History Division, for their efforts in making my research in the manuscripts a much easier task. Thanks also go to Dr. John M. Dawson, Director of the Morris Library, University of Delaware, and his staff, especially Dr. Charles W. Mason, Rachel Elliott, and Elizabeth Russell. Joanne Davis earned her stripes as a yeoman for typing the manuscript and correcting my many typos. Lastly, my thanks go to my wife, Ann, who spent countless hours in traveling to

Washington, D.C., and editing, blue-penciling, and reading the manuscript.

James M. Merrill
University of Delaware

Contents

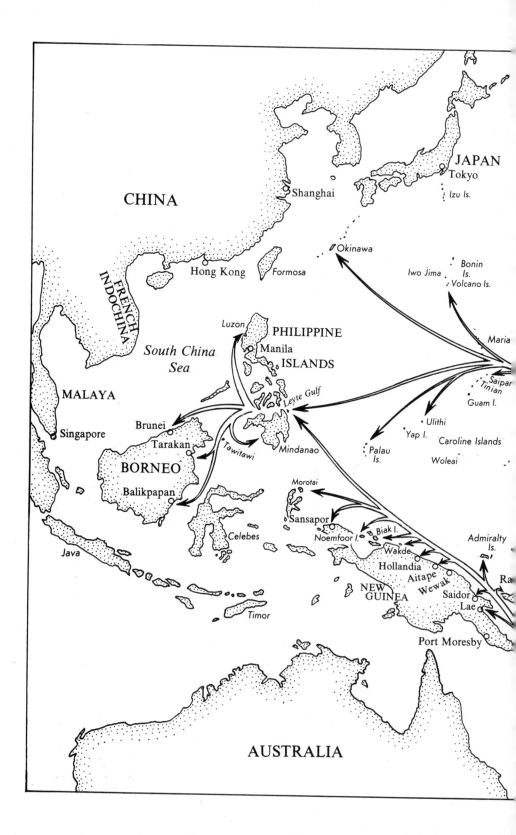

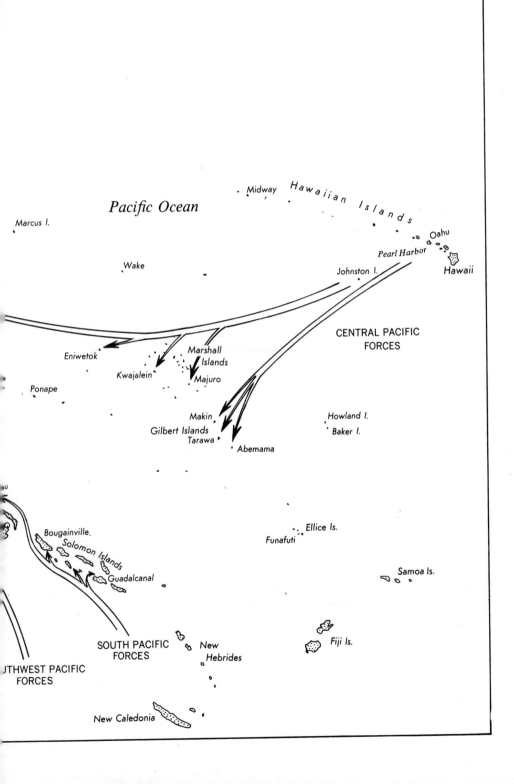

Marcus I.

Pacific Ocean

. Midway *Hawaiian Islands*

Oahu

Wake

Pearl Harbor

Johnston I.

Hawaii

Eniwetok

CENTRAL PACIFIC
FORCES

Marshall
Islands

Kwajalein

Majuro

Ponape

Makin

Howland I.

Gilbert Islands
Tarawa

Baker I.

Abemama

Bougainville.

Ellice Is.

Solomon Islands

Funafuti

Guadalcanal

Samoa Is.

SOUTH PACIFIC
FORCES

New
Hebrides

Fiji Is.

UTHWEST PACIFIC
FORCES

New Caledonia

[I]

"This Is No Drill"

ON 27 NOVEMBER 1941, Admiral William F. Halsey, Jr., USN, in command of the Aircraft Battle Force in the Pacific, was at Fleet Headquarters in Pearl Harbor, Oahu. Along with other high-ranking officers, he sat behind closed doors marked Commander in Chief, Pacific Fleet, known as CINCPAC in the Navy's endless maze of initials, listening to Admiral Husband E. Kimmel. Kimmel was brutally frank as he discussed the "war warning" from the Chief of Naval Operations in Washington.

War with Japan was imminent. The Navy Department expected a Japanese attack "at any moment" against the Philippines, Malaya, or Borneo. Focusing attention on Japan's capabilities of mounting an offensive to the southward from the home islands, Washington discounted her capacity to move eastward against the Hawaiian Islands. Kimmel's intelligence, too, pointed to an attack by the Japanese to the southward, either against the Philippines or the Malay Peninsula. While Kimmel did not rule out Pearl Harbor, the mass of evidence pointed in another direction.

Dressed in faultless whites, Kimmel recited the catalog of chilling details. As he probed for answers, his staff and force commanders contributed their expertise. The Pacific Fleet was inferior to that of the Japanese in many categories, but especially in carriers. Ten Japanese flattops faced three American—the *Enterprise*, then at Pearl Harbor; the *Lexington*, returning from Midway; the *Saratoga*, at San Diego, undergoing overhaul and repair.

Still, Kimmel's voice remained hearty and confident. Halsey thought him an extraordinary officer, one who had climbed the promotion ladder all the way to four stars in rapid fashion.

"How far do you want me to go?" Halsey asked Kimmel.

Kimmel replied, "Goddammit, common sense!"

The meeting concluded, Halsey hastened to his flagship, the *Enterprise,* which had been loaded with a squadron of Marine fighter planes for delivery to Wake Island. His task force consisted of three cruisers, nine destroyers, and the *Enterprise.* On board the latter, as soon as the group cleared Pearl Harbor, pilots in khakis or in flying suits filled the deep comfortable chairs in the ready room. After a few brief remarks, the squadron commander handed out green mimeographed sheets, Halsey's Battle Order No. 1, which began: 1) The *Enterprise* is now operating under war conditions; 2) At any time, day or night, we must be ready for instant action; 3) Hostile submarines may be encountered. . . . "Steady nerves and stout hearts are needed now." Halsey ordered all planes armed with torpedoes and bombs and relayed to his pilots, "Sink anything you sight!"

Halsey had already been informed that no American or Allied shipping was in the waters between Pearl Harbor and Wake. The admiral, Commander Miles Browning (Halsey's Chief of Staff), and Major Paul Putnam, commanding Marine Fighting Squadron 211, were the only men on board who knew the *Enterprise*'s destination. "So my order," said Halsey later, "burst on the task force like a thousand-pounder."

That day, Commander William H. Buracker, Operations Officer, brought the order to Halsey and asked, "Admiral, did you authorize this thing?"

"Yes."

"Do you realize this means war?"

"Yes."

"Goddammit, Admiral," Buracker protested, "you can't start a private war of your own! Who's going to take the responsibility?"

Halsey replied, "I'll take it! If anything gets in my way, we'll shoot first and argue afterwards."

Since it was vital for the delivery of the Marine planes to go undetected by the Japanese, Halsey stood ready to destroy their aircraft or ships before they could radio the task force's position. Therefore, the Americans maintained radio silence, flew antisubmarine patrols during daylight hours, and every morning and evening searched the ocean for 300 miles around. Halsey believed that war was a matter of days, possibly hours away, and that if they had to fight, their only chance of survival—and of even getting off an alert to the Commander in Chief before their ships were annihilated—was to strike the first blow. He felt completely justified in striking it.

While the *Enterprise* force pounded on toward Wake Island, a Japanese fleet was steaming eastward for Hawaii. In the broad expanses of the Pacific, unsearched miles of water stretched out and the two forces, one American, one Japanese, passed unmindful of each other in peace.

Delivering the Marine fighter planes to Wake Island without incident, Halsey's force started its return run to Pearl Harbor on 4 December.

Sunday, December 7, 1941, dawned bright and windy. The *Enterprise* was roughly 150 miles west of Oahu, less than an hour's flight time. Rising early, Halsey scanned the night's accumulation of dispatches and downed a scalding cup of coffee. Then he went to the flag bridge and watched two Dauntless dive bombers take off at 0615 for Ford Island, Pearl Harbor. Other planes of Squadron Six roared off the flight deck at 0637 to conduct air searches ahead of the *Enterprise*.

When closing the shore of Oahu, Commander Howard ("Cy") L. Young in his Dauntless dive bomber noticed planes circling the Marine airfield at Ewa, but supposed them to be Army aircraft and paid no more attention. Just as he was wondering why the anti-aircraft guns were blazing from Ford Island, Japanese planes attacked him. He quickly evaded them, but, with insufficient fuel to return to the *Enterprise,* he flew the gauntlet of Ford Island's ack-ack fire, the excited gunners failing to notice his recognition signals. He screeched down the runway, bullet holes through his wings. Ten minutes later fifteen other planes from Squadron Six, also encountering heavy ack-ack fire, landed. Five were shot down.

At 0755 on board the *Enterprise,* Halsey was sitting in his wardroom, drinking coffee, when the Communications Officer rushed in and thrust him a dispatch.

From: CINCPAC
To: ALL SHIPS PRESENT
AIR RAID ON PEARL HARBOR X THIS IS NO DRILL

Angrily, Halsey sprang up, shouting, "My God, they're shooting at my own boys!"

All hands were instantly notified over the loudspeakers. General Quarters sounded.

At 0823 Halsey received another dispatch.

From: CINCPAC
To: ALL SHIPS PRESENT
ALERT X JAPANESE PLANES ATTACKING PEARL AND AIRFIELDS ON OAHU

At 0903,

From: CINCPAC
To: ALL SHIPS PRESENT
HOSTILITIES WITH JAPAN COMMENCE WITH AIR RAID ON PEARL

The *Enterprise* and her escorts swerved northward to search for the Japanese fleet. Halsey heard a Honolulu radio station spewing out information. News from Pearl continued bad—many ships sunk or damaged, casualties in the thousands. Suddenly, the station went dead.

The *Enterprise* group combed a large area west of Kaula Rock, 150 miles from Pearl Harbor. Dispatches kept pouring in. "So many false reports were received from unknown sources concerning the presence of enemy ships, carriers, transports, and submarines," wrote Halsey's flag secretary, "that it was very difficult to glean the true from the false." One of the first of these dispatches stated that a patrol plane had sunk an enemy submarine off the entrance to Pearl. This proved true, but the others were false almost without exception.

Late in the afternoon four cruisers and a few destroyers from

Pearl joined the *Enterprise*. When Halsey received a report stating that enemy units were located to the southwest of Honolulu, he formed a scouting line of all ships in the task force, except the *Enterprise* and her destroyer escorts, and ordered them to search and to open fire on contact. Then came another report—a Japanese carrier was south of Pearl Harbor. The only weapons that Halsey had left were twenty-one planes of Torpedo Squadron Six. They hurriedly took off, but discovered nothing.

That night the *Enterprise* group proceeded independently. "The confusing and conflicting reports that had poured in on us all day," Halsey wrote, "had succeeded only in enraging me. It is bad enough to be blindfolded, but it is worse to be led around the compass. I waited all night for the straight word, and all night I reviewed my situation. Suppose that the enemy was located, and suppose that I could intercept him: what then? A surface engagement was out of the question, since I had nothing but cruisers to oppose his heavy ships."

"On the other hand," he continued, "my few remaining planes might inflict some damage, and by the next forenoon the *Lexington*'s task force coming from Midway would reach a position from which her air group could support an attack. If only someone would give us the straight word!" His ships woefully short of fuel, Halsey changed course for Pearl.

At dusk on 8 December the *Enterprise* and the destroyers steamed through the submarine nets at Pearl Harbor, maneuvering through water coated black with oil and floating debris. They passed the fire-blackened, bomb-blasted, listing, and overturned battlewagons of the Pacific Fleet. The *Arizona* and *Oklahoma* were complete losses. The *West Virginia, Tennessee, Maryland,* and *California* were severely damaged. Along the shoreline of Ford Island loomed the skeletons of charred Navy planes and ruined hangars. Surveying the scene from the flag bridge, Halsey turned suddenly to a staff officer and said quietly, "Before we're through with 'em, the Japanese language will be spoken in hell!"

The smoking ruins of Pearl Harbor reinforced Halsey's belief that the battleship was no longer the capital ship of the world's navies. Japanese carrier-based bombers and torpedo planes had consigned the old doctrine of the battle line to the past.

Halsey was in such a hurry to see Admiral Kimmel that he commandeered the first boat he found. Edgy machine-gunners were still firing at everything that moved, and bullets whizzed past him and his staff all the way to CINCPAC's landing, but the blackout saved them from harm.

When Halsey arrived at Fleet Headquarters, confusion was surging around Kimmel, still in his Sunday uniform, now crumpled and splotched. Despite the hysteria, Kimmel was, remembered Halsey, "a marvel of cool efficiency." He felt compassion for this gray-faced man, a man suddenly saddled with the blame for America's greatest naval tragedy.

Reports were flooding into headquarters: eight Japanese transports were seen rounding Barbers Point; Japanese gliders and paratroopers were landing on the east coast of Oahu. Upon hearing the latter, Halsey broke out laughing.

"What the hell is there to laugh about?" Kimmel demanded.

Halsey replied, "I've heard a lot of wild reports in my life, but that's the wildest I *ever* heard! The Japs can't possibly tow gliders here from their nearest base, and certainly they're not going to waste their precious carrier decks on any such nonsense. My God!"

Bill Halsey had been raised in the naval tradition. Born on 30 October 1882 in Elizabeth, New Jersey, he came from a long line of seafarers, beginning with Captain Eliphalet Halsey who, from Sag Harbor in 1815, sailed the first Long Island whaler around Cape Horn. Halsey's father, a Naval Academy man, class of 1873, retired from the service with the rank of captain. His son, William F. Halsey, Jr., spent his childhood as a Navy junior, attending prep schools in California, Pennsylvania, and Maryland before entering the Academy in 1900. Halsey stood in the middle of his class academically, was a two striper in the Battalion, a member of various committees, president of the Athletic Association and fullback on an often defeated Navy team. The Academy yearbook, *The Lucky Bag*, described him as "a real old salt. Looks like a figurehead of Neptune. Strong sympathizer with the YMCA movement. Everybody's friend. . . ." *The Lucky Bag* neglected to mention that he also was the winner of the Thompson Trophy Cup, awarded annually to the first classman "who has done most during the year for the promotion of athletics at the Naval Academy."

Halsey was a young ensign when his ship, the *Kansas*, steamed around the world as part of President Theodore Roosevelt's White Fleet. He rose rapidly in rank and, in December 1909, married Frances ("Fan") Cooke Grandy in old Christ Church, Norfolk, Virginia.

Soon after the United States entered World War I, Halsey joined the American Destroyer Force based at Queenstown, Ireland, commanding the *Benham*, then the *Shaw*. The destroyers engaged in North Sea patrols and escorted American convoys to and from England.

During the war Halsey kept a personal log. On 7 June 1918, he noted, "At 3:45 A.M. got a radio from the P-68 [British patrol ship] that she had just bombed a sub that had sunk a ship 8 miles from Trevose Head. Headed over at 25 knots to join the party. Fritzi had done a good job. Busted the ship wide open. Nothing left but kindling wood and a huge amount of oil.

"Quite an inter-Allied event—one blimp, two aeroplanes, two P-boats, two trawlers, and the *Shaw*. One trawler picked up a boat containing four men, one dead. Exchanged signals with the blimp and hustled oil wakes for 2½ hours but could see nothing definite. Finally had to return to station for escort duty.

"About 10:30 A.M. was taking a nap in the chart house when the O.O.D. reported, 'Submarine on surface dead ahead!' Best thrill I have had since my arrival in the war zone! Made the bridge in two jumps and found the for'd gun manned and pointed at sub, with the pointer's finger itching on the trigger and not giving a damn what kind of a sub she was. About to give the order to fire when the quartermaster, who was watching her thru a long glass, reported he could see her letters and she was a U.S. sub.

"Made the challenge to him, but he did not reply. By that time could see her letters with the naked eye: AL 10. Finally she fired the recognition signal. In the meantime we had been following her close, ready to open up and ram in case she made a false move. Needless to say, we were very much let down."

For his services as a destroyer commander during the war, Halsey was awarded a Navy Cross with the following citation: "For distinguished service in line of his profession as Commanding Officer of the USS *Benham* and the USS *Shaw,* engaged in the important, exacting, and hazardous duty of patrolling the waters infested with enemy submarines and mines, in escorting and protecting vitally important convoys of troops and supplies through these waters, and in offensive and defensive action, vigorously and unremittingly prosecuted against all forms of enemy activity."

Halsey said later, "There was a very wide distribution of the Navy Cross to commanding officers of naval vessels during World War I. It did not have the prestige then that has attached to the award in World War II."

Just before the end of the war in 1918, Halsey relinquished command of the *Shaw* and returned to the United States. He vacationed with Fan and the two children in Atlantic City for three weeks, then reported to Cramp's shipyard in Philadelphia to take command of the new destroyer *Yarnall.* The *Yarnall* was soon escorting President Woodrow Wilson's ship to Europe. Once Wilson went ashore at Brest on 13 December, the *Yarnall* was assigned to messenger service, chiefly between Brest and Plymouth.

A mess attendant, second class, remembered Halsey during those days: "There was that time in Lisbon when there was a terrible storm. Halsey was given orders to go out in spite of it. He didn't want to, but he loosened the ropes and started. It was so bad three men were washed overboard and lost. Halsey swore after that he'd use his own judgment on weather conditions when the lives of his men were at stake. There was a great man. And there was a slight indiscretion that got me in trouble in Brest. Halsey took my side and got me out of it. Yes, he's a great man."

Once the Paris Peace Conference ended in June 1919, President Wilson reembarked on the *George Washington,* and the *Yarnall* was part of the destroyer escort.

After World War I the United States Navy endured public disinterest, usual of any post-war decade. With paltry appropriations the fleet was relegated to its classic role of "showing the flag."

"Just after World War I," wrote Halsey in 1947, "there weren't many people then who figured that we'd ever have to fight again. They failed to see any reason for maintaining armed forces of any size, or why we should experiment with new equipment and weapons. Fortunately, the officers of the naval service were able to study the problem impartially. They looked at the facts, they looked at history and they studied their maps. From these things they were able to determine the situation we would face if we should be involved in a war in the Pacific and what we would have to do to win it."

After operating with the new Pacific Fleet in the *Yarnall* for a year, Halsey, then a commander, was ordered to Washington for duty in the Office of Naval Intelligence. After a few German lessons Halsey and his family set off for Germany, where he became naval attaché at the American Embassy.

"A naval attaché has a double duty," wrote Halsey. "He is an aide and advisor to the ambassador, and he keeps his department informed on naval developments in the country to which he is accredited. This doesn't mean that he is a spy! Everything he does is perfectly aboveboard and with the consent of his hosts, and the information he obtains is what they see fit to grant."

Halsey toured numerous German industries, in which the Navy was keenly interested—the Zeppelin works at Friedrichshafen, the Zeiss and Goetz optical works, and the Krupp plant at Essen. He was also accredited to the American legations in Denmark, Sweden, and Norway.

In June 1924 Washington ordered Halsey to command the destroyer *Dale* and later, the *Osborne,* two of six American destroyers still operating in European waters. "Malta," wrote Halsey, "was a special milestone on this cruise, because there I saw my first aircraft carrier, HMS *Hermes.* To an officer used to destroyers, she was an off-center, ungainly bucket, something a child had started to build and had left unfinished. In years to come, though, when not only American carriers but British, too, were under my command, I realized that they had a grace and beauty of their own."

Raymond Spruance relieved Halsey in November. Halsey collected his family from Switzerland, sailed back to the States and, in January 1926, reported for duty as executive officer of the *Wyoming*. That spring Halsey was selected for the rank of captain, took his examination in the summer, and in February 1927, sewed on his fourth stripe. By then he had been ordered to the Naval Academy as commanding officer of the *Reina Mercedes,* a prize from the Spanish-American War. Receiving ships, ships that hold sailors in transit awaiting orders, were the only ones on which a commanding officer's family was permitted to live. The Halseys had comfortable quarters in the after part, with a cook and steward. ''Athletic and social events at the Academy,'' wrote Halsey, ''furnished a pleasant background to my not too arduous duties, and if we found Annapolis dull, Washington and Baltimore were less than an hour away. I remained on this duty for three years and five months, and it was one of the most delightful tours in my career.''

In the spring of 1927, the *Reina* became the base for the Academy's first permanent aviation detail, ''and my whole naval career changed right there.''

Halsey had flown before but, at Annapolis, ''I became fascinated with it.'' He flew as often as he could and learned how to handle the controls of the clumsy planes of the period. ''Soon I was eating, drinking, and breathing aviation, and I continued to do so during the remainder of my duty on the *Reina.*''

Al Williams, then a navy pilot at Annapolis, recalled, ''Halsey quickly sensed the 'take any chance' spirit that was heading me towards an inevitable payoff. Without arousing my suspicions, he took me in hand, and with some sound common sense, established a bit of reason in my mind.''

''As Halsey tried to knock some caution into my head,'' Williams continued, ''I began to work on him to forsake temporarily the seagoing navy and apply for duty in naval aviation. We younger naval aviators knew we needed some more high ranking officers and that we were going to get them. Thus when we spotted a real right guy, we started our missionary work to bring him over with us. It didn't take long to convince me that Halsey was that kind of a real right guy we needed in naval aviation. I can't claim credit for getting him into Aviation, but I sure worked like a beaver at it. . . .''

Realizing Halsey's avid interest, the Chief of the Bureau of Navigation, Rear Admiral James O. Richardson, asked him if he would take a course at Pensacola. Halsey replied quickly and affirmatively. Unfortunately, he flunked the rigorous physical examination because of poor eyesight.

In June 1930 Halsey was detached from Annapolis and ordered to command a squadron of destroyers in the Atlantic. "Returning to sea duty was wonderful after more than three years on the beach," he wrote, "and I was particularly pleased to return to my favorite ships." Halsey continued to indulge in flying. Planes were now an integral part of the fleet. By early 1932 Halsey's destroyers were operating in the Pacific, where the major part of the fleet was then concentrated.

He said goodbye to destroyers forever when he was ordered to the Naval War College at Newport, Rhode Island, for instruction, and, afterwards, to the Army War College in Washington. Shortly before his year in Washington ended, the Chief of the Bureau of Aeronautics, Admiral Ernest King, offered Halsey the command of the carrier *Saratoga* if he would take an aviation observer's course at Pensacola. "The world of aviation," he said, "reopened to me; I was so excited that I regarded the privilege of commanding the *Sara* merely as a pleasant bonus."

At ground school in Pensacola, Halsey studied engines, radio, aerial navigation, gunnery, bombing, and torpedoes. He was not content, desperately wanting his designation changed from "student observer" to "student pilot."

"From the standpoint of simple safety," he said, "I considered it better to be able to fly the plane myself than just to sit at the mercy of the pilot." With a carrier command ahead of him, he wanted a clear understanding of a pilot's problems, not an observer's. To overcome his failure to pass the eye tests, Halsey gained a temporary waiver upon the recommendation of the Bureau of Aeronautics.

Qualifying as a pilot in the spring of 1935 at the age of fifty-two, Halsey took command of the *Saratoga*.

Fortunately for the United States Navy, shipbuilding had begun to increase sharply. President Roosevelt realized the seriousness of the deteriorating world situation and recognized that navies could not be improvised in crisis situations. Naval appropriations grew year by year, finally approaching a billion dollars annually. In addition to new construction, older vessels were modernized. There was marked emphasis upon naval aviation and carriers.

In the fall of 1935, the *Saratoga* went to Bremerton Navy Yard for a four-month overhaul. "It is to be regretted that we are so short handed during this critical overhaul period," Halsey wrote Vice Admiral H. V. Butler. "At present we are 234 men short of our allowance. . . . This necessitates keeping an appreciable number of young men, averaging 20 years old, working in the voids and double bottoms for the full four months of the overhaul. This does not help morale, but it is unavoidable. To combat this, we are stressing athletics, and I have been making headway in arousing interest in this important activity. At present we have not shown ourselves world beaters in competition but we anticipate being amongst the top notchers in the near future."

Just before the overhaul period ended, Halsey wrote a friend, "Our stay here has been too long for all of us. We are tired of the eternal noises and dirt. However, considering the lack of money the Yard has really done a fine job and given us particularly all the essentials. Our post trial went off nicely, and we expect to leave here soon."

After Bremerton, the *Saratoga* steamed to Panama on a winter cruise, then returned to her base at Long Beach, California.

Halsey was relieved of command in June 1937 and ordered to Pensacola as commandant, "the best shore job in the Navy." He had been selected for rear admiral the previous December, but because promotion took effect only when there were vacancies in grade, Halsey did not "make his number" for fifteen months, until after he had reported to Pensacola.

After a year at the naval air station, Halsey took command of Carrier Division Two (part of Aircraft Battle Force, commanded by Admiral Ernest King). One day during spring maneuvers in the Caribbean, through an error of a lieutenant, Halsey's flagship, *Yorktown,* was slow in launching planes.

King signaled, "Report to me name of officer responsible for this delay."

Halsey characteristically replied, "Responsibility is mine."

As one staff officer commented, "He's got broad shoulders. He takes it without passing it on. For my money, that's the mark of greatness in a naval officer. It's also the stuff that loyalty is built on."

In the summer of 1939 Halsey's carriers sailed for the West Coast. Meanwhile the carrier divisions and their commanders were reshuffled, and Halsey was made Commander Carrier Division One with his flag on the *Saratoga*.

Halsey, like most Americans, was deeply troubled about the outbreak of war in Europe. In an article, "The Navy—Security—and Neutrality," he pointed out that hemisphere defense rested with the Navy, which had the responsibility to engage and defeat any attacker at sea beyond the range of the enemy's bombers.

If American carrier doctrine had not come of age by the time the United States entered World War II, it was because a large number of high ranking officers had not fully grasped the carrier's potential. Many thought that the next conflict would be fought in the same way as World War I. Fleet battles would remain gunnery duels between battleships and cruisers. During the 1930s, in accordance with established procedure, carriers steamed astern of the battle line.

In 1939 when Halsey's carrier division joined King's division in the Pacific, the two admirals experimented by operating flattops together and running into the wind simultaneously to launch aircraft. They also experimented with carrier task groups, using cruisers and destroyers to escort and defend the carriers when they left fleet formation to execute flight operations. King strongly recommended that cruiser-destroyer screens be assigned to carriers so that the carriers and their escorts could learn to work effectively together.

Battleship admirals, members of the so-called "Gun Club" or the "Black Shoe Navy," refused to comply, insisting that cruisers and destroyers could not be spared from the main formation. Carriers should have only a scouting-observation function, remaining "the eyes of the fleet."

In the spring of 1940 Halsey was detached from the command of Carrier Division One and designated Commander Aircraft Battle Force with the rank of vice admiral. He now commanded all the carriers in the Pacific Fleet and their air groups. Seven months later as part of a general shakeup of flag officers, his friend and classmate Rear Admiral Husband E. Kimmel was relieved of his command of the Cruiser Battle Force and appointed Commander in Chief of the Pacific Fleet, with rank of admiral.

In Tokyo during the early months of 1941 political leaders had deliberated upon a war that would gain for Japan dominance over the entire Far East. The Army insisted on moving into Southeast Asia and the Dutch East Indies, supported by the Navy. Admiral Isoroku Yamamoto, Commander in Chief of the Japanese Combined Fleet, agreed in principle but he could not permit the United States Pacific Fleet, moored at Pearl Harbor, to cross the Pacific and attack his left flank. To immobilize these battleships, the admiral had devised a daring plan for a carrier air attack against Pearl Harbor. If American sea power were knocked out, the Japanese could capture the British base at Singapore and the American bases in the Philippines, then sweep into the East Indies, utilizing their resources for a drive to finish up China.

In the fall of 1941 Japanese warlords completed detailed plans for an attack on Pearl Harbor and made the decision to wage war against the United States. Japan's decision was predicated on Germany's and Italy's position in Europe. By the fall of 1941 the German Afrika Korps was threatening Egypt and German armies were driving toward Moscow. The Japanese gambled that the United States, confronting the dilemma of an Axis victory in Europe or Japanese dominance in Asia, would elect to put its resources into the European theater. Japan would be free to overrun Southeast Asia and establish a defensive barrier of island air and naval bases so powerful that the United States would not risk attack.

On 8 December, the day following Pearl Harbor, President Roosevelt appeared before Congress to ask for a declaration of war against Japan. It was voted with one dissenting voice in the House and unanimously in the Senate. Three days later Germany and Italy declared war on the United States. The American government replied in kind the same day, 11 December.

In the following months, the Japanese engulfed more than a

million square miles of the Pacific Ocean. They conquered Guam, Wake, the Philippines, Thailand, Burma, the Malay Peninsula, Singapore, most of New Guinea, the Solomons, and the Dutch East Indies. Australia and New Zealand braced against invasion.

The United States had a two-ocean war to fight with a one-ocean Navy. It was the most appalling crisis the nation had faced since the preservation of the Union had been achieved in 1865. The treacherous attack on Pearl Harbor aroused the American people, ended their smug assurance of military superiority, and brought home the ruthlessness of the enemy.

There were, however, bright spots in the situation for the Pacific Fleet. In zeroing in on the ships at Pearl Harbor, Japanese bombers had disregarded the machine shops, leaving repair facilities virtually unimpaired. They had neglected to destroy the four million barrels of oil exposed in tank farms. Without that oil, ships could not have operated from Hawaii for months. American carriers had avoided destruction and only a few cruisers and destroyers had been hit.

In Washington officials restructured the command system. President Roosevelt relieved Admiral Kimmel from active duty and designated Admiral Chester W. Nimitz, then Chief of the Bureau of Navigation, as Commander in Chief, United States Pacific Fleet and, later, Commander in Chief, Pacific Ocean Areas, giving him control over the entire Pacific theater of operations except for General Douglas MacArthur's Southwest Pacific Area and the then inactive Southwest Pacific Fleet. Roosevelt appointed Admiral Ernest J. King, former Commander, United States Atlantic Fleet, as Commander in Chief, United States Fleet, and issued Executive Order 8984 "Prescribing the Duties of Commander in Chief of the United States Fleet and the Cooperative Duties of the Chief of Naval Operations."

Among the many decisions made by Roosevelt during the early years of the war, few had more telling effect upon naval operations than this executive order. It stemmed from the concept that all oceans, Atlantic and Pacific, must be regarded as one area so that effective coordinated control and the proper distribution of naval power might be realized. In every sense King became "the most powerful officer the Navy had ever had'' and responsible both for the planning of long range operations and for supervision of their execution.

King's first instructions to Nimitz underscored his duties: 1) to hold the Hawaii-Midway line and keep open communications with the West Coast; 2) to maintain communications between the United States and Australia, chiefly by securing the Hawaii-Samoa route. American strategy also called for guarding a line running from the Aleutian Islands through Midway to Samoa, thence to New Caledonia and to Port Moresby, New Guinea.

Sir Winston Churchill, Prime Minister of Great Britain, arrived in Washington to meet with President Roosevelt. Upon the advice of high military and naval officers, they decided to carry on the war defensively against Japan since Germany was still the primary enemy and her defeat was the key to over-all victory. Once Germany was crushed, Italy would collapse. This strategic decision was the genesis of the United States Navy's gravest quandary—how to apply its limited capability in the Pacific to keep pressure on Japan. Accepting the concept of defeating Germany first, Admiral King in subsequent international conferences strenuously spurred his colleagues to push toward the war in Europe so that the United States Navy and Army might secure adequate forces for their commitments in the Pacific.

[II]

"Haul Ass with Halsey"

ON 9 DECEMBER 1941, after a quick night refueling, the *Enterprise* sortied before dawn with orders to hunt submarines north of the Hawaiian Islands. Bill Halsey spent a hectic five days searching. The lookouts, he said, "were spying periscope feathers in every whitecap and torpedoes in every porpoise." He signaled his task force: "If all the torpedo wakes reported are factual, Japanese submarines will soon have to return to base for a reload, and we will have nothing to fear. In addition, we are wasting too many depth charges on neutral fish."

The testy admiral was fighting to hold his temper in check when an officer rushed up to the flag bridge and frantically pointed to an escorting destroyer and cried, "She's sinking! Look, there she goes!" When the destroyer rode up on the crest of the next wave, Halsey exploded, "If you ever make another report like that, sir, I'll throw you over the side!"

At dawn on 10 December, the task force was cruising 200 miles from Pearl. A plane from the *Enterprise* spotted a submarine and, making a dive-bombing run, inflicted severe damage. Later another plane discovered a surfaced submarine, dive-bombed, and sank her. The *Enterprise* dodged a torpedo but although destroyers depth-charged the submarine, they failed to sink her. After two more days spent chasing false leads, Halsey's force re-entered Pearl Harbor on 15 December to refuel.

To Halsey's dismay, he discovered that Kimmel had been relieved of his command as a result of the Pearl Harbor holocaust. High ranking naval officers, including Halsey, were sure that the disaster would be formally investigated. "But I'll take my oath," said Halsey, "that not one of us would have guessed that the blame would fall on Kimmel, because not one of us believed that he deserved it—any part of it."

Even after the war, Halsey maintained, "In all my experiences, I have never known a Commander in Chief of any United States Fleet who worked harder, and under more adverse circumstances, to increase its efficiency and to prepare it for war; further, I know of no officer who might have been in command at that time who would have done more than Kimmel did." *

Kimmel was sacrificed to public opinion. The fact that in November 1941 a fleet exercise had presupposed a Japanese air attack on Oahu meant little. In the public eye, there was no excuse for Kimmel.

At Fleet Headquarters Acting Commander in Chief Admiral William S. Pye (Nimitz had not yet arrived) gave Halsey instructions to proceed to sea with his *Enterprise* force, cover the northern flank of Oahu from possible Japanese attack, and help land reinforcements at beleaguered Midway. Meanwhile Task Force Eleven (the *Lexington* group), commanded by Admiral Wilson Brown, and Task Force Fourteen (the *Saratoga* group), commanded by Admiral Frank Jack Fletcher, were steaming southwestward to support Wake Island, then under heavy attack from Japanese naval forces. However, Washington decided that the stakes were too high to risk a carrier group at Wake Island, which was now considered a military liability. Evacuation was impossible. Washington pressured Admiral Pye to recall Task Forces Eleven and Fourteen. When Halsey returned from Midway on 31 December, he was furious over abandoning Wake Island to Japanese amphibious troops. "Task Force 14 could have been at Wake," said Halsey, "raising hell with the Jap occupation. Why we were diverted I still don't know. All we knew was that the war was only days old, and we had already lost Wake."

* During the Congressional hearings regarding the Pearl Harbor disaster, Halsey was asked how he himself happened to be ready for the Japanese attack. "Because of one man," he replied, "Admiral Kimmel."

Admiral Chester Nimitz, the new Commander in Chief, Pacific Fleet, slipped out of Washington for Pearl Harbor with confidential reports in his wife's commandeered sewing bag. Under the name of "Mr. Wainwright" and in civilian clothes, the tow-haired, blue-eyed Texan traveled by train to San Diego and then by plane to Hawaii, arriving on Christmas Day, 1941. At an historic meeting with Admiral Kimmel, Nimitz shook hands cordially with the friendly remark, "You have my sympathy—the same thing could have happened to me."

On 30 December Nimitz, who had not yet assumed command, received an urgent dispatch from Admiral King in Washington. Nimitz was to protect the Hawaii-Midway line and maintain sea communications between the west coast of the United States and Australia by holding the Hawaii-Samoa-Fiji line.

Nimitz delayed no longer in assuming command. At 1000, 31 December, he pinned on his four stars, went to Fleet Headquarters, and relieved Admiral Pye. To most of the senior officers at Pearl Harbor, who had been picked by Kimmel, it seemed likely that Nimitz would replace them. But Nimitz felt sure, from first-hand observation, that the standard of any major group of United States naval personnel was, by definition, high; and that while the Pearl Harbor disaster might have impaired the efficiency of fleet officers by lowering morale, the way to correct this was not to collect a new crew, but to encourage the men he had. Professing faith in Kimmel's staff, he asked all of them to stay on and serve under him. Once this was decided, Nimitz set to work to pick up the pieces of the shattered Pacific Fleet and to work out plans for eventual victory.

To the question, "What is the Pacific Fleet doing?", Nimitz responded in Hawaiian, *"Hoomana wa mei"* (Be patient).

Bad news continued to pour into Fleet Headquarters. Canton Island, an important port of call on the Oahu-Samoa-Fiji route, only 960 miles from enemy-held Makin Island, lacked planes and its personnel consisted of seventy-eight Army engineers with no guns, no radar, "no nothing." An enemy submarine shelled the United States naval installation at Pago Pago, Samoa, suggesting that a Japanese move in that direction was imminent. Another submarine torpedoed the *Saratoga*. The carrier struggled back to

Pearl, where repairs would keep her out of commission for five crucial months.

Besides the limited number of carriers in the Pacific, Nimitz had to struggle along with sub-standard aircraft, a sad testimony to American unpreparedness for war. The basic Navy fighter plane was the Grumman F4F Wildcat, good, but not up to the capabilities of the Japanese Zero. The dive bomber was the Douglas SBD Dauntless, rugged and dependable, and versatile enough to act as a fighter, scout, and bombing plane. The torpedo plane was the Douglas TBD Devastator, antiquated and slow. The Navy had already contracted for its replacement.

On 1 January Admiral Frank Jack Fletcher was at San Diego, California, preparing to take his task force, built around the *Yorktown* (recalled from the East Coast) to Pago Pago, escorting three transports loaded with 5,000 troops, two cargo ships, and an oiler. On 3 January Task Force Eleven (the *Lexington*) returned to Pearl Harbor from guarding the Oahu-Palmyra-Johnston triangle. Halsey with Task Force Eight (the *Enterprise*) was south of Oahu practice firing.

Over the strong objections of his conservative staffers, Admiral Nimitz decided to send a carrier force to strike the Japanese where it would hurt—in their Marshall Islands bases in the Central Pacific. When Task Force Eight returned to Pearl Harbor for fuel, Nimitz sent for Halsey.

Nimitz detailed the Japanese advances in the Pacific. With the enemy in control of the British Gilbert Islands, it appeared that they were ready to launch an invasion of Samoa, 1,300 miles farther southeastward. If successful, they would command the American line of communications with Australia and New Zealand unless the Navy jolted them hard. But how? American amphibious forces were at that moment ill-prepared to invade Japanese-held islands. It was up to the carriers.

The Marine garrison at Samoa was to be reinforced with troops, being escorted from San Diego by Admiral Fletcher and his *Yorktown* force. Nimitz suggested that Halsey get under way for Samoa with the *Enterprise* and, as soon as the Marine reinforcements had landed, he was to lead the *Yorktown* and *Enterprise* forces in a raid against the Marshall and Gilbert Islands.

The attack units could inflict "a disproportionate amount of damage," by destroying enough shore objectives so as to prevent, or at least hinder, Japan's use of those bases. "It's most desirable," Nimitz said, "that the Pacific Fleet take some offensive action but an attack by ship-based aircraft against shore-based aircraft bases, except when the element of surprise is present, partakes of the nature of an attack on shore fortifications with long range guns and may result in serious losses." Yet such a raid, if successful, would divert the enemy for defense purposes and boost American morale.

When Nimitz asked him how the plan sounded, Halsey replied enthusiastically, "It's a rare opportunity." On their way to Samoa Halsey's ships seemed jinxed. The destroyer *Blue* lost a man overboard. A seaman was killed in a turret accident on the *Salt Lake City*. A plane crash-landed on the *Enterprise*'s flight deck, killing a machinist's mate. A torpedo plane failed to return. A scout plane made a direct hit on a Japanese submarine, but the bomb failed to detonate. The destroyers *Fanning* and *Gridley* collided in a heavy storm with such damage to their bows that they both returned to Pearl Harbor.

The Marine landings at Samoa completed, the task forces of the *Enterprise* and *Yorktown* began their run northwestward to attack the Japanese-held islands. The submarine *Dolphin,* making a reconnaissance of the Marshalls, reported on 27 January that the entire group of islands were lightly defended and that the greatest concentration of aircraft and shipping were at Kwajalein Atoll, the center of the archipelago.

Halsey divided his task force into three groups—*Enterprise,* escorted by three destroyers, was to send planes against Wotje, Maloelap, Kwajalein; Rear Admiral Raymond Spruance, Halsey's close friend, in the heavy cruiser *Northampton* with *Salt Lake City* and one destroyer was to bombard Wotje; Captain Thomas M. Shock in the *Hester* with two destroyers was to shell Maloelap. Admiral Fletcher in the *Yorktown* accompanied by light cruisers and destroyers planned to hit Makin in the Gilberts and Mili and Jaluit in the southern Marshalls.

After frustrating patrols, Bill Halsey was at last going on the offensive, running his task force deep into enemy territory. He was a risk-taker who welcomed such hazardous missions. For years he had been an apostle of naval air power—touting its importance, its effectiveness, its flexibility. Planes could bring the battleground into "streets and gardens far removed from the scene of a formalized surface engagement." In the kind of war that the vast expanses of the Pacific dictated, strong, fast carrier forces were indispensable since they could strike with surprise at long range. "We do the unexpected," said Halsey. ". . . . We expose ourselves to shore-based planes. We don't stay behind the battle with our carriers. But . . . whatever we do, we do fast."

Lightly armored with its long flight deck raised at least fifty feet above the water to permit planes to take off in foul weather, the carrier was extremely vulnerable to enemy attack. For protection the flattop relied on elaborate compartmentalization and a speed of thirty knots. Below its flight deck were a maze of hangar decks, machine shops, gas and oil tanks, storage spaces for extra planes, engines, propellers, and guns. With its high percentage of plane handlers, mechanics, radiomen, and gunners, its personnel was unlike the crew of any other type of Navy ship.

Halsey displayed a shrewd confidence in the extreme mobility of the fast carrier task force, appraising it as a force which could gain command of the air at a required time and place to establish the conditions necessary for amphibious operations. Independent of the investment in personnel and shipping required for the construction of airfields and facilities on islands, which would soon be left far behind the rapidly advancing front, the carrier's flexibility gave its planes the advantage of continuous initiative and surprise.

The *Enterprise*'s crew, in fact all men who had served under him, revered the admiral. They liked his kind of discipline. Although he ran a taut ship, he was not an unreachable, unknowable commander. Ordinary seamen with whom he came in contact he called by their first names. He asked no man to face perils that he would not face himself. He passed no bucks. He did not saddle his men with unnecessary regulations and permitted officers to wear khaki without ties and even blue dungarees to dinner. To Halsey, the time lost in tying and untying neckties represented a "tremendous loss of manpower." He himself appeared on the bridge, his gray hair bristling in the wind, outfitted in a huge brown sheepskin coat over a khaki shirt without a tie. In foul weather he wore a raincoat with ADM (Admiral) stenciled on its back.

At 1830, 31 January 1942, Halsey's and Fletcher's forces parted company for their runs in from the eastward. When a Japanese scouting plane passed over the *Enterprise* without sighting the task force that afternoon, Halsey dictated a message to the Japanese admiral on the Marshalls. "It is a pleasure to thank you for having your patrol planes not sight my force." The message, translated into Japanese and printed, was ordered to be dropped by the *Enterprise*'s pilots together with their bombs.

Halsey pushed on at thirty knots during the night, although his only available charts were old and incomplete. The possibility of reefs and minefields haunted his navigators. Lookouts strained their eyes, gazing into the blackness. Halsey fidgeted. He shut himself up in his emergency cabin, out of sight. Sleep was impossible. He drank coffee, read mystery stories, chain-smoked. "One of the hardest things in command," he said, "is sending men into action to die when you'd much rather go yourself. You can't manufacture blood, you can't grow it and you can't mine it."

On the *Enterprise*'s bridge, the staff duty officer felt particles stinging his face. He rubbed them between his fingers—sand!

He quickly reported to Halsey. The charts showed no islands nearby, but could they be trusted? The duty officer licked his fingers. The sand tasted sweet. Dimly on the range finder platform, forward, he saw a sailor stirring a cup of coffee.

At 0300 the *chong-chong-chong* of General Quarters sounded. Men tumbled to their battle stations. Pilots received last-minute instructions in the ready rooms and dashed for their planes. The flight deck was still a pitch-black platform along which the pilots were guided by bluejackets bellowing plane numbers. Pilots had memorized the positions of their planes from charts in the ready rooms to locate them in the darkness. One by one they clambered into their cockpits, fastened shoulder harnesses, buckled seat belts, plugged in radio connections. The bullhorn boomed: "Stand by to start engines"; and a minute later,

"Stand clear of propellers"; and then, "Start engines." Pilots flipped switches, slapped primer switches three or four times, held down the starter switch, and listened. A startling roar. The *Enterprise* straightened out her turn and headed into a freshening wind. The first plane sat on the starting line. The pilot advanced his throttle. The roar grew to a shrill, ear-splitting thunder. The pilot took his feet off the brake pedals and the plane headed toward the pitching bow of the flight deck. At 0443 the bullhorn blared out again above the thunder of revving engines. "Launch aircraft." Other planes roared skyward. Blue flames dotted the sky, the planes converging into formation, disappearing toward the targets.

Nine torpedo planes streaked toward Kwajalein; forty-seven dive bombers, toward Roi, one of the chief islands in the Kwajalein chain. The dawn mist blurred the atolls and the dive bombers failed to locate Roi until 0705. Anti-aircraft batteries pumped away, while Japanese pilots scurried to their planes and took off to intercept.

The American squadron commander had barely released his first bomb when he was shot down by ack-ack. Three more planes were lost. The squadron blasted several installations around Roi airfield, destroyed an ammunition dump, and damaged three enemy aircraft.

At Kwajalein, the torpedo planes encountered no fighter opposition and the atoll offered plenty of targets.

Halsey launched a second strike of nine more torpedo planes at 0731.

Mechanics and refuelers on the *Enterprise* prepared for the return of aircraft. The planes circled above the carrier and swept down into the landing circle. Then the precise pattern up the groove and the welcome sight of Fly One, the landing signal officer, paddles in hand, waving them on, across the stern and onto the deck and into the wires. Then came the quick, jolting, satisfactory jerk as the tail hook caught and the plane was hauled to a standstill.

Sailors attached bombs, loaded ammunition, and rushed damaged planes below for repairs. Pilots reported sinking a transport,

a net tender, a subchaser, and damaging two converted gun-
boats, a minelayer, a transport, a light cruiser, and an ammunition ship. They had destroyed thirteen planes and crippled four.
Other *Enterprise* planes raided Wotje, but sank nothing.

On board the *Salt Lake City,* part of Admiral Spruance's
group, which was bombarding Wotje Atoll, a news correspondent watched the dots and dashes of white and orange gun-
bursts from batteries all along the shore. American planes hurtled
across the island, bombing and strafing. The cruiser's guns
flashed. Enemy dive bombers attacked.

"My ears couldn't even believe themselves in all that hell with
all the guns going," the correspondent said. "There was that
chilling whoosh of huge explosives, ending in a dull ominous
WHOOMPH. Planes were diving in high from several directions.
The huge morning sun seemed spotted with them. But for the
time being neither bombs nor shore batteries were effective
against us."

The cruisers and destroyers dumped shells into the island in a
never ending stream. "We could see more fires springing up on
the island under the ceaseless fire of the ships."

Twenty-one times that day the *Enterprise* launched strikes.
"These young pilots," said Halsey, "acted as if they were playing football. They'd fight like the devil, then take a short time-
out, and get back into the fight again."

All day long, clad in a leather windbreaker and an old white
sun helmet, Halsey watched from the flag bridge and listened to
his pilots chattering excitedly over their phones—"Get away
from that cruiser, Bill, she's mine!" "We sure got that big bas-
tard, didn't we?"

Halsey was extremely lucky. For nine hours he had maneuvered his force without plane protection in a rectangle only five
by twenty miles, mostly within sight of Wotje. One news correspondent charged Halsey with recklessness, but the admiral retorted later, "Aggressive, yes; audacious, yes; but not reckless."

When the *Enterprise'* s aircraft returned at 1300, Commander
Miles Browning, Halsey's Chief of Staff, said, "Sir, I've been
thinking it's time we hauled out of here."

Halsey nodded, "You know, Miles, I've been thinking the same thing myself." The force retired at high speed. This started the legendary club, "Haul Ass with Halsey."

That afternoon the enemy retaliated with their few remaining planes. Five twin-engined bombers dropped from the clouds. The gunnery officer of the *Enterprise,* stationed in the control room atop the mast, yelled, "Here they come, give 'em hell!"

Anti-aircraft guns swung into action. Twenty heavy bombs splashed and exploded in the water, port side of the *Enterprise.* The lead plane, disabled, attempted to crash into the hull. An aviation mechanic jumped into the rear seat of a plane on the flight deck and opened fire with its machine gun. This action, together with a "hard right rudder" command from the Officer of the Deck, caused the bomber to hit the port side of the flight deck and fall harmlessly over the side. Two more bombers swept in toward the carrier, but AA guns shot them down.

Once clear of the area, Halsey told his crew and pilots, "I've never been so damn proud of anybody as I am of you."

Miles Browning said later, "Surprise was complete and I think it may honestly be said that Pearl Harbor was fairly well repaid, except for the absence of the foul note of treachery."

Meanwhile, the more cautious Frank Jack Fletcher had led his *Yorktown* force against the southern islands. Eleven torpedo planes and seventeen dive bombers attacked Jaluit. Thunderstorms hit, concealing the atoll. Only two ships off Jabor Town were damaged, and a minimum amount of destruction was done ashore. Six planes failed to return to the *Yorktown.* At Makin Island nine planes hit only a mine layer. The attack on Mili was equally unfruitful.

It is unfair to gauge this raid by its meager results. The two carrier forces had gained valuable combat experience and the overly optimistic accounts of the damage inflicted had symbolic importance. Halsey, hitting the heart of the Japanese defenses in the Central Pacific, was suddenly acclaimed the nation's first naval hero of the war.* In popular imagination, he became something of a superman.

* The press called him "Bull"; his close friends, "Bill"; his devoted staff, "Admiral Bill."

American newspapers heralded Halsey's success. The New York *Times* commented, "This feat shows that we can strike far into the Western Pacific. It assures protection for the route between the American coast of the Pacific and New Zealand and Australia. Above all, it proves the value of attack. . . . We can be sure that this successful raid is only the first of many blows which will pay in full for Pearl Harbor, for lost ships and for treacherously taken lives."

When he heard the news of the Marshall raid, a naval air commander wrote Halsey: "When we heard of the first reports of your successful action in the Marshalls all of us picked up our heads with renewed pride in our service. Now that the whole story has been released we are prouder than ever and especially so because our aviation Admiral was in command. You did a lot for the Navy as well as the country. Congratulations, sir, and thanks!"

From Pearl Harbor Nimitz informed Halsey that he had just received the following message from the Secretary of the Navy.

THE PRESIDENT HAS THIS DATE AWARDED THE DISTINGUISHED SERVICE MEDAL TO VICE ADMIRAL HALSEY JUNIOR U S NAVY WITH THE FOLLOWING CITATION QUOTE FOR DISTINGUISHED SERVICE IN A DUTY OF GREAT RESPONSIBILITY X AS COMMANDER OF THE MARSHALL RAIDING FORCE UNITED STATES PACIFIC FLEET AND ESPECIALLY FOR HIS BRILLIANT AND AUDACIOUS ATTACK AGAINST MARSHALL AND GILBERT ISLANDS ON JANUARY THIRTY ONE X BY HIS GREAT SKILL AND DETERMINATION THIS DRIVE INFLICTED HEAVY DAMAGE TO ENEMY SHIPS AND PLANES.

Nimitz concluded his message by sending his CONGRATULATIONS . . . ON A WELL DESERVED AWARD.

To celebrate the raid, Halsey ordered all ships of his force to fly their largest flags and pennants when entering Pearl Harbor. Cheers from ships and shore welcomed the *Enterprise*. Nimitz did not wait for the carrier to lower a ladder. He came over the side in a bos'n's chair. "Nice going, Bill! Nice going!"

After Nimitz awarded Halsey the Distinguished Service Medal, Halsey called in his staff. "This is as much for you as it is for me. You made it possible."

Halsey sensed a mood of optimism. The shock of Pearl Harbor had made the Americans gloomy, negative, and defensive. When the task forces sortied for the run for the Marshalls, "you could almost smell the defeatism around Pearl. Now the offensive is re-established; officers and men are bushy-tailed again."

That night on the *Enterprise,* the crew watched movies on the hangar deck. When Halsey suddenly appeared, the bluejackets gave him a rousing ovation, calling for a speech. He rose before them, saying simply, "I'm so proud of you I could cry." To one captain, the roar of approval they gave Halsey was "the most moving demonstration I ever witnessed."

[III]

"All That
Took Guts"

ALONG THE DOCKS at Pearl Harbor and Ford Island seamen labored through the hot days and cool nights. Heavy cranes swung the materiel of war over the ships' sides and down into the holds—ammunition, bombs, fifty-calibers, thirty-calibers, twenty-millimeters, forty-millimeters. Then came toothpaste and shaving gear, meat and medicine, clothing and canned foods.

At Fleet Headquarters the staff pondered the problems of the Southwest Pacific, where intelligence reported definite signs of a "widespread and coordinated" Japanese buildup, indicating a major offensive in that zone and, possibly, raids against Midway, Oahu, New Hebrides, and northeastern Australia. Admiral King in Washington was pressuring Nimitz to alleviate the situation in the Southwest Pacific by aggressive action in the mid-Pacific, mentioning Wake and the northern Marshalls as possible targets.

For two days Nimitz, the staff, and Halsey searched for suitable objectives. "It is very difficult to select a target within reach of the fleet (extended by oiling at sea) which would result in any considerable diversion of enemy forces from the Southwest Pacific." One staffer proposed that Halsey's force make a sweep as far as Rabaul. Another suggestion was to hit Tokyo, but Nimitz ruled this out as being "too precarious due to bad weather for fueling." The decision was finally reached for Halsey to raid Wake and Marcus islands. While both Halsey and Nimitz feared that such actions could not divert much enemy strength from the southwest, it was as strong an aggressive move as could be undertaken at that time.

After only a week at Pearl Harbor, Halsey's ships slipped their moorings and moved down channel. Pilots lining the flight deck watched as the *Enterprise* cleared Pearl Harbor and followed a westward course past Barbers Point.

At dawn on 24 February the force struck Wake Island. Cruisers and destroyers lobbed in shells, destroying buildings, but were unable to silence enemy shore batteries. The *Enterprise* closed in that night and launched forty-two planes at sunup. Although this strike proved to be good practice, the destruction meted out was hardly worth the loss of an American dive bomber with its crew.

Halsey next raided Marcus Island, an area less than a square mile, 1,000 miles from Tokyo. Planes struck before sunrise on 4 March in full moonlight. They observed no enemy aircraft, but AA fire was severe and one scout bomber was shot down.

Both the Wake and Marcus raids were diversions and there is no evidence that these strikes pulled any forces of the enemy up from the South Pacific. As one officer remarked, "The Japs didn't mind them any more than a dog minds a flea."

Yet the Pacific Fleet was getting into the war, and Admiral Halsey and his staff were learning. In the Marcus raid, Halsey for the first time relied on radar to find his own aircraft on their way to their objectives and to correct their navigation. He also discovered that his planes needed incendiary bullets to strike land targets effectively. He reported he needed a supply of reserve pilots, especially since the *Enterprise* might be at General Quarters around the clock, with pilots flying five-hour missions, then returning only to take off again to fly search-and-patrol missions.

Although the damage inflicted on Wake and Marcus was minimal, newspapers publicized the raids. The New York *Times* extolled, "This is welcome news. . . . While the damage done to the enemy was limited in extent, the actions show that our Navy is continuing to take the initiative in the waters between Hawaii and the main islands of Japan. We may be certain that the hammering thus begun will not cease until Wake is once more back in American hands and converted into a base for offensive operations.''

By early March 1942, the military situation in the Far East was black for the Allies. A combined American, British, Dutch, and Australian naval force was disastrously defeated in the Java Sea by enemy units. The United States Navy's first carrier, *Langley,* was bombed and sunk. The Japanese bombing of New Guinea, including Port Moresby, and Tulagi in the lower Solomons indicated to Allied intelligence a further advance to the southeast. To counter such a move, a task force built around the *Lexington* and *Yorktown* was ordered to strike Rabaul, which the Japanese were developing into a major naval base. But a report of Japanese landings on 8 March at Lae and Salamaua on the northern side of New Guinea caused the *Lexington* to shift its attack against these points. Launching its planes south of Papua, aircraft achieved surprise by winding in over the Owen Stanley Mountains and scoring successes against Japanese ships.

By April the command structure in the Pacific was permanently established. The Allied nations set up two huge commands, the Southwest Pacific Area and the Pacific Ocean Areas. The Southwest Pacific included Australia and adjacent waters, all the Dutch East Indies except Sumatra, and the Philippine Islands. The vast Pacific Ocean Areas included nearly all the remainder of the Pacific Ocean. Unlike the Southwest Pacific, which was one unit, the Pacific Ocean Areas were divided into three sections—the South, Central, and North Pacific. The North Pacific included the ocean that reached north of latitude 42 North; the Central Pacific lay between 42 North and the Equator.

The South Pacific Area, which lay south of the Equator, east of longitude 159 East and west of longitude 110 West, was an immense stretch of water including the islands of New Zealand, the French colony of New Caledonia, and the British-French condominium of the New Hebrides, Santa Cruz, Fiji, Samoa, Tonga, the Cook Islands, the Society Islands, and the Marquesas. The boundary dividing the South and Southwest Pacific areas (longitude 159 East) split the Solomon Islands.

General Douglas MacArthur became Commander in Chief of the Southwest Pacific Area with headquarters at Brisbane, Australia. Nimitz was appointed Commander in Chief of the Pacific Ocean Areas as well as Commander in Chief of the Pacific Fleet. Nimitz exercised direct control over the North and Central Pacific Areas but, in accordance with the Joint Chiefs of Staff instructions, appointed a subordinate as Commander of the South Pacific Area, Admiral Robert L. Ghormley, with headquarters first at Aukland, New Zealand, and later at Noumea, New Caledonia.

Among the problems Ghormley faced was the fact that New Zealand, Noumea in New Caledonia, and Fiji fell within Nimitz's command, while the area where the Navy had been actively engaged, the area around the Solomons and New Guinea, fell actually in MacArthur's zone.

A few days after Halsey returned from the Marcus raid, Nimitz called him to Fleet Headquarters for a conference with Rear Admiral Donald ("Wu") Duncan, just arrived from Washington.

Duncan related that a top secret operation was under way. Colonel James H. Doolittle, USAAF, had trained sixteen Army air crews in Florida to take B-25s off a carrier's flight deck, and the Navy had promised to launch them for Tokyo. The risks were high for a strike by Navy planes, but an attack on Tokyo from carriers by Army bombers flying on to Chinese airfields would not only damage Japan but provide planes for the Chinese national defense.

Nimitz turned to Halsey and asked, "Do you believe it would work, Bill?"

Halsey replied, "They'll need a lot of luck."

"Are you willing to take them out there?"

"Yes, I am."

"Good!" said Nimitz. "It's all yours!"

Halsey suggested that the mission would run more smoothly if he could discuss it personally with Colonel Doolittle. Nimitz agreed, and signed orders for Halsey and his Chief of Staff, Miles Browning, to proceed to San Francisco.

On 31 March in a quiet restaurant in San Francisco's Fairmont Hotel, Halsey and Browning waited for their guest. As Doolittle strode in, the admiral greeted him with a wide grin. They shook hands, sat down, and started off the evening with drinks, then ordered dinner. The booths on each side were empty. When they finished their dessert, and more coffee arrived, Halsey waved the waiter away and the three men got down to business.

Halsey reported that his force would consist of two carriers, *Enterprise* and *Hornet,* four cruisers, eight destroyers, and two tankers. The B-25s would be hoisted on board the *Hornet* (Captain Marc A. Mitscher commanding), then in San Francisco harbor. The carrier, escorted by half the task force, would rendezvous in mid-Pacific with the *Enterprise* group from Pearl Harbor. If they escaped detection, the carriers would make a high speed run to within 400 miles of the Japanese coast. The plan suited Doolittle. The three men shook hands, and Halsey wished Doolittle luck.

Halsey expected to be back in Pearl Harbor on 2 April in time to work out final details for the raid, but strong winds grounded all westbound planes. Bad weather continued and, on 5 April, Halsey notified the *Hornet* to postpone her rendezvous for twenty-four hours. Halsey and Browning left San Francisco for Pearl Harbor on the 6th.

The *Enterprise* got under way from Pearl Harbor at 1120 on 8 April and threaded her way down channel together with the cruisers *Salt Lake City* and *Northampton,* the destroyers *Balch, Benham,* and *Fanning* and, once at sea, sortied with the destroyer *Ellet* and the oiler *Sabine.* They steamed on a course to a point thirty miles southwest of Nihoa Island in the Hawaiian chain. From there the force shifted course to 310°.

On 13 April at a point between Midway Island and the western Aleutians, the *Enterprise* rendezvoused with Mitscher's *Hornet* group. As the two forces merged, the ships maneuvered to take up station. The *Hornet* with the Army planes was in the center, trailed by the *Enterprise* and oilers. The cruisers and destroyers screened ahead and on the flank.

As the task force steamed westward, classroom work started for both Army and Navy pilots. Charts and photographs were removed from safes and spread across tables in the ready rooms. Complicated drawings were executed, showing exact locations and procedures to be followed in case of emergency landings. In the blackout recognition rooms pilots sat and memorized details as silhouettes of enemy planes flashed on the screen. On the

hangar decks mechanics manipulated screwdrivers and wrenches
until the machine guns performed with the precision of Swiss
watches. Well into the night, electricians labored over complicated arrays of wires, and radiomen checked and rechecked in-
struments.

When 1,000 miles east of Tokyo, 17 April, the tankers began
refueling the carriers and cruisers in foul weather. One naval lieutenant remembered that the wind and sea were "the God-
damnedest I've ever seen." The tankers' hoses were barely withdrawn before winds hit gale force.

At 1430 the *Hornet* and *Enterprise* and four cruisers stepped
out at a speed of twenty-eight knots for the final run. The
destroyers and tankers dropped astern to conserve fuel and permit
high speed operations.

It dawned murky and gray, 18 April. Navy aircraft from the
Enterprise searched the sea. A scout plane spotted a Japanese patrol vessel. The plane did not attack, complying with Halsey's
orders, and attempted unsuccessfully to avoid detection. Plummet-
ing over the *Enterprise,* the pilot dropped a message reporting
contact.

To eliminate the possibility of enemy craft sending a message,
Halsey ordered the *Nashville* to sink her and quickly. The cruiser
opened up. But in the angry sea, accuracy was difficult. The Japanese radio operator got off a message.

The *Nashville*'s rapid-fire salvoes were fearsome, but the Japanese craft went unscathed. Gaping in astonishment, Halsey angrily ordered the *Nashville* to close to point blank range. Finally,
the *Nitto Maru No. 23,* after evading 924 shells, was sunk after
an engagement of twenty-nine minutes.

Radio intelligence on the *Enterprise* indicated that the picket
ship had already broadcast the position and the number of ships
in the task force. Japanese radio traffic built up. News of the carriers' approach had been received in Tokyo.

Halsey was dangerously exposed. His carriers were within
range of shore-based bombers and open to attack by surface
units. The problem, he reasoned, was to weigh and balance accurately the risks to his naval and air units.

Two controlling ideas dominated tactics: the enemy should not be given a chance to hit the carriers; Doolittle's bombers must have enough fuel after the raid to give them a fighting chance for reaching the Chinese coast. The prime consideration was to launch the Army planes before the arrival of shore-based Japanese bombers. The task force was 668 miles from Tokyo. Doolittle's original plan had been to take off late that afternoon, but Halsey decided on a premature launch.

At 0800 blinker lights flashed from the *Enterprise,* LAUNCH PLANES. TO COL. DOOLITTLE AND HIS GALLANT COMMAND GOOD LUCK AND GOD BLESS YOU.

At 0825 Doolittle led his squadron off the deck of the *Hornet.* Halsey related that "there wasn't a man topside in the task force who didn't help sweat him into the air."

The last plane was airborne at 0924, and minutes later Halsey's staff duty officer wrote in his log, "changed course and axis to 090, commencing retirement from the area at twenty-five knots."

Several days later Halsey wrote Doolittle. "The hats of the Task Force are on high to you. Superb! The takeoff was splendid. The conditions were trying for our trained carrier pilots, and for men who had never taken off from a carrier deck before, is little short of marvelous. . . .

"I hated to dump you off at that distance, but because of discovery there was nothing else to do. . . . I stated to my Staff, that on landing you should have had two stars pinned on each shoulder, and the Medal of Honor put around your neck. . . . I am highly honored in having had you, and the very gallant and brave lads with you, serve under my command for a short period of time. It is something I shall always remember. I do not know of any more gallant deed in history than that performed by your squadron. . . ."

"God knows," concluded Halsey, "when or where this will reach you, but if and when it does, I would appreciate hearing of your experience. This, of course, at your leisure. Again my hearty congratulations. Keep on knocking over those yellow bastards."

The Japanese pursued Halsey's task force. Whenever the group's radar tracked enemy search planes, Halsey was tempted to send out fighters. However, he realized that it was more important not to reveal his position than to shoot down two or three scouts. The enemy dispatched a task force after the *Enterprise* and *Hornet;* submarines attempted to intercept them. With the help of foul weather and devious course changes, Halsey eluded enemy air and surface units and returned to Pearl Harbor on 25 April.

Halsey later learned that thirteen of Doolittle's B-25s had bombed Tokyo, Nagoya, Osaka, and Kobe and, inflicting only minor damage, had flown on toward China, where the planes, short of fuel, had crash-landed or their crews had parachuted out. Eight men landed in enemy territory and of these, three were executed for bombing Japanese residential areas.

A friend was with Halsey when he received word that three fliers had been executed. It was the first time he had ever noticed the birthmark on Halsey's neck. "I saw it," he said, "because it turned purple. He stuck out that ram-bow jaw and he ground his teeth. Those eyebrows of his began to flail up and down. . . . All he could choke out was 'We'll make the bastards pay! We'll make 'em pay!' "

The South Pacific theater was warming up. The carriers *Lexington* and *Yorktown* were guarding the area against more Japanese thrusts southward. Nimitz ordered Halsey to the South Pacific to reinforce Task Force Seventeen, Admiral Frank Jack Fletcher, and, while en route, to land a squadron of Marine fighter planes on Efate Island in the New Hebrides group.

Halsey's force, including the *Hornet* and *Enterprise,* got under way from Pearl Harbor. On 7 May, while Halsey was still 1,000 miles away, Japanese and American naval units fought the Battle of the Coral Sea in the South Pacific. Although the carrier *Lexington* was sunk, the Americans, in a strategic sense, won the battle. The enemy's planned invasion of Allied-held Port Moresby, New Guinea, collapsed and Japanese ships retired to Rabaul. The battle also marked the most distant advance southward of the enemy and saved Australia and New Zealand from possible invasion. On 11 May Halsey's force sent two planes ahead to see if Efate field was ready to receive the squadron. They discovered it was not, so Halsey ordered the fighters off to

Admiral William F. Halsey, Jr., Commander South Pacific Force, Pacific Fleet, being sworn in by his Chief of Staff, Captain Miles R. Browning, November 1942. (U.S. Navy photo)

Eleanor Roosevelt visits New Caledonia, August 1943. Left to right, Lieutenant General Millard F. Harmon, Mrs. Roosevelt, Halsey. The plane in the background is the C-47 in which she traveled while at this base. (Navy Department, National Archives)

38

RIGHT Admiral Ernest J. King and his two principal Pacific subordinates, Admiral Chester W. Nimitz (left) and Halsey, after a conference at Pearl Harbor, September 1943. (U.S. Navy photo)

BELOW Halsey on an inspection tour of Barakoma Island in the North Solomons, November 1943. Left to right, Commander J. L. Cotton, Major General G. E. Barrowclough of New Zealand, Halsey. (U.S. Navy photo)

Halsey with Admiral John S. McCain in Los Angeles for a conference, January 1944. (Navy Department, National Archives)

ABOVE Admiral Nimitz (left), Lieutenant General R. C. Richardson, and Halsey review units of the 7th Division at Schofield Barracks, Hawaii, May 1944. (U.S. Navy photo)

BELOW Halsey holding a staff conference on the *New Jersey*, 1944. At right, Admiral Robert B. Carney, Chief of Staff. (Navy Department, National Archives)

Halsey takes good-natured kidding from his officers on board the *New Jersey*. (Navy Department, National Archives)

Noumea, New Caledonia, then swung northward along the 170th meridian, scouting 200 miles on each side.

Conscious that the Japanese forces which had fought the Battle of the Coral Sea had vanished, Halsey wanted to make sure that they were not regrouping to break through between New Hebrides and Fiji. Several days later Nimitz ordered Halsey's force to return to Pearl.

Working under stress and in the heat and humidity of the South Pacific, Halsey had developed an itching skin disease. His sweat glands had become irritated and swollen and he had a fine pebble-like rash on his waistline, neck, chest, back, and armpits, accompanied by intolerable itching.

Halsey experimented with a variety of remedies, including oatmeal baths, but nothing worked. He was unable to eat or sleep and became completely exhausted, nervous, and ill-tempered. Dr. Hightower placed him on the binnacle list, but the admiral refused to stay in bed. When he went to Fleet Headquarters, after his return from Efate, Nimitz took one look at him and ordered him into the hospital.

Even before the Battle of the Coral Sea and Halsey's return, Nimitz had been aware through intelligence sources that the Japanese were planning to mount a major naval offensive in the Central Pacific in June and was convinced that the principal target would be strategically located Midway Island, a tiny atoll at the tip of the Hawaiian chain.

After checking the list of possible commanders who could replace Bill Halsey, and recalling Halsey's words of praise for Admiral Raymond Spruance, Nimitz chose Spruance to lead the Halsey task force into action.

Even before Halsey had reached Pearl Harbor, he had expressed faith in his intimate friend, Raymond Spruance, in an official letter. "Admiral Raymond Spruance has consistently displayed outstanding ability combined with excellent judgment and quiet courage," wrote Halsey. "I consider him fully and superbly qualified to take command of a force comprising mixed types and to conduct protracted independent operations in the combat theater in wartime."

Quiet, meticulous, and methodical, Spruance was not a pilot, but he had deep respect for the fast carriers of the Pacific Fleet.

Although "itching to get into a fight," Halsey reported to the hospital. One afternoon Spruance visited him. Halsey lay naked in his bed, his body covered with ointment. Although extremely cheerful, he was uncomfortable, his body itching all over. Rather than talk on war matters, they spoke as old friends, one ailing, the other wishing him a quick recovery.

On 28 May Halsey watched from his hospital window as Spruance's ships sortied. "Missing the Battle of Midway," he said later, "was the greatest disappointment of my life."

The Battle of Midway signaled a turning point in the Pacific war. Personally assuming command, Admiral Yamamoto deployed almost every capital ship of the Japanese Navy. If his force could capture Midway Island, the Japanese could use it as a staging point for air raids to bomb Pearl Harbor. Yamamoto also penciled in Attu and Kiska islands in the western Aleutians as secondary targets, islands which would anchor his northern defense line. But Admiral Yamamoto's primary objective was to lure Nimitz into battle with his numerically inferior fleet.

On 4 June 1942 the carrier battle opened when Japanese fighters splashed thirty-five of the forty-one torpedo bombers in the first attack. Then, American dive bombers hit three Japanese carriers, leaving them blazing and exploding. The fourth enemy carrier, *Hiryu,* launched planes which knocked the *Yorktown* out of commission. American planes struck back and demolished the *Hiryu.* Later a torpedo from a Japanese submarine sank the *Yorktown* as she was under tow.

Losing his four best carriers, Yamamoto ordered his armada around. Midway was safe, but Kiska and Attu had been seized by the Japanese.

The Battle of Midway ended the major Japanese drive across the Pacific and both sides retired to repair their losses. Neither the Japanese nor the Americans could seek open action since neither side could afford more losses.

After the victory at Midway, Washington planned a limited offensive to check further Japanese advances and to guard the line of communication with Australia. On 2 July 1942 the Joint

Chiefs of Staff sent out a directive, declaring that the first major objective in the South Pacific was to capture Rabaul, the big new Japanese base on the island of New Britain in the Bismarck Archipelago. General MacArthur, Allied Commander in the Southwest Pacific, planned to move in a series of swift operations up the Solomon Islands and New Guinea to seize Rabaul. Since his land-based Army Air Force bombers could not reach that point without constructing airfields, MacArthur wanted Nimitz's carriers to cover his flanks. He regarded the carriers as expendable auxiliaries to his advance on Rabaul, a stepping-stone back to the Philippines.

Admirals King and Nimitz declined. Having lost two carriers (*Lexington* in the Coral Sea, *Yorktown* at Midway) and many aircraft, they were hesitant to expose flattops, which needed operating room, to the confined waters of the Solomon Sea where the carriers would be helpless targets for enemy land-based planes and submarines. They also believed it poor strategy to place the few remaining flattops at the disposal of MacArthur, who did not appreciate their uses as mobile, long range strategic capital ships.

The Navy agreed to a compromise in the South Pacific. The Solomons-New Guinea zone was divided into two parts: the South Pacific Force commanded by Nimitz's deputy, Admiral Robert L. Ghormley; and the Southwest Pacific Force, commanded by MacArthur. Both groups would cooperate in a limited offensive toward Rabaul. Immediately, the Navy would deploy its carriers to cover Marine Corps landings at Tulagi and Guadalcanal in the southern Solomons. MacArthur would use the Army, Allied air forces, and his own small Seventh Fleet to move up the Papuan peninsula of New Guinea.

On 7 August 1942, 19,000 leathernecks stormed the beaches of Guadalcanal, Tulagi, and adjacent inlets. Americans and Japanese fought savagely in the steaming, fetid jungles. Soon after the marines hit the beaches, the Japanese fleet inflicted on the United States Navy one of its worst defeats in the Battle of Savo Island near Guadalcanal. Not since the Pearl Harbor attack had American or Allied forces been taken so unaware. In the dead of night Japanese cruisers dashed past American patrol vessels. The destroyer *Patterson* sounded the alarm by voice radio but it was too late. Before Allied ships could bring their guns to bear, Japanese torpedoes had blown off a part of the cruiser *Chicago*'s bow and smashed in the side of the Australian heavy cruiser *Canberra*. The *Patterson* was hit and severely damaged. The cruiser *Astoria* was hit by gunfire. The cruiser *Quincy* capsized. The cruiser *Vincennes* also capsized and sank. Badly impaired, the destroyer *Ralph Talbot* limped back to Tulagi. Suffering only minor damage to their cruisers, the Japanese retired.

At Pearl Harbor the dispatches that flooded in from the South Pacific were confusing. Nimitz realized he had suffered serious losses. He gathered from the requests for more aircraft that there was not enough air cover in the Solomons, but he could do nothing about it. A week and a half after the battle, Nimitz still did not know the extent of the damage, but he was beginning to believe from the South Pacific reports that the outcome of the battle was disastrous. "Our losses were heavy and there is still no explanation why. The enemy seems to have suffered little or no damage. . . ."

The invasion of Guadalcanal had looked easy until the Battle of Savo Island. Yet in the second week in August, Major General A. Archer Vandegrift and his marines realized that the fight was going to be a long and bloody one. The Japanese retained control of the sea and air around Guadalcanal and they were determined to reinforce their troops left on the island.

To send more men and arms into Guadalcanal, Japanese destroyers and small transports steamed to the island at night so regularly that the marines began to refer to them as "The Tokyo Express." After unloading, they would lob shells into the airstrip and be safely out of reach of Marine bombers before daylight.

[IV]

"Jesus Christ and General Jackson!"

B I L L H A L S E Y S P E N T an impatient two months in hospitals at Pearl Harbor and at Richmond, Virginia. Doctors finally certified him to be fit for active duty and, in early September, he was in San Francisco to meet with Admirals King and Nimitz and their advisors, who were there to discuss the Pacific situation. These meetings took place in the Federal Building in the office of Vice Admiral D. W. Bagley. They lasted all day for several days, broken only by luncheons at the Bohemian Club.

King was tough, brilliant, a supreme realist, and a taskmaster who inspired respect. Once an officer gained his confidence, King, writes historian E. B. Potter of the Naval Academy, "would drop his rigid demeanor and could be delightfully informal. . . . His relations with those he admitted into his intimacy were warm and friendly."

At the 8 September meeting, Halsey stepped out of the room momentarily, and King and Nimitz changed the discussion to the deteriorating situation at Guadalcanal. The overall responsibility for the Savo Island defeat fell upon the Commander of the South Pacific Force, Admiral Ghormley. Nimitz and King considered relieving him. King criticized Ghormley severely, especially over the poor night dispositions during the Guadalcanal operations. Had the best use been made of the forces available? No. Had the surprise attack by the Japanese been a result of inefficiency? King thought so. He and Nimitz decided to strengthen the South Pa-

47

cific Force by sending Halsey down as Task Force Commander, a subordinate to Ghormley. Meanwhile, Nimitz said he would check into the Ghormley problem and report back.

The Japanese were about to mount another effort to recapture Guadalcanal. In the Coral Sea where American carriers continued to patrol, enemy submarines were taking a heavy toll. On the last day of August torpedoes ripped into the *Saratoga,* putting her out of commission for three crucial months. Two weeks later, within a quarter of an hour, torpedoes sank the *Wasp* and badly damaged the new battleship *North Carolina* and the destroyer *O'Brien.* That day's series of disasters left the Americans with only one operational carrier, the *Hornet,* and one undamaged new battleship, the *Washington,* in the entire Pacific Ocean. Morale was low and Nimitz was not sure what had to be done to set it right and get operations there moving more quickly. He was cheered, however, by the return of Bill Halsey to the Pacific.

On the 12th, Nimitz invited him to a medal-awarding ceremony on board the *Saratoga* at Pearl Harbor. Nimitz, ordering Halsey to stay out of sight temporarily, stepped to the microphone and said, "Much has been accomplished since those critical days of the war, but much remains to be done. At this moment our forces . . . are . . . stubbornly resisting the powerful efforts of the Japanese to eject us from the hard-won positions in the Southeastern Solomons. Slowly but surely we are tightening our grip—not without losses, but with losses disproportionately small compared with those of the enemy. . . . We have losses, and we must not be dismayed at such prospects. . . . We will win this war only by fighting."

After Nimitz had presented the medals, he went back to the microphone and said, "Now I have a surprise for you" and, turning toward the cabin where Halsey had been waiting, he called, "Come out, Bill!"

When Halsey walked out, his cap, as usual, at a rakish angle, a grin splitting his weather-worn face, officers and men alike forgot decorum and cheered and whistled. A news correspondent wrote, "It is the writer's belief that the American sailor is the straightest-shooting, best naval fighting man in the world when he is led by officers in whom he has confidence. Of all the admirals afloat in the Pacific, this correspondent believes, none would be more certain to inspire their loyalty and command their respect than Admiral Halsey. His return to active command is the best news for months.''

Until Halsey organized his staff for the South Pacific, he was placed on temporary duty at Pearl Harbor.

Meanwhile, Nimitz and members of his staff flew out of Pearl Harbor in a Coronado flying boat for an inspection tour of the South Pacific. On 28 September at Noumea harbor, New Caledonia, they were on board Admiral Ghormley's flagship, the *Argonne*. In the flag mess Ghormley sat at the head of a green-baize-covered dining table. Nimitz was on one side, along with General Omar Pfeiffer, who worked in CINCPAC's War Plans Section. Across the table were Ghormley's staff officers. Nimitz asked Ghormley probing questions about logistics, air support, and morale. He wanted to know who was responsible for the dispositions and actions in the Battle of Savo Island. ''Such a blow cannot be passed over, and we owe it to the country to do our best to fix responsibility for that disaster, and to take the action necessary to prevent a recurrence.''

Admiral Daniel J. Callaghan, Ghormley's Chief of Staff, came into the room with a dispatch which he handed to Ghormley. He scanned it and muttered, ''My God, what are we going to do about this?'' Then a communications officer entered with another message. Ghormley pushed away with evident distaste the first dispatch to read the second. ''My God,'' he said, ''what are we going to do about this?'' ''Nimitz,'' said Pfeiffer, ''was thus able personally to observe the decision-making ability or non-ability of his then-subordinate in command of the South Pacific Area.''

After visiting various island facilities, Nimitz returned to New Caledonia and resumed his discussions with Ghormley. The more questions Nimitz posed, the more Ghormley squirmed. Back at Pearl Harbor Nimitz's intelligence staff were writing a summary of South Pacific operations. ''The situation . . . is far from satisfactory. We are strengthening our positions in the southern SOLOMONS but the logistic and personnel replacement programs remain to be put on a satisfactory basis. . . . There is overwhelming evidence that the enemy's intention is to try to cut us

off from Australia and then capture or neutralize that continent.
. . . The enemy's most probable next moves are the recapture of
the southern Solomons, and the extension of control in New
Guinea. It now seems that the effort in the Solomons and in New
Guinea will be in the nature of a gradual infiltration followed by a
major assault. Whether the final effort in the Solomons will be
concurrent with that in New Guinea is not known.''

Nimitz arrived back in Pearl Harbor distressed about the
morale problem in the South Pacific, and Admiral Ghormley's performance. On 8 October he sent a letter to Ghormley
saying that Halsey would soon be arriving in Noumea. Halsey
would inspect the South Pacific area first, and then take command
of Task Force Sixteen. Halsey, Nimitz said, would be under
Ghormley's operational control as long as he was in the South
Pacific.

On 11 October an American force was patrolling an area not
far from Cape Esperance in the Solomon Sea. That night it
engaged Japanese surface units. The destroyer *Duncan* was sunk,
the cruiser *Boise* was hit, and the *Salt Lake City* damaged. The
enemy lost the heavy cruiser *Furutaka* and the destroyer *Fubuki*.
Two more Japanese destroyers were sunk the next day. The victory boosted American morale, but it failed to prevent the enemy
from escorting more ships loaded with troops and guns to Guadalcanal.

On 13 October Japanese battleships bombarded American-held
Henderson Field on Guadalcanal. On the next day six Japanese
transports landed soldiers on Guadalcanal in broad daylight.

At Pearl Harbor, leafing through the dispatches, Nimitz concluded that American forces could not gain command of the sea
in the southern Solomons. Although ''the situation was not hopeless, it was critical.'' On 15 October Nimitz and his staff discussed the entire South Pacific operation and considered the possibility of relieving Admiral Ghormley, who, in their opinion,
was not aggressive enough.

Nimitz wanted his staff, who had been with him at Noumea, to
give their opinion of the command situation there. Those officers
who had noted Ghormley's reaction to the two dispatches were so
emphatic in their opinion that Nimitz said, ''All right, I'm going

to poll you" and he pointed to each staff member and said, "Is it time for me to relieve Admiral Ghormley?" Each officer replied, "Yes."

Nimitz sent a dispatch, highest priority for "King Eyes Only," asking for authority to detach Ghormley from command and to order Halsey to replace him.

That same night King answered, "Affirmative."

On that same day, 15 October, a Navy Coronado had taken off from Pearl Harbor, carrying Halsey and a few of his staff for an inspection tour of the South Pacific. At Canton Island, Halsey was handed a dispatch from Ghormley, suggesting that Halsey bypass his planned itinerary and proceed immediately to Noumea. Halsey replied that he intended to keep to his schedule and sent a copy to Nimitz. An officer awakened Halsey at 0200 the next morning to read Nimitz's answer: PROCEED SUVA AND NOUMEA.

During the afternoon of the 18th, the clumsy flying boat, dipping sharply, began its steep descent into Noumea's lagoon. Because of the chop, it hit the water hard, bounced twice, and pushed to taxiing speed as it neared the mooring. As Halsey emerged from the Coronado's wide flung hatch, a whaleboat came alongside and Ghormley's flag lieutenant saluted and handed the admiral a sealed envelope. Inside it was a second sealed envelope marked SECRET. Halsey ripped it open. The dispatch from Nimitz read, YOU WILL TAKE COMMAND OF THE SOUTH PACIFIC AREA AND SOUTH PACIFIC FORCES IMMEDIATELY.

Halsey reread the dispatch, then said, "Jesus Christ and General Jackson! This is the hottest potato they ever handed me!" It was an entire new poker game for Bill Halsey.

Back in Pearl Harbor, Nimitz told reporters, "For his effect on morale, Bill Halsey is worth a division of fast battleships."

The whaleboat took Halsey across the lagoon to the flagship, *Argonne*. He met Ghormley as he stepped on the quarter-deck. Ghormley, shaking hands warmly, remarked, "This is a tough job they've given you, Bill."

Halsey replied, "I damn well know it!" Halsey regretted relieving Ghormley, who had been a friend for forty years, ever since the days when they had played together on the Naval Academy football team.

Ghormley arrived in Pearl Harbor, extremely upset about the manner in which he had been relieved and called on Nimitz.

"Bob," said Nimitz, "I had to pick from the whole Navy the man best fitted to handle that situation. Were you that man?"

"No," replied Ghormley. "If you put it that way, I guess I wasn't."

Later Nimitz secured Ghormley's appointment as commander of the Fourteenth Naval District in Hawaii.

The coming of Halsey to the South Pacific was a shot of adrenalin to morale. Now, said the marines and sailors, operations would get cracking.

The press was delighted with the appointment. Headlines in the New York *Times* proclaimed, "Halsey Replaces Ghormley in the Solomons—Pacific Command Shake-Up Is Laid to Guadalcanal Crisis—Shift to Offensive Is Seen in Washington in Selection of 'Fighting' Admiral Halsey as Commander in the South Pacific."

The *Times* reported that Halsey now had "direct responsibility for pursuing the Solomons attack" and could be "expected to turn the venture from a currently defensive operation into an aggressive fight."

Halsey himself was apprehensive. He knew little about the military and naval situation in the South Pacific except that it "was desperate." "Ashore on Guadalcanal," Halsey said, "our troops are locked in a savage struggle to maintain their foothold. A crisis is obviously imminent and we will have to meet it." The admiral acknowledged that the war against Japan might be the largest and deadliest in human history. How could the Japanese ever be dislodged from their "unsinkable carriers," the chain of islands swarming with land-based planes?

"I early placed emphasis on the principle of unity of command," Halsey wrote. "I insisted that each commander of a task force must have full authority over all components of his force, regardless of service or nationality. I believe the wholehearted efforts of all hands to create one South Pacific fighting team proved the key to success in overcoming many obstacles in the conduct of later operations, involving the use of Task Forces of varied compositions.''

Halsey's slogan was ''Kill Japs, Kill Japs, Kill More Japs.'' No sailor or marine in the South Pacific forgot it. The slogan was painted on buildings, hung over the fleet landing at Tulagi, and in a few common urinals in Officers Clubs throughout the South Pacific.

Halsey's ''Keep 'em dying'' attitude, his ''bloodthirstiness,'' was not just a put-on to gain headlines. He strongly believed that by denigrating the enemy he was counteracting the myth of Japanese martial superiority which developed in the wake of Pearl Harbor and the early Japanese victories in the Pacific. His bellicose statements made him a symbol of combative leadership, a vocal Japanese-hater. He was outspoken because he believed that the vast majority of the soldiers and sailors in his command was buoyed by his disparagement of the enemy.

His assessment of the morale factor was at variance with that of Admiral Spruance, who later said, ''I did not think we should call our enemies a lot of names the way Bill does.'' To Spruance, belittling the fighting capabilities of the Japanese was no way to prepare the country for the long and hard war which lay ahead.

Since it was impossible for Halsey to leave Noumea for a trip to the Guadalcanal front, he ordered men who knew the situation best to fly to New Caledonia to describe their predicament. They met on board the *Argonne* on the night of 20 October. General Vandegrift, commanding the Marine division on Guadalcanal, told bitter stories. As Halsey sat smoking, Vandegrift reviewed the campaign. He impressed upon Halsey the poor physical condition of the marines—the inevitable result of two and a half months of restricted diet, sleepless nights, and diseases, and underscored the effect of frequent surface and air bombardments.

Halsey asked, ''Are we going to evacuate or hold?''

Vandegrift answered, ''I can hold, but I've got to have more active support than I've been getting.''

Halsey nodded, ''You go back there, Vandegrift. I promise to get you everything I have.''

Halsey delayed construction of an air base on Ndeni in the

Santa Cruz Islands and dispatched Army troops destined to occupy that island to Guadalcanal instead. Another airfield to be built at Aola Bay on Guadalcanal was also canceled. Construction crews who had already started work there were sent to reinforce Vandegrift's forces near Henderson Field on Guadalcanal.

As Halsey analyzed the problem, Guadalcanal was the key to the entire campaign in the South Pacific. The Japanese were pouring in men and materiel almost nightly and sending submarines, planes, and surface units to sever the American supply line. They also were massing a powerful armada—four carriers, four battleships, twoscore cruisers and destroyers, together with transports and auxiliaries. To counter them, Halsey had his Third Fleet. Admiral Norman Scott commanded two cruisers, three destroyers, and the battleship *Washington*. Admiral George D. Murray's force included the *Hornet,* cruisers *Northampton, Pensacola, San Diego,* and *Juneau* and the destroyers *Morris, Anderson, Hughes, Austin, Russell,* and *Barton*. A third task force built around the *Enterprise* and battleship *South Dakota* was en route from Pearl Harbor.

The situation was grave. "I would have," recalled Halsey, "a motif of a rusty nail and a frayed shoestring. It was certainly the way we felt about it in those days and we had very little prospects of getting anything more. There was a great feeling among all hands that the South Pacific Forces were forgotten men."

Although Halsey realized that Allied strategy was to defeat Germany first and Japan second, he said, "It is hard to convince those of us . . . why we should not have some of the gravy that is being shipped in great quantities to Europe."

Halsey did not know it, but Roosevelt was also concerned. In a memo of 24 October to the Joint Chiefs of Staff, the President wrote, "My anxiety about the Southwest Pacific is to make sure that every possible weapon gets into that area to hold Guadalcanal."

At 1245 on the 24th the *Enterprise*'s group met the *Hornet*'s northeast of the New Hebrides. Halsey now had a fighting chance. He sent the combined carrier forces northward to a position off the Santa Cruz Islands, where they would be beyond reach of the enemy's land-based aircraft, yet capable of hitting the Japanese flank when they closed on Guadalcanal.

The battle ashore on Guadalcanal intensified. Before dawn on 25 October, enemy cruisers and destroyers landed more troops and supplies, then bombarded the island. American dive bombers from Henderson Field on Guadalcanal and B-17s from Espiritu Santo scored direct hits on a cruiser and a destroyer.

American patrol planes reported enemy surface forces moving southward. From Noumea Halsey ordered Rear Admiral Scott's *Washington* force to sweep around Savo Island. They failed to discover the enemy but, to Halsey, "action was now . . . obviously a matter of hours." He sent a dispatch to all units: AT-TACK REPEAT ATTACK. The admiral anxiously watched the outlines of the operation take shape.

The Battle of Santa Cruz, 26 October, was a carrier duel. The Japanese jumped Halsey's forces by launching planes twenty minutes before the Americans did. The enemy concentrated on the *Hornet* force. Five bombs hit the *Hornet*'s flight deck, several dropping deep into the hull before detonating. Torpedoes ripped in and exploded in her engine spaces. The *Hornet,* dead in the water, was ablaze and listing. Her planes, far to the northwest, broke through enemy air patrols to pummel the cruiser *Chikuma* and knock the carrier *Shokaku* out of commission.

Japanese planes discovered the *Enterprise* group. Savage anti-aircraft fire, especially from the *South Dakota,* limited damage to the *Enterprise*. A bomb wiped out a turret on the *South Dakota*. A torpedo plane smashed into the deck of an American destroyer. The *San Juan* was damaged.

The crippled *Hornet,* left without air cover, became the primary target of repeated air strikes. The flattop listed dangerously. The commander ordered "Abandon Ship." Two destroyers were left to sink the carrier, but they failed and, when darkness fell, they retired. The Japanese force approached the blazing *Hornet,* but, unable to take her in tow, sent her to the bottom.

In the Battle of Santa Cruz, the American forces received the heaviest blows, but the Japanese lost 100 planes, the Americans but seventy-four. To Halsey this meant that the enemy's four air groups on its carriers had been cut to pieces and that the Japanese naval forces would be unable to provide effective support of their troops on Guadalcanal. The battle also convinced Halsey of the absurdity of operating flattops in confined waters, so he ordered the last carrier, *Enterprise,* to retire southward.

Though Halsey's forces had, at a very heavy price, won important long-term gains, it was the soldiers and marines on Guadalcanal who saved the immediate situation. They held firm while the Japanese attack rose to a crescendo and finally petered out on the 26th. Henderson Field remained in American hands, and enemy casualties were roughly ten times the American losses. Enemy ground forces would no longer pose so serious a threat.

Despite the losses incurred in the Battle of Santa Cruz on 31 October, Halsey promised Nimitz that "it will be my utmost endeavor to patch up what we have and go with them. In other words I will not send any ship back to Pearl Harbor unless it is absolutely necessary."

"As you may well imagine," continued Halsey, "I was completely taken aback when I received your orders on my arrival here. I took over a strange job with a strange staff and I had to begin throwing punches almost immediately."

"We need tankers and more tankers and more tankers," he reiterated. His forces needed repair ships and repairmen. "The biggest and best thing is the army. They have made available to us various mechanics, electricians and welders, and I would like to see it widely advertised that the army is helping us here. I have never seen anything like the spirit there is in this neck of the woods. It is a real United States service.

"We are in need of everything we can get, planes, ships, escort vessels, men, and so on ad nauseam. You are well aware of our needs and this is not offered in complaint or as an excuse but just to keep the pot boiling. We are not in the least downhearted or upset by our difficulties, but obsessed with one idea only, to kill the yellow bastards and we shall do it. . . ."

In another letter to Nimitz, Halsey said, "I never thought that you could get me working but you really have. And how I am enjoying it. The days are not long enough for everything we feel we should do, but somehow we muddle along. Have been able to get ashore each afternoon about 5 or frequently not before 6. If early enough I take a walk. It gives me a chance to reorient myself. . . .

"It will be necessary, and very shortly, to put in a request for a number of officers. I am not trying to pad things, but the need for experienced Naval officers here is crying. . . . My growls and grouches are the privileges of an old sailor-man." And he repeated, "We are not in the least downhearted and are going to continue to lick hell out of the yellow bastards."

During the lull in operations Halsey decided to tour Guadalcanal as he wanted to get a first-hand impression, unobtainable from scanning reports. General Vandegrift remembered that Halsey "flew in like a wonderful breath of fresh air." During the tour of the area, Halsey showed extreme interest and enthusiasm in all phases of the Marines' operations, concurring with Vandegrift's existing positions and future plans. More importantly, Halsey talked to large numbers of leathernecks, and saw their gaunt, malaria-ridden bodies, their faces lined from what seemed a "nightmare of years," "the most fatigued looking men I have ever encountered."

Halsey could not say enough in praise of these Marines who invaded the island and held without reinforcements for more than a month. He was especially proud of the Army, Navy, and Marine fliers who controlled the air over the island against heavy odds. "I think they are the most superb gang of people I have ever known. I knew they were good, but they are so damn good they have surprised the hell out of me." He said to them, "Kill Japs, kill Japs, and keep on killing Japs." He predicted that "eventual victory will not be won without an invasion of the Japanese home islands. I hope so. I want to be there."

The next morning Halsey, standing in front of Vandegrift's headquarters, decorated thirteen officers and men of the Marines who had distinguished themselves in the recent fight. He said, "I wish to God that every man, woman, and child in our great country could know and see what you are doing. God bless you." As he pinned on the medals, Halsey had a word of praise for each man. To Private Joseph D. Champayne, who had won the Navy Cross, Halsey expressed the conviction that "you will undoubtedly be more than a private the next time I come here."

At Fleet Headquarters in Pearl Harbor, Nimitz sensed that Halsey had turned the situation around in less than a month. "The situation is critical," Nimitz wrote, "but the determination, efficiency, and morale of our people there is so fine that even the most pessimistic critics must concede that we will win out in the end. . . ."

"It is now definite that the enemy suffered heavy attrition losses during October," he continued, "and considerable damage to striking forces on October 25th. Thus, they could not continue what seems to have been the start of a grand scale attack on GUADALCANAL. While the enemy may still retain the balance of sea power in the SOLOMONS area, the margin seems too small to risk a grand offensive."

To King, Nimitz wrote: "We are more than justified in having made the change in that area."

When Halsey returned to Noumea on 9 November, after inspecting a base hospital at Efate, Miles Browning was waiting with news that the enemy was already mounting an offensive. Intelligence reported that planes would strike Guadalcanal on the 11th; naval forces would bombard Henderson Field on the 12th; and, after a carrier raid on the 13th, ground forces would land. Reports indicated that the enemy fleet included two carriers, four battleships, five cruisers, thirty destroyers, twenty transports with 20,000 troops. The Japanese intended to retake Guadalcanal.

Halsey's units consisted of Admiral Scott's force of one cruiser and four destroyers, which was escorting cargo vessels to Guadalcanal. Admiral R. Kelly Turner had two cruisers and four destroyers, also protecting a convoy moving toward the island. Admiral Daniel J. Callaghan's force of three cruisers and six destroyers planned to rendezvous with Turner on 11 November. Admiral Willis A. ("Ching") Lee's group—the battleships *South Dakota* and *Washington,* two cruisers, and eight destroyers—was still moored at Noumea, where the *South Dakota* was undergoing repairs. This group, however, was about ready to sail.

If the Japanese kept on schedule, Halsey realized that his supply vessels would have to discharge and retire from Guadalcanal before the night of the 12th so that the fighting ships could be free of that responsibility.

Scott's ships began unloading at their anchorage off Lunga Point at 0530 on 11 November. The enemy struck with dive bombers. Anti-aircraft fire shot them all down, but three cargo vessels were hit, one seriously. While the ships continued to unload, Scott moved his warships into Indispensable Strait and joined Callaghan's unit, which had cruised ahead of Turner's. They swept eastward and westward of Savo Island, but failing to flush out the enemy, they retired at dawn on the 12th to protect the unloading of Turner's transports at Kukum Beach.

The Japanese had already brought their fleet down from Truk to a position north of Santa Isabel Island. Admiral Kondo dispatched Vice Admiral Hiroaki Abe southward with his bombardment group.

Scout planes notified Turner of the approaching enemy force. Turner hurried the unloading and might have finished by nightfall, but work was interrupted for two hours to fight off a strike of torpedo planes. Turner's transports were ninety percent empty when he ordered them withdrawn, escorted by destroyers and minesweepers.

Callaghan was left with the heavy cruisers *San Francisco* (flagship) and *Portland,* and the light cruisers *Atlanta* (Scott's flagship), *Helena,* and *Juneau,* and eight destroyers. Callaghan failed to issue a battle plan or to provide for any means of scouting ahead. The Americans faced overwhelming odds.

On board the *Argonne* in Noumea, Halsey fully realized a battle was brewing. He hoped that the action of Callaghan would delay the Japanese long enough for them to be within reach of the *Enterprise*'s planes the next day, 13 November.

Halsey glanced at the words on little slips of yellow paper clipped into cardboard folders, reports from his battle forces. One news correspondent remembered that Halsey's face was "like a battlefield." Time after time Halsey said, "Now if these were Japs, this is how I would strike."

"The waiting was hard," Halsey said of the night of 12/13 November. "I walked the decks, re-examined reports and charts, and conferred with my staff. I must have drunk a gallon of coffee and smoked two packs of cigarettes. When the tension became unbearable, I skimmed through the trashiest magazine I could find.''

Under a moonless but starry sky Callaghan's force moved into Lengo Channel at midnight. Radar picked up three groups of enemy ships. Almost before the Americans knew it, their column steamed into the Japanese forces. Suddenly guns roared, and Callaghan was under fire at point blank range. Methodically, the Japanese and American ships pumped salvo after salvo.

The action lasted twenty-four minutes. All formations broke and the engagement became a series of individual actions. After the battle, the forces retired, each side desperately battered. The enemy lost two destroyers, and the battleship *Hiei,* struck by more than fifty shells, was helpless north of Savo, where planes from Henderson Field raked her over until she sank. Admirals Callaghan and Scott were both killed. Four American destroyers were lost. The cruiser *Portland* and a destroyer lay dead in the water. The riddled and blazing *Atlanta* had to be sunk. The *Juneau,* retreating from the melee, was torpedoed and sank with the loss of 700 men. All but one of the other American ships were damaged. But the United States Navy, despite the odds, had by sheer courage carried out its objective—turning back the Japanese battlewagons and transports.

The Japanese were not finished. Admiral Gunichi Mikawa's Cruiser Bombardment Group in the early hours of 14 November shelled Guadalcanal. By daybreak American scout planes reported two Japanese forces—the Cruiser Bombardment Group and the Reinforcement Group with its transports. The *Enterprise*'s planes, shuttling out of the airfield at Guadalcanal together with the bombers, swarmed down on the Japanese cruisers, sinking one and damaging three others. Joined by Army B-17s from Espiritu Santo, they hit repeatedly the Reinforcement Group. The planes sank seven transports carrying 1,000 soldiers each. But with remarkable valor the Japanese pushed on toward Guadalcanal with four damaged transports.

Another force—the battleship *Kirishima,* four cruisers, and nine destroyers—headed southward. They blasted *Washington* and *South Dakota* and four destroyers. During the night there were bright flashes all down the Japanese battle line. Two American destroyers were knocked out of commission. To avoid colliding with the crippled destroyers, the *Washington* swerved while the *South Dakota* shifted to starboard toward the enemy. The broadsides of the *Kirishima* and two heavy cruisers broke loose on the *South Dakota*. The battleship staggered under the blows. Shells tore huge holes in her superstructure, driving red hot fragments everywhere. The *South Dakota* retired from action.

The *Washington* faced the entire Japanese fleet. Her five- and sixteen-inch guns crashed out against the *Kirishima*. Splashes and flashes, smoke and spray made the *Kirishima*'s outline uncertain. But after seven minutes, the Japanese battlewagon was helpless. The *Washington* withdrew to the south. Admiral Kondo ordered the *Kirishima* and a battered destroyer to retreat northward.

Minutes after the American victory was confirmed, Halsey sent a message to every unit in his command. The word went out by radio, by signal blinker, by hand courier to all men who served under him. YOUR NAMES HAVE BEEN WRITTEN IN GOLDEN LETTERS ON THE PAGES OF HISTORY, AND YOU HAVE WON THE EVER-LASTING GRATITUDE OF YOUR COUNTRYMEN X MY PRIDE IN YOU IS BEYOND EXPRESSION.

The Japanese campaign to retake Guadalcanal, which triggered numerous battles, was complicated. The important naval events can be summarized as follows. On 7 August the marines invaded Guadalcanal and, two days later, the United States Navy sustained serious losses in the Battle of Savo Island. In mid-October in the Battle of Cape Esperance, the destroyer *Duncan* was sunk, and the cruisers *Boise* and *Salt Lake City* were damaged. The Japanese lost three destroyers in this surface action and one heavy cruiser. On 18 October Halsey relieved Ghormley. In the Battle of Santa Cruz Islands, a carrier action, the *Hornet* was lost.

During November there were more surface actions. On the 13th the Japanese lost two destroyers and the battleship *Hiei*, while four American destroyers and the cruisers *Atlanta* and *Ju-*

neau were sunk. Admirals Callaghan and Scott were killed. In another battle the *South Dakota* and *Kirishima* sustained heavy damage. The latter finally sank.

The Japanese failed to reconquer Guadalcanal because, in essence, they could never transport sufficient manpower, artillery, and supplies to the island to wrest Henderson Field from the entrenched Americans. By mid-November the enemy's situation there was hopeless.

[V]

"We Are Well Dug In"

G U A D A L C A N A L   W A S   S A V E D . The enemy risked no more capital ships in the Solomons campaign.

At Pearl Harbor, Nimitz initialed CINCPAC War Diary for 15 November: "It is now definite that the enemy offensive was completely stopped. It is probable that damage we inflicted on the enemy is greater than received by us. The striking forces of both sides have retired from the Guadalcanal area and can hardly be in large scale action in the near future."

Vandegrift on Guadalcanal hurried a dispatch to Halsey: TO SCOTT, CALLAGHAN, AND THEIR MEN GOES OUR GREATEST HOMAGE X WITH MAGNIFICENT COURAGE AGAINST SEEMINGLY HOPELESS ODDS, THEY DROVE BACK THE FIRST HOSTILE STROKE AND MADE SUCCESS POSSIBLE X TO THEM THE MEN OF GUADALCANAL LIFT THEIR BATTERED HELMETS IN DEEPEST ADMIRATION.

"With the Navy's victory . . . came the turning point of the war," Halsey recalled. "Japanese aggression was stopped."

After the Americans' feat at Guadalcanal, Halsey became a focus of hope. A new confidence gripped the forces fighting in the South Pacific. Nimitz acknowledged this: "Halsey's conduct of his present command leaves nothing to be desired. He is professionally competent and militarily aggressive without being reckless or foolhardy. . . . He possesses superb leadership qualities which have earned him the tremendous following of his men. His only enemies are Japs. . . . For his successful turning back of the Jap attempt to take Guadalcanal . . . he has been nominated by the President for the rank of Admiral, which reward he richly deserves.''

At a press conference at Pearl Harbor, Nimitz asserted that the "victory surpassed anything of the kind that the United States Navy had done before in its history." He stated that "the United States [had] eliminated the immediate danger to our hold on Guadalcanal so that now we can begin the reinforcement, consolidation and onward offensives." When one reporter replied that the Navy was still "behind the eight ball," Nimitz retorted, "I'd say we've gotten some distance away from the eight ball now." Nimitz continued, "Needless to say, we are delighted with what transpired, but it was no more than we expected of Admiral Halsey, his officers and men, and our ships, planes and all the Army, Navy and Marine forces. I am sure this action will result in an immediate strengthening of our hold on the area we now control on Guadalcanal and the eventual expulsion of the enemy from the island."

A reporter mused that the Japanese were undoubtedly holding a conference at Rabaul. Nimitz replied, "I'd hate to sit in on that— I'd hate to have to explain what they have to."

One correspondent concluded that the Navy in the Pacific had "entered a new phase, in which 'attack' was the watchword."

In Washington President Roosevelt, at his regular Tuesday press conference, termed the engagement in the Solomons as "a major victory, to the Navy itself, where outward confidence had been greatly nullified by doubts as to the manner in which the Navy would meet formidable Japanese odds. Those doubts no longer exist."

The Secretary of the Navy wrote Halsey, "The whole nation has been lifted and inspired by the magnificent victory which you and your men and those of the Army and Marine Corps have won over a powerful enemy whose forces exceeded your own in ships and men. Speaking for myself and for the entire Navy, I wish to convey to you the thrill of satisfaction and pride which the service feels as a result of the resolution and courage displayed. Our gallant exploits of recent days have enriched the record of the American Navy for all time."

Halsey replied, "I have received your kind message . . . and have passed it on to the gallant men who have fought so courageously. In the Southern Pacific neither we of the Navy nor those of the Army and Marine Corps recognize any division between the services. All are united in service to the United States. It is with a feeling of humility for myself as their commander and a deep sense of pride for our heroes of this service that I accept your generous tribute."

At Melbourne, Australia, Prime Minister John Curtin, remarking on the Solomon Island naval victory, said, "These forces are carrying out gallantly resistance which has the immediate effect of sparing our cities from raids."

In Noumea Halsey grieved over the loss of American lives. In answer to a mother who had lost a son on the cruiser *Juneau,* Halsey wrote, "Words are of little avail, either in bringing you real help and comfort at this time or in expressing our own feelings when face to face with one of the war's many tragic situations. I know what Frederick's loss means to you and Mr. Bainbridge and I confess that this sad picture of a home mourning for a son missing somewhere in action is perhaps the heaviest burden of one who finds himself in command of so many in time of war."

"The *Juneau* went down in action, suddenly," Halsey continued, "thus the loss of life was extremely high, leaving few survivors. . . . I want you and all of Frederick's friends to know that he was at a hero's station . . . a member of a gun crew, serving his country nobly and bravely at the time the *Juneau* was destroyed. There is no medal which could be given you in his memory which could commensurate with what he has given. . . . In closing I would speak again of how insufficient I know words to bring consolation to your home in this dark and lonely hour."

At the same time, Halsey was deluged with congratulatory letters. In answer to a friend's letter, he replied, "These yellow bastards are beasts alright and it's not me, but the greatest fighting men this country ever produced that are teaching them their manners. . . . We are trying to keep our swords sharp on these yellow bellied sons of bitches and will continue to give them Hell every time they want it. The day is not in the too distant future when we will be able to go after them and kick them off the face of the earth. In order to save the world, I am going to advocate at the peace table for the yellow bellies that are left—emasculation for the males and spaying for the females."

In answer to a letter from a naval friend, Halsey wrote, "You know and I know how much luck enters into this. I am surrounded by excellent people who do the planning and the 'fightingest' fighting men this country has ever produced to do the fighting. With such a gang to use it would be difficult not to accomplish something. I feel, however, that I am getting too much recognition and that they are not getting enough. I hope that we can soon get together again and hoist a few for old times sake and to each other."

Washington promptly promoted Halsey to four stars. Secretary Knox termed Halsey "One of the few great naval leaders of history." This promotion to admiral placed Halsey on a par with Nimitz and made him the sixth full admiral.*

American surface forces in the South Pacific increased in numbers. The *Enterprise, Washington,* and the cruiser *San Diego* were moored at Noumea. Anchored at Nandi in the Fijis were the *Saratoga,* the battleships *North Carolina, Colorado,* and *Maryland,* and the cruiser *San Juan.* The cruisers *Northampton, Pensacola, New Orleans, Minneapolis,* and *Honolulu* were at Espiritu Santo.

After the Guadalcanal action Halsey, although an advocate of fast carrier striking power, strongly believed that the day of the battleship was "far from a thing of the past. . . . They certainly inflicted terrific damage. . . . The use we made of them defied all conventions; narrow waters, submarine menace, and destroyers. . . ." The admiral was impressed by the actions of the crews of the PT boats, combatting Japanese destroyers. "The young fellows are full of 'pee and ginger.' "

---

* The other full admirals were King, Harold R. Stark (Commander Naval Forces Europe), William Leahy (Chief of Staff to the President), and Royal Ingersoll (Commander of the Atlantic Fleet).

The Japanese prepared a new defensive line by constructing a pair of airfields on Kolombangara and New Georgia in the central Solomons. They maintained their garrison on Guadalcanal merely to frustrate the marines and soldiers. Japanese destroyers kept it alive by floating drums of supplies offshore and then hurrying northward before daylight. To halt these operations, Halsey dispatched cruisers and destroyers. Southeast of Savo Island, Americans sank one enemy destroyer in the Battle of Tassafaronga on 30 November. Tragically, the *Northampton* was torpedoed and went down. Three other American cruisers were also torpedoed, but managed to sneak back into port. Halsey was dissatisfied. "I see nothing to criticize from the reports submitted, but I have an intuitive feeling it was not well handled." The engagement was Japan's last surface effort against Guadalcanal. Except for desultory aid brought the beleaguered Japanese troops by destroyers, they were abandoned to die from disease or starvation or at the hands of the marines and soldiers.

After Tassafaronga there was a lull. "It is the first breathing spell we had," Halsey wrote Nimitz. Halsey could now turn his attention for the first time to organizing his command and settling in for the long struggle ahead. He believed strongly in delegating authority. He called in his staff and said, "There's a lot to be done. Look around, see what it is, and do it." Yet the "job swamped even them, and I had to supply them with more assistants." The overcrowded *Argonne* was hopelessly inadequate for the increase in personnel.

Commanding Destroyer Division Forty-Three, Arleigh Burke was deeply concerned about his ships, which were badly in need of overhaul. The destroyers had been "fighting some tough battles without major maintenance, and were in rough shape; just about everything that could go wrong with them already had." Also, morale had suffered. To make matters worse, the battle-weary men had no beer, no whiskey, no recreation. Burke bombarded Halsey's office with letters, "raising hell because we weren't getting what we needed." Burke did not know it, but Halsey had no choice. He had nothing to give anybody and was only too aware that his thin line of ships stood between the marines on Guadalcanal and disaster.

In desperation Burke drew up orders sending the ships to Sydney for repairs and radioed Halsey that they were leaving. Back came the reply: "Keep them in the Solomons."

A boiler on the destroyer *Saufley* was in such bad shape that Burke finally decided to send her to Sydney without telling Halsey. The men and officers in Burke's command collected money and gave it to the *Saufley*'s skipper. While the destroyer's boiler was being repaired, he would buy beer and whiskey for the entire squadron.

Only when the *Saufley* was on her way back to the Solomons did Burke tell Halsey what he had done. A message soon arrived, asking Burke to drop in on the admiral next time he happened to be in Noumea.

When the commander walked into Halsey's office, he found the admiral seated with his back to the door, staring at the bulkhead. Halsey turned around and said, "Oh, Burke." He looked down at some scribbled notes on his desk. "*Saufley*," he muttered. Suddenly, he sat bolt upright and looked straight at Burke.

"Why in God's name did you take it in your own hands to send the *Saufley* to Sydney?"

"Sir," Burke began, "my boys haven't had any beer or whiskey for months."

"You mean," Halsey interrupted, "you sent that ship down for *booze?*"

"Yes, sir, the captain did pick up a lot of liquor, but. . . ."

Halsey's face relaxed. "All right, Burke, you win. Your boys have been doing a great job, and I can't condemn you for going out on a limb for them. But don't do it again."

Halsey leveled his finger at Burke and continued. "If you had told me that you sent *Saufley* for *repairs*, I'd have had your hide."

"That's when I knew," recalled Burke, "I would follow Admiral William Halsey anywhere in this world and beyond. And so would thousands of other sailors, from the lowliest apprentice right on up the line."

Halsey and his staff eventually established themselves on Noumea in a cluster of buildings constituting "a miniature International Settlement"—two Quonset huts (nicknamed "Wicky-Wacky Lodge"), a run-down house ("Havoc Hall"), and the former Japanese consulate. "We are well dug in," Halsey wrote to Nimitz. "I wish the Mikado could know that I am occupying the house of his former Consul at this port. We are enjoying his silverware, china, and many other comforts. Unfortunately the furniture (chairs, sofa, etc.) was designed for those bandy legged bastards. We must perforce sit on the back of our necks." The house was thoroughly comfortable and modern and it had a magnificent view of the harbor.

"The Harbor," wrote a commander just arrived, "is full of ships, many merchantmen among them. Dock facilities are poor, at best, and long delays in unloading are the result. The facilities of the Army, Navy and Marine Corps ashore are crude to say the least. In comparison, Reykjavik, Iceland, is Nirvana."

"What a dump!" he wrote the next day, after inspecting Noumea. "Splay-footed Melanesians chattering a patois, some fly-blown stores with their shelves empty, and a general air of dejected lassitude prevail."

Halsey assembled a first-rate set of advisors, efficient, hardworking, intelligent. Decision-making was uncomplicated.

"The Admiral and his staff," wrote Captain Ralph Wilson, a staff member, "were a team in the truest sense. He kept himself fully informed of all important details. He expected his staff to handle normal routine and make minor decisions, but was quick to override if his judgment dictated." Major decisions were reached after informal discussions with key members of the staff. Each participant had full opportunity to be heard in a warm, friendly atmosphere. "Halsey made the ultimate decision," continued Wilson, "but in a manner which made each individual present feel he had a part in it. It was the smoothest organization I have ever experienced."

Once a decision was made, it meant "get going." Halsey's staff labored hard and enjoyed being called "The Dirty Tricks Department."

Later in the war a British officer went to see Halsey. He arrived at sundown and discovered the admiral sitting on the veranda, barefoot, dressed only in shorts and khaki shirt without insignia. Halsey mixed a cocktail for the visitor and sat and swatted mosquitoes as they talked. "I remember," said the Britisher, "thinking that he might well have been a parson, a jolly one, an old time farmer, a Long John Silver. But when I left him and thought of what he had said, I realized that I had been listening to one of the great officers of the war."

Bill Halsey was not one of the Navy's intellectuals. His official reports are couched in commonplace. His speeches, private correspondence, and reports reveal that he often thought in clichés, that his vocabulary was narrow, and that he had trouble with syntax. His letters confirm his contempt for the Japanese in locker-room jargon. Despite his sophomoric shortcomings, he had the knack of appointing extremely intelligent officers to his staff upon whom he relied for decision making. On only rare occasions did he overrule them.

"Another of Halsey's traits," remembered another staffer, "was the fierceness with which he defended his staff, even his men. He gave them credit for the victories won, he blamed himself for the losses." He would ship out officers who "goofed" assignments or who displayed disloyalty to him, but a loyal officer, who did his job, Halsey vigorously defended.

"Halsey possessed to a magnificent degree," said Arleigh Burke, "the intuition that let him know just how to get the best out of his people under any conditions." After the *Saufley* affair, Burke's officers and men in the destroyers kept going and fought the Japanese as hard as they could. Halsey sensed this, and never bothered Burke with unnecessary instructions. One night the admiral warned Burke that a number of enemy destroyers were coming his way. PROCEED. YOU KNOW WHAT TO DO. was all the message said.

"Admiral Halsey's strongest point," wrote a staff officer, "was his superb leadership. While always the true professional and exacting professional performance from all subordinates, he had a charismatic effect on them which was like being touched by a magic wand. Anyone so touched was determined to excel."

Admiral Spruance described Halsey as "a grand man to be with," a "splendid seaman," able to "smack them [the enemy] hard every time he gets a chance."

Occasionally, Halsey's support of a staff officer was inadequate, as in the case of his Chief of Staff, Miles Browning. Although his career had been punctured by controversy and failures, Browning worked well under Halsey. But he drank too much and had the capacity for insulting behavior. Browning antagonized Secretary of the Navy Knox when he visited Noumea and from then on Admiral King pressured Halsey until Browning was reassigned.

The staff teased Halsey continually about his raucous swim trunks, the terror he inspired when he took the controls of an airplane, and the junk he collected and carried along with him. Any gift, no matter how insignificant, he treasured. In his trousers he carried a New Zealand coin presented to him by the Governor General. In his wallet was a four-leaf clover mounted in isinglass. He cherished a Hawaiian symbol of good luck.

Bill Halsey was convivial. For his own personal use and "for entertaining" he received ten cases of Scotch and five cases of bourbon—tax free—a month. Later this was upped to seventeen cases of Scotch and six of bourbon. In Halsey's personal papers there is a file of such shipments covering the years 1942–44. In one letter dated 19 June 1944 a captain of the Service Force informed Halsey's aide that he had "paid up an outstanding indebtedness with liquor companies amounting to $441.15."

Recalled a staff officer, "He liked to drink and go to parties, but never did this interfere with duty either ashore or afloat."

Halsey employed the principle that a bottle of Scotch on the table "always bore fruit in our dealings with other commands. . . . [It] always gave us an entry where others feared to tread." His favorite toast was:

> I've drunk your health in company;
> I've drunk your health alone;
> I've drunk your health so many times,
> I've damned near ruined my own.

On occasion Halsey liked to sip beer or a martini, but his staple was Scotch and water. The admiral was quoted as saying, "There are exceptions, of course, but as a general rule, I never trust a fighting man who doesn't smoke or drink." A non-believer in the strict Navy regulations against liquor on board ship, he carried 100 gallons of bourbon for his pilots. "To a man who has just had a tense, hazardous flight or a wet watch," Halsey remarked, "there is no substitute for a tod of sound spirits, as the Royal Navy well knows."

When the Methodist Board of Temperance learned the admiral's drinking habits, their *Clipsheet* carried a six-column spread beginning "Shocking! . . . an astonishing breach of Naval discipline."

One man wrote the White House: "Why don't you fire William F. Halsey? . . . Any man who is in charge of responsibilities such as assigned to Halsey should by all means be opposed to drinking much less advocating it."

Halsey retorted that drinking on board United States naval vessels was a court-martial offense, but that the liquor for pilots was "bonded medical stores" and "administered by competent medical men in small amounts."

"There is no doubt," said a Halsey aide, "concerning its beneficial effects on the pilots under strain of combat."

During those days in Noumea Halsey was tormented again with a skin disease—"a little trouble with my hands, feet and scrotum." To his doctor in Richmond, Virginia, Halsey wrote, "I've started injecting your serum. I'm sure that it will clear it up in no time. It really has amounted to nothing so far but I don't want it to get away from me. They sent me a lotion from San Francisco which has cleared up my hands and feet almost entirely."

After months in the South Pacific, Halsey's sailors experienced a morale letdown. To inspire his men, the admiral consented to a press interview in which he employed the Knute Rockne locker-room technique. He predicted that 1943 would see the "complete, absolute" defeat of the Axis Powers in Europe and American forces in Tokyo. "And," he continued, "here's a few messages I wish you would send to Japan for me. To [Emperor] Hirohito 'as emperor and leader of a traitorous and brutal Japan during the years of your foul attacks on peaceful peoples, your time is short.'

"To [Premier Hideki] Tojo: 'When you unleashed your cowardly attack on December 7 you started something you can't finish. Beneath your thin veneer of civilization lies the dominant instinct to kill. Because of this you have released the greatest instinct to fight in the American people ever in history. We have good evidence of your atrocities and know where they were perpetrated. They'll be properly repaid!'

"To [Admiral Isoroku] Yamamoto [commander of the Japanese Fleet who predicted that he would make peace in the White House]: 'You will be present at the peace if you are still alive. That peace will be in the White House, but the White House will not be as you envisaged. . . .'

"To the Japanese people: 'That heavy rumbling you hear now will gradually grow into a shock of bursting bombs, the shrieking of shells and of the clashing of swords on your own soil. You had better stop now before it is too late.' '' *

"Do we have enough materiel here to conduct . . . an offensive?'' asked a reporter.

"No man in military history ever had enough men and materiel, but he has always gone ahead and done it just the same.''

"Have we passed from the defensive to the offensive?''

"Definitely.''

In a letter to a congressman, Halsey reiterated that the war could be won in the Pacific within the year. "The kind of men we've got out here *can* take these birds in less than a year if we make the breaks work for us. I agree fully with you on the necessity for breaking through the Jap perimeter defense and getting a knife through his liver as soon as we can.''

In another interview a correspondent questioned Halsey's "low estimate of the Japanese service man.'' The admiral replied, "When we first started out I held one of our men equal to three Japanese. I now increase this to twenty. They are not supermen, although they try to make us believe they are. They are just low monkeys. I say monkeys because I cannot say what I would like to call them.''

Such remarks created a storm of criticism. The State Department argued that it was not becoming an American admiral to

---

* "The remarks that appeared in print,'' said Halsey later, "were a diluted version of what I actually said. . . . [My staff] edited them and watered them down.''

sling epithets at the Japanese Emperor and his Prime Minister. "The State Department," said Halsey, "may be right in its argument . . . but the correspondents had asked my opinion, not for my guess at what State hoped it was. So I said what I thought: The Japanese are bastards." The record does not show what Secretary Knox or Admirals King and Nimitz thought of Halsey's outburst.

The severest criticism centered on his prophecy that American troops would march through Tokyo by late 1943. Production leaders in the United States were terrified that their labor forces would take the admiral's words as gospel and quit their war jobs. Draft authorities complained as did other officials. They accused Halsey of "everything from recklessness to drunkenness." "God Almighty," stormed Halsey, "I knew we wouldn't be in Tokyo that soon! I knew we wouldn't be there even by the end of 1944."

"What the civilian bigwigs should consider," he continued, "is this: my forces were tired; their morale was low; they were beginning to think that they were abused and forgotten, that they had been fighting too much and too long. Moreover, the new myth of Japanese invincibility had not yet been entirely discredited. Prior to Pearl Harbor, the United States in general had rated Japan as no better than a class-C nation. After the one successful sneak attack, however, panicky eyes saw the monkeymen as supermen. I saw them as nothing of the sort, and I wanted my forces to know how I felt. I stand by the opinion that the Japs are bastards."

As early as 30 November 1942 Admiral King complained to Nimitz that he was "uneasy" about the slowness of Halsey's forces moving northward up the Solomons toward Rabaul. He indicated that the South Pacific Force was exerting too much strength against the remaining Japanese forces on Guadalcanal; in effect, Halsey was "bogged down" in a frontal operation when he might better cut off the Japanese forces on Guadalcanal by seizing the bases from which they were being supported.

Both Halsey and Nimitz responded quickly. To move up the Solomons, Halsey explained, required a huge buildup on Guadalcanal and Tulagi, an increase in air and logistical support, and the seizure or neutralization of Japanese-held Munda and Rekata. The enemy had by no means abandoned Guadalcanal, and was still attempting to reinforce its troops there. Before the next American offensive, Halsey said, it was absolutely essential to have more ships and troops to "exploit immediately the initial landings and follow through."

From Pearl Harbor Nimitz wrote King that the necessity for "getting along with the war" was well recognized by CINCPAC and Halsey, and that every possible "short cut" was being investigated. Certain conditions delayed a northward move, notably the lack of troops and shipping. "Although the Guadalcanal campaign has progressed favorably," he said, "I consider that we are now in the period which is, as was foreseen, one of building up our strength while taking advantage of every favorable opportunity to cut down the enemy's. In regard to the latter, the enemy is apparently going to continue to expose his forces in the Guadalcanal area—a situation over which we should perhaps not be impatient until we have effected the superiority which will make it suitable to similarly expose our forces in operations against his bases."

In initiating an offensive, Nimitz continued, "Any considerable step forward will require a superiority in sea forces, aircraft and troops, and our supporting bases must be sufficiently developed and reasonably secure. The superiority must not only be local, but there should be sufficient strength to support our new base and its supply lines against the forces the enemy will throw against them. . . . While we have been successful in the Guadalcanal campaign, I do not consider that we have yet superiority in surface forces. Such superiority will be brought about by our new construction and by further losses we cause the enemy, especially in his further efforts against Guadalcanal."

[VI]

"These Yellow Bastards Are No 'Super Men' "

AT NOUMEA HALSEY COMPLAINED to Nimitz about the critical shortage of destroyers in the command, the limited unloading areas and equipment on Guadalcanal and Tulagi, and the lack of maintenance which caused material casualties. "At present," Halsey said, "part of our heavy striking forces are immobilized and the remainder suffer gravely reduced battle efficiency due to what I have outlined."

During those months Halsey as well as Nimitz and King charted strategy for the South Pacific, weighing alternatives for the next targets. "We are looking at the situation," Halsey told Nimitz, "and making up our ideas."

"The situation with the Nips at this moment is as obscure to me as it is probably to you," Halsey continued. "All indications point to a Japanese buildup on the coast of New Guinea. However, we must be prepared for the possible attempt at breaking through from the Coral Sea to the Southward and Westward of the Solomons. I have disposed my available combatant ships. . . . They are also in a position to attack in case they move down the Solomons."

In July 1942 the Joint Chiefs of Staff had issued a directive, outlining in broad detail the strategy for the South Pacific and Southwest Pacific campaigns. Task One was the seizure and oc-

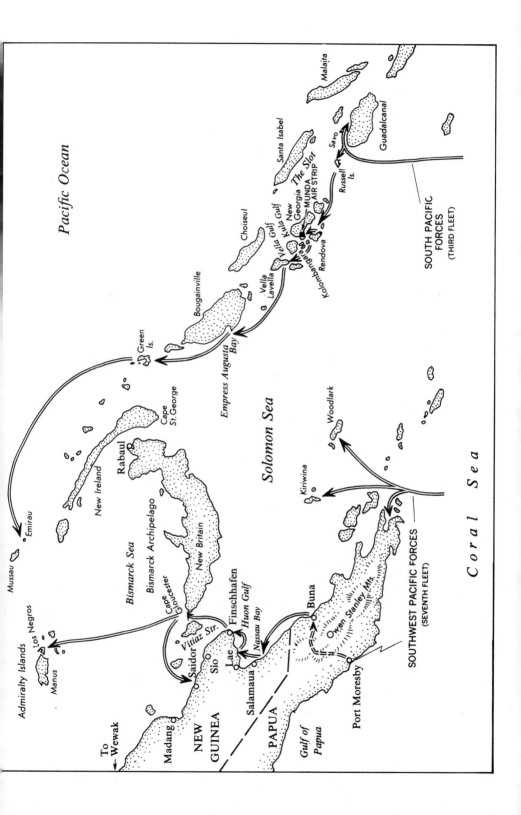

cupation of Guadalcanal and Tulagi. The Marines and Army had almost completed this operation. Task Two was the capture of the remaining Solomon Islands and of Lae, Salamaua, and other points on the northeast coast of New Guinea. Task Three was the assault by both Halsey and MacArthur upon Rabaul, the great Japanese bastion on New Britain Island in the Bismarck Archipelago, 700 miles south of Truk. Bristling with warships and aircraft, it threatened the line of communications from the United States to Australia and it blocked any Allied advance along the north coast of New Guinea to the Philippines. Reduction of Rabaul was therefore the primary mission of both the South Pacific and Southwest Pacific forces.

"Our common objective," Halsey wrote, "is RABAUL. Until Jap air in New Britain and the northern Solomons has been reduced, risk of valuable naval units in the middle and western reaches of the Solomon Sea can only be justified by a major enemy seaborne movement against the south coast of New Guinea or Australia itself."

"I am," he continued, "reinforcing Gaudalcanal . . . and expediting means of operating heavy air from there. . . . I believe that my greatest contribution to our common effort would be to strengthen my position and resume the advance up the SOLOMONS as soon as possible, while continuing to maintain a naval force in being on the flank of any possible Japanese large-scale advance against Australia or southern New Guinea."

Later, the Joint Chiefs of Staff in Washington suggested that American forces in the South and Southwest Pacific accomplish Task Two at once, moving northward along the shores of New Guinea and the Solomons.

Halsey looked on Munda Point on the southwest corner of New Georgia Island in the central Solomons, less than 200 miles from Henderson Field on Guadalcanal, as the most likely first objective for his forces under Task Two. The Japanese had started an airfield at the Australian Methodist Mission on Munda in November 1942 when their attempts to recapture Henderson Field had failed. In Allied hands, Halsey believed, Munda would be invaluable for continuing the advance against Rabaul.

To Halsey, Rabaul was "the logical objective towards whose

seizure or neutralization all efforts of both the South and Southwest Pacific forces would be directed. Until Rabaul was seized, or at least naval and air control of the New Britain area was established, the planned advance of the Southwest Pacific Forces along the New Guinea coast toward the Philippines was impracticable.''

"A tempting thought, we have toyed with," Halsey wrote Nimitz, "is to bypass everything up the line and hit direct at Rabaul. If it can be done, we would save large numbers of lives, time and materiel. I believe with Rabaul in our hands the war in the Pacific is approaching an end."

Certain factors, though, pointed toward conservatism. Except for those in New Guinea, the entire system of Japanese bases— Kavieng, Rabaul, Buka, Kieta, and Buin—were mutually supporting and none, thought Halsey, even Rabaul, could be considered a keystone, which, if captured, would cause the rest of the system to collapse. The communication line of any base that the South Pacific Force seized would unavoidably be flanked by the enemy bases it bypassed. To establish a base successfully with one or more enemy bases in the Americans' rear, or to capture two or more positions simultaneously, Halsey needed a preponderance of strength which he did not possess.

Halsey believed that the need for continuing the American offensive and keeping the pressure on the enemy was paramount. There was not time to wait until the South Pacific Force had built up an overwhelming superiority to enable it to bypass any strong base of the enemy.

Intelligence reported that the enemy had greater troop strength in the South Pacific, but as time went on, and the American training and rehabilitation program took effect, it would gain the advantage. Enemy surface superiority would continue at least through April, but their shore-based air was no longer supreme in the Solomons and American advantage would increase markedly.

Halsey was vehemently opposed to the doctrine of defense. "The present war," he said, "has forced us to abolish such a concept, but for years the entire world, with the exception of our Navy, the Royal Navy, the German Army, and the Jap Military establishment was hypnotized by the idea of defense. . . . At the present time our entire military establishment is following the principle of offense and a careful plan of education is necessary so that after this war the post-war public is continually impressed with the fact that if forced to fight we will carry the war into enemy territory wherever it may be.''

Halsey and his staff finally crystallized their strategy for the coming months. ''We have the initiative in the Solomons area,'' Halsey wrote Nimitz, ''and my plans are to press against the Rabaul area as fast as our means permit.'' On 21 February Halsey planned to occupy Russell Island in the central Solomons, a stepping-stone to New Georgia, then land there sometime in April. ''Jap reaction to these operations will be indicative to his attitude, and the extent to which he dares withdraw his fleet units.''

Since intelligence reported no Japanese buildup in the South Pacific, Halsey accepted an invitation to visit New Zealand. On 2 January 1943 Halsey and his staff took off from Noumea in a Navy Coronado. Peter Fraser, the Prime Minister, met them at the dock and escorted them to their hotel. There Halsey met reporters. Questioned about the enemy, Halsey replied, ''Like everything else about them, they are tricky, but not too hard to fathom. There is nothing to be worried about in their tactics. Any normal naval officer can lick them.''

Asked about Japanese tactics, the admiral said, ''Japan's next move will be retreat. A start has been made to make them retreat. They will not be able to stop going back.''

On the next day Halsey toured various installations at Auckland, including American hospitals, which overflowed with wounded Marines and soldiers from Guadalcanal. Halsey then flew to Wellington for a similar tour, returning to Noumea on 7 January.

No sooner had he arrived than he flew to Espiritu Santo to meet Secretary Knox and Nimitz, who were on an inspection tour of the South Pacific. Halsey met them on board the tender *Curtiss*.

After conferences with Knox and Nimitz, Halsey settled into his bed. Suddenly bombs exploded. The enemy's raid was minimal, but Halsey couldn't help wondering whether the strike's coincidence with his arrival was luck or leakage.

The following night, at Guadalcanal, the group was bombed again. Halsey had "very little stomach for bombs. There were no foxholes on the *Curtiss,* but there were plenty on Guadalcanal. When I heard the first *boom!,* I left my comfortable hut and dove into the ground, with Mr. Knox."

Although by January more ships and aircraft were arriving in the South Pacific, Halsey reported that "the shoestring was still frayed; the total forces available were still so sparse that we had to strip the planes from three new escort carriers and send them to beef up the shore-based squadrons on Guadalcanal; but now for the first time we felt strong enough to attempt a modest offensive."

On the 23rd at Halsey's compound in Noumea, Nimitz, Halsey, and their staffs met to review the situation and to exchange views. "No decisions will be reached," Nimitz pointed out. "Indeed we may not agree on all points."

Nimitz first wanted to know about progress on Guadalcanal. Halsey let his staff reply to most of the questions. General Dewitt Peck, Halsey's Chief of War Plans, predicted, "The Japs will be eliminated by 1 April. We do not believe that the Japs will strike further at Guadalcanal, but will hold the defensive in order to contain our force there in greater number for them." However, Peck stressed that the 1 April date was optimistic. "The Japs may use delaying tactics which will prolong the business."

Turning the discussion to future operations, "The staff has been exploring the use of Russell Island," Peck said. "Our idea is to take it with one raider battalion and part of a defense battalion and to use it as a staging point for our landing craft, for a P.T. boat base, and to deny it to the enemy. It will be in the nature of a minor movement preparatory to an advance on Munda, and its possession will add to the security of Guadalcanal. Russell is eighty miles from Guadalcanal."

The subject changed to other matters but later Nimitz turned to Guadalcanal again. "How will the island be used next?"

Peck replied, "It will be used as a supporting base for further advancing movements in the Solomons."

"It is my idea," Nimitz cut in, "that no permanent installations should be erected there. The only construction should be what is necessary, and there should be a reduction in the rear areas. Everything should be predicated on a forward movement.''

The staffs talked about other installations, then returned to the problem of future strategy.

Nimitz: "Will it help to go into Munda?"

Peck: "Yes. By the time we expect to go into Munda it will require a division of troops because the Japs will have land-based aircraft by that time."

Nimitz: "You will need naval surface craft to get into Russell?"

Peck: "Yes, and after the landing we shall require ships for a few days to get supplies in. I estimate the enemy strength in the Russells to be between 200 and a battalion. We plan to use the Third Raider Battalion against them."

Nimitz: "When do you think that you can move against Munda?"

Peck: "April 1st."

After more discussions about details of other maneuvers, the conference broke up, and Nimitz returned to Pearl Harbor.

On 5 February a lone Army bomber, at the extreme limits of its 800-mile search, spied a strong Japanese force moving down from Truk—carriers, battleships, cruisers, and destroyers. At Noumea, Halsey expected the enemy to make a final, desperate effort at Guadalcanal. Immediately, he dispatched his task groups to meet the challenge. While Halsey waited, Japanese destroyers made three runs to the island and evacuated their half-starved troops. The main Japanese naval force never closed in. The campaign for Guadalcanal had ended. On 10 February General Alexander Patch, USA, who had replaced Vandegrift, sent the following message to Halsey: ORGANIZED RESISTANCE ON GUADALCANAL HAS CEASED.

Halsey replied: WHEN I SENT A PATCH TO ACT AS TAILOR FOR GUADALCANAL, I DID NOT EXPECT HIM TO REMOVE THE ENEMY'S PANTS AND SEW IT ON SO QUICKLY X THANKS AND CONGRATULATIONS.

Halsey wrote Nimitz: "Far from being an orderly retreat, it was a complete rout. While I regret that many of their higher officers got away . . . it should not be a total loss. These yellow bastards are no 'super men' and they will yap as much as our own people do. The news will undoubtedly infiltrate through the Jap forces of the Hell these people went through. . . . We are . . . cheerful and optimistic. Perhaps that indicates a lack of sense, but at least it is better than going around with long faces.''

The enemy's evacuation of Guadalcanal, after six months of bitter fighting on land, sea, and in the air, was by no means an indication that the Japanese intended to retire from the Solomon Islands. Intelligence reported that they would hold fast to their positions. Since enemy airfields on Munda Point, New Georgia, and at the mouth of the Vila River (on the southern tip of Kolombangara Island) threatened positions on Guadalcanal, American aircraft blasted these airstrips repeatedly.

Meanwhile the Combined Chiefs of Staff had met at Casablanca to plan future operations. For the first time Allied prospects seemed favorable. The Russians had turned the tide at the decisive Battle of Stalingrad. Egypt had been saved. Allied air and naval forces were fast being built up in Morocco and Algeria. The Allied chiefs gave the United States the green light to start Nimitz and MacArthur on an offensive against the Japanese and allocated more men and materiel to the Pacific. Later they accepted the ''Strategic Plan for the Defeat of Japan.'' The enemy would be defeated by 1) blockade, severing Japan's access to the oil of the East Indies; 2) air bombardment of Japan's cities; 3) the invasion of the enemy's home islands.

Nimitz's Central Pacific Force would move westward from Hawaii; Halsey's South Pacific and MacArthur's Southwest Pacific forces would cooperate in a drive on the Japanese fortress on Rabaul. Once this base was secured units would move along the north coast of New Guinea toward the Philippines.

Admiral King later clarified naval organization by numbering the fleets. Fleets maneuvering in the Atlantic and Mediterranean bore even numbers; those in the Pacific, odd numbers. Under King's scheme, the Pacific naval forces consisted of the Central Pacific Force, based at Pearl Harbor (Fifth Fleet); Halsey's South Pacific Force (Third Fleet); MacArthur's miniature Southwest Pacific Naval Force (Seventh Fleet).

Halsey was concerned that the command structure between his

forces and those of General MacArthur's would result in interservice rivalry. The Joint Chiefs of Staff had fixed the boundary between the South and Southwest Pacific areas at longitude 159 East.

General MacArthur, responsible for the overall strategy in the South and Southwest Pacific, was frequently consulted; but he gave Halsey a completely free hand. Halsey insisted on exercising unity of command over all forces in the South Pacific and enforced this concept right on down. To make sure no spirit of rivalry penetrated his ranks, Halsey called in all of his subordinate commanders and said, "Gentlemen, we are the South Pacific Fighting Force. I don't want anybody even to be thinking in terms of Army, Navy, or Marines. Every man must understand this, and every man *will* understand it, if I have to take off his uniform and issue coveralls with 'South Pacific Fighting Force' printed on the seat of his pants."

Halsey enjoyed the greatest respect of Army commanders who served under him. "For one thing," Halsey recalled, "I didn't meddle in their affairs. I had the highest regard for their ability. In joint operations for which I was responsible it was my job *to define the objectives and outline the mission.* I was never concerned for one minute with the *administration* of their forces . . . those were rightfully *their* problems. That's the way we worked out there."

Halsey and his subordinates had begun planning and preparing for New Georgia in January 1943, before the end of the Guadalcanal campaign. This process, which involved air and naval bombardments, the assembly of supplies, and reconnaissance of the target areas together with the preparation and issuance of operation plans and field orders, continued through the spring.

New Georgia is the name for a large group of islands in the central Solomons, which includes Vella Lavella, Kolombangara, New Georgia (the main island of the group), and Rendova.

New Georgia Island was difficult to reach by sea except in a few places. Reefs and a chain of barrier islands blocked much of the coastline, which was frequently covered with mangrove swamps. The best deepwater approach was Kula Gulf, which had a few inlets, but Japanese destroyers and seacoast batteries protected much of the shoreline of the gulf. There were also protected anchorages in the southeast part of New Georgia at Wickham Anchorage, Viru Harbor, and Segi Point. Munda Point, the airfield site, was inaccessible to big vessels.

On 28 February, only seven days off the original target date, American forces landed unopposed on Russell Island. This shortened the air distance to Munda by sixty-five miles and provided torpedo boat and landing craft bases to assist in the capture of all New Georgia. Construction crews immediately began building an airfield, stockpiling fuel and ammunition, and preparing for the eventual invasion of Munda Point.

"Everything down here is, in general, progressing happily," Halsey wrote Secretary Knox. "The occupation of the Russells without difficulty or opposition was fortunate. . . . We hope that our worthy (?) opponent is punch-drunk at the moment, but we are not placing too much confidence in that hope."

Certain officials in Washington criticized Halsey for not seizing strongly held New Georgia instead of getting sidetracked in a minor operation. Halsey's response was that "the Russells occupation is a step in the direction of New Georgia and is in a sense the completion of the first stage of the New Georgias. I do not consider the Russells as anything but a stepping-stone toward the New Georgias."

Halsey was "rarin' to go" against New Georgia and "to get some more Monkey meat." "My ambition remains to populate Hell with yellow bastards."

Munda Point was, physically, one of the best sites for an airfield in the Solomons. Strategically, it was well-situated to support the invasion of Bougainville, which would be necessary if American planes were to bomb Rabaul effectively. Halsey would have to use carriers to move directly from Guadalcanal to Bougainville, but possession of Munda Point would enable them to advance progressively with support of land-based fighters and bombers and negate the need to use the precious carriers close to enemy-held islands.

In March the Joint Chiefs of Staff directed that the South and Southwest Pacific operations in 1943 be limited to Task Two and dispatched orders to Halsey and MacArthur. They were to establish air bases on Woodlark and Kiriwina islands off the south-east coast of New Guinea, to capture the Lae-Salamaua-Finschhafen-Madang area of New Guinea and occupy western New Britain Island, and seize and occupy the Solomon Islands as far as southern Bougainville. These operations were to inflict maximum losses on the enemy, to contain Japanese forces in the Pacific by retaining the initiative, and to prepare for the final reduction of Rabaul. The offensive in the Solomons was to be commanded by Halsey, who would operate under MacArthur's strategic direction. Except for those elements assigned by Washington to task forces engaged in these campaigns, all units of the Pacific Ocean Areas would remain under Nimitz.

To discuss the upcoming New Georgia campaign with Mac-Arthur, Halsey flew to Brisbane. At this, their first personal meeting, Halsey and MacArthur immediately established cordial relations of mutual respect, which were destined to deepen into a friendship. Later discussing their meeting, Halsey recalled that after five minutes with him, "I felt as if we were lifelong friends. I have seldom seen a man who makes a quicker, stronger, more favorable impression."

"All during the war," Halsey said, "I recall no flaw in our relationship. We had arguments, but they always ended pleasantly. Not once did he, my superior officer, ever force his decisions on me. . . . When I disagreed with him, I told him so, and we discussed the issue until one of us changed his mind. My mental picture poses him against the background of these discussions; he is pacing his office, almost wearing a groove between his large, bare desk and the portrait of George Washington that faced it; his corncob pipe is in his hand (I rarely saw him smoke it); and he is making his points in a diction I have never heard surpassed."

MacArthur found Halsey "blunt, outspoken, dynamic." The general discovered that "the bugaboo of many sailors, the fear of losing ships, was completely alien to his conception of sea action. I liked him from the moment we met."

At this conference, timing and coordination in New Guinea with the New Georgia operation were discussed. They agreed that the initial landing at New Georgia would take place at the same time as the invasion of Woodlark and Kiriwina instead of after the establishment of MacArthur's forces on the Huon Peninsula as the Southwest Pacific officers had been advocating. The plan of operation decided on by MacArthur was the same as that set forth in previous plans—mutually supporting advances along two axes, converging finally on Rabaul.

Halsey planned to keep pressure on New Georgia, especially the Munda airfield, by air bombardment and by hit-and-run raids on outposts. "If, as a result of the pressure of continuous combat, reconnaissance indicates the Jap is withdrawing forces from New Georgia or is being so weakened that Munda can be taken without major operations and can be logistically supported and built up by us in strength for operations against Bougainville," Halsey told the Joint Chiefs of Staff, "I propose moving ahead."

Meanwhile, Navy code experts had learned that Admiral Isoroku Yamamoto, the Commander in Chief of the Imperial Japanese Navy, was to visit the upper Solomons. Yamamoto, who had conceived the attack on Pearl Harbor, was due to arrive in Ballale Island, just south of Bougainville, at 0945 on 18 April.

To top intelligence officers at Pearl Harbor, Nimitz addressed the question: Would the elimination of Yamamoto help the Allied cause? Did the enemy have anyone better to replace him? To the latter inquiry, Intelligence answered "No!" Nimitz "gave the green light" and directed Rear Admiral Marc A. Mitscher, Commander Air Solomons, to get the job done.

As had been predicted, Yamamoto and members of his staff took off in two bombers from Rabaul at 1100, 18 April, covered by nine fighter planes, for Kahili Airfield, Buin. Sixteen fighters from Henderson Field were already flying low up along the west coast of New Georgia. Yamamoto arrived over Buin at 1135. So did the Americans. Exactly as planned, the plane commanded by Captain Thomas G. Lanphier, USAAF, swept in under the departing Japanese fighters as the two bombers were about to land. Lanphier shot down one, Lieutenant Rex T. Barber, USAAF, disposed of the other. The first, which carried Yamamoto, crashed in the jungle north of Buin; the other, carrying Vice Admiral Ugaki, his Chief of Staff, plunged into the sea and sank. Yamamoto and five or six key staffers were killed; Ugaki was critically injured. To the Japanese Navy, the loss of its ablest commander was equivalent to a major tragedy.

When the news reached Noumea, Halsey reported the incident to his staff, who "whooped and applauded." But Halsey said, "Hold on. . . . What's so good about it? I'd hoped to lead that scoundrel up Pennsylvania Avenue in chains, with the rest of you kicking him where it would do the most good!"

When Halsey returned from his conference with MacArthur, the Third Fleet was preparing for the invasion of New Georgia.

"As I see the general situation," Nimitz wrote Halsey, "the Japs have gone over to the strategic defensive, consolidating their economic and military gains within their present perimeter of control. I expect that they will take vigorous offensive measures to harass us and to prevent us breaking through at any point in the periphery. In the Pacific war the bottlenecks are ships, aircraft, and amphibiously trained troops, but the greatest is ships. Washington wants every possible method explored to that end that we get the most economical use of shipping."

Again Nimitz wrote, "I wish you all success with the coming operations, and you may rest assured that my staff and I'll continue to look out for your interests, although it may appear to some of you occasionally that your Force has been forgotten. We have a good over-all picture of what is happening in the Pacific, and will see that you are not left without tools when the time comes."

"I have no doubt," Nimitz concluded, "that . . . Tojo is beginning to have doubts about the future. You have certainly done your share to make Tojo doubtful about Japan's place in the sun!"

Halsey replied, "I see no reason why the plan will not go through as indicated. I agree with you that the Japs are definitely on the strategic defensive. I question whether they will make vigorous defensive measures. My opinion is they will wait for us to make the next move. I further believe that when we start up NEW GUINEA and SOLOMONS that they . . . will come down on us with everything they can muster afloat in the usual 'save-face' attitude. I am strongly of the opinion that they will do everything they can to maintain their positions, particularly in Rabaul. . . . We are expecting and hoping when we start to move that we will bring their surface ships down so once again we will have a chance of killing YELLOW BASTARDS.''

To a friend, Halsey wrote, "We know we are better than the YELLOW BASTARDS on the sea, under the sea, on land, and in the air. It is just a question of men and equipment before we will run them into Hell where they belong.''

Final plans and orders for the invasion of New Georgia were ready—a simultaneous capture of Rendova, Viru Harbor, Wickham Anchorage, and Segi Point. The general plan of attack called for assault troops from Guadalcanal and the Russells to move to Rendova, Segi Point, Wickham Anchorage, and Viru Harbor on transports, cargo ships, minesweepers, and minelayers. Segi, Wickham, and Viru would be seized by small units to secure the line of communications to Rendova, while the main assault troops captured Rendova. Howitzers on Rendova and the barrier island and guns on the warships were to bombard Munda Point.

Several days following D-Day the slower landing craft, the LSTs and LCIs, would transport more troops and supplies, traveling by night to avoid detection. When enough men had assembled, landing craft were to bring the troops from Rendova across Roviana Lagoon to New Georgia to begin the thrust against Munda Point.

Halsey's basic plan also organized the task forces, prescribed their general missions, and directed Admiral Turner to coordinate the planning of the participating forces.

Word arrived from MacArthur that he could not meet the D-Day deadline for the invasion of Woodlark and Kiriwina (15 May) and ordered its postponement to 30 June. It made little difference to Bill Halsey as preliminary attacks had already been under way with cruisers and destroyers blasting Munda's airfield. "Those Jap bastards don't know what hit them," Halsey wrote. Interspersed with the bombardments, planes struck the area and, four days before D-Day, they pounded Munda with special severity, damaging aircraft, supplies, and killing and wounding personnel.

The Japanese retaliated. One hundred and twenty fighters and bombers bore in on Guadalcanal. American Army, Navy, and

Marine planes roared off runways to gun down 107 at the cost of six. Halsey remembered that months earlier he had told correspondents that one American was equal to twenty Japanese. Halsey now mused, "I seem to have been slightly off my estimate. The actual ratio is not quite eighteen."

Prior to the invasion of New Georgia, Nimitz made a hurried trip to Noumea to discuss future operations with Halsey. After his departure, Halsey toured his bases and was impressed with the Navy's installations on Russell Island. "They've done extremely well up there and have a going concern." On his return the admiral wrote Nimitz about the forthcoming New Georgia campaign. "The witching hour is rapidly approaching. It is not a pleasant occupation to sit around and think. However, that is my job."

On 21 June Marine Raiders landed without firing a shot at Segi Point, New Georgia, 400 miles from Munda. Army units reinforced them the next day. Work crews began building an airstrip and, in less than two weeks, planes were taking off from what had originally been virgin jungle.

On 29 June an attack force of cruisers, destroyers, and minelayers moved past New Georgia and into the Buin–Shortland Islands sector off southern Bougainville, 200 miles further up the line. Two destroyers headed into Kula Gulf, which separates New Georgia and Kolombangara, and shelled Vila-Stanmore, while minelayers sowed explosives across the southern entrance to Bougainville Strait to obstruct Japanese raids on Halsey's Munda forces. Cruisers and destroyers shelled Japanese anchorages and installations on the Shortlands, Faisi, Poporang, and Ballale.

On D-Day, two hours after troops disgorged from transports and landed on Rendova, American 105-millimeter howitzers crashed out against Munda Point. By 1500 the transports, completing their unloading, stood down Blanche Channel for their return to Guadalcanal. Twenty-five enemy fighters and torpedo bombers hurtled through the American air screen. The transports' ack-ack and American aircraft shot down all twenty-five, but not before a torpedo ripped into the transport *McKinley*.

While the main forces landed on Rendova, lesser units captured Viru Harbor and Wickham Anchorage off Vangunu Island.

After the invasion of Rendova, the next task was the move to New Georgia mainland, and the advance to Munda Point. On 2 July Halsey, encouraged by ineffective Japanese resistance, directed Admiral Turner to proceed with the plans for the thrust against Munda.

On D-plus-2 landing craft ferried troops from Rendova to the mainland at Zanana. Holding a line along the Barike River, they moved slowly forward under cover of five-inch shells from the destroyers in Blanche Channel.

To prevent the enemy from reinforcing New Georgia, American cruisers and destroyers operating in Kula Gulf pounded the shores of Kolombangara. Once this bombardment ended, the ships withdrew, but were ordered to swerve back at full speed to strike enemy warships. The battle of Kula Gulf lasted four hours and resulted in the loss of the cruiser *Helena* and two Japanese destroyers. A week later an American task unit again caught Japanese surface elements at night. In the brief battle of Kolombangara the destroyer *Gwin* went down and three American crusiers were crippled. The Japanese fled northward with the loss of only one cruiser.

These two engagements were expensive, but they helped protect the New Georgia operation and denied the enemy further use of Kula Gulf as a supply line for their troops.

Meanwhile on New Georgia, American troops gained a mile a day until the main Japanese defense slowed them to a standstill. There were attacks and counterattacks. Casualties mounted. "At least fifty percent of these individuals requiring medical attention or entering medical installations," said a surgeon, "were the picture of utter exhaustion, face expressionless, knees sagging, body bent forward, arms slightly flexed and hanging loosely . . . feet dragging, and an over-all appearance of . . . physical exhaustion."

Supported by air and ship bombardment, the American advance inched forward and, eventually gaining momentum, troops secured the island on 31 July. General Oscar W. Griswold, commanding the New Georgia Occupation Force, radioed Halsey, "Our ground forces today wrested Munda from the Japs and present it to you . . . as the sole owner. . . ."

Halsey replied with "a custody receipt for Munda. . . . Keep 'em dying."

When Nimitz learned the news, he hastily wrote Halsey, "Congratulations on the successful accomplishments of the New Georgia operation. . . . As usual the surface and air forces under your direction turned in splendid accounts of themselves."

Construction battalions started the work of widening, resurfacing, and regrading the airfield at Munda. Power shovels dug coral out of Kokengolo Hill and bulldozers and earthmovers spread and flattened it. By 7 August the field, although rough, was operational for emergency wheels-up landings.

As a result of the bloody New Georgia campaign, the Americans forced the enemy to abandon its naval base in the Kahili-Buin-Shortlands area off southern Bougainville; gained air bases for the neutralization of Japanese airfields on Bougainville; and brought Rabaul into range.

The New Georgia campaign had been lengthy and costly. American casualties numbered 1,094 dead and 3,873 wounded. These figures, however, do not include casualties resulting from disease or from combat fatigue or war neuroses. Japanese casualty figures are not known, but Americans counted 2,483 dead soldiers.

Simultaneously with Halsey's invasion of New Georgia, Mac-Arthur's Southwest Pacific forces had landed without opposition on Kiriwina and Woodlark islands, and, in September, captured the Japanese fortress at Lae on the mainland.

[VII]

"We Were Biting Our Nails"

DURING THE SUMMER of 1943 Nimitz remained relatively idle at Pearl Harbor, waiting for newly commissioned warships to arrive. Carriers could do little in the confined waters of the Solomon Sea and both King and Nimitz wanted to take no chances in repeating the losses suffered during the campaign for Guadalcanal. Therefore, land-based planes fought in the South Pacific, while the new flattops moved to Hawaii and, eventually, to the Central Pacific, the strategic choice for the major offensive, as in this area enemy island airfields and the Japanese fleet commanded all approaches. Here the United States Pacific Fleet could entice its enemy into combat and thus open the way for a drive against the Japanese homeland.

The Joint Strategic Survey Committee recommended that American strategy in the Pacific be changed from MacArthur's Southwest Pacific command to Nimitz's Central. MacArthur and others argued that the Southwest Pacific and the Army would be subordinated to Nimitz and the Navy. Yet General George Marshall, Army Chief of Staff, agreed that the armada of carriers could not be permitted to wither. The Joint Chiefs of Staff alerted MacArthur that Nimitz's Central Pacific forces would strike the Marshalls and perhaps the Gilberts in November 1943. In the South Pacific, Halsey's units were to neutralize or secure Rabaul by 1 February 1944. The Central Pacific forces would then turn toward Truk, anchorage of the Japanese Fleet in the eastern Carolines. Simultaneously, MacArthur's Southwest Pacific Force would push across northern New Guinea to attack Hollandia from the sea on 1 August 1944. The Central Pacific Force would then invade Truk and move on to the Palau Islands in the western Carolines on 30 December 1944. The primary targets of the Central and Southwest forces' advances were that stretch of sea between the Chinese mainland from Hong Kong to Amoy, the island of Formosa, and Luzon in the Philippines. By occupying the Chinese coast or Formosa or Luzon in 1945, Americans could stop the flow of raw materials in enemy ships from the East Indies to the Japanese home islands. After this operation, Americans could seize Malaya to the west and the Ryukyu Islands in the north. The final offensive against Japan would commence in 1947–48. Everything, of course, was predicated on an Allied victory in Europe in 1944.

During the spring and summer of 1943 seamen at Pearl Harbor were awed by the sight of new carriers maneuvering into the harbor from the States. These arrivals had been made possible by the success and speed of America's ship construction program. In 1941, the carrier strength had numbered seven first-line ships and one escort carrier converted from a merchant ship. Since then, the *Lexington* had been sunk in the Battle of the Coral Sea; *Yorktown* at Midway; *Wasp* in the South Pacific; *Hornet* in the Battle of Santa Cruz. At one crucial period in the winter of 1942–43 only three carriers were in commission—the *Ranger* in the Atlantic and the *Saratoga* and *Enterprise* in the Pacific.

When America entered the war, contracts had already been signed for building large carriers of the new Essex class and for converting cruiser hulls and merchant ships. The urgent need of increasing naval air power and of replacing the losses suffered in the Pacific led to a stepped up program for building flattops.

On 30 May 1943, the *Essex,* the first of the new class of 27,100-ton flattops, steamed into Pearl Harbor; a month later, the light carrier *Independence* (converted from a cruiser hull), displacing 11,000 tons. Soon more ships of these classes reported to Pearl Harbor at the rate of almost one a month through the summer. By December 1943, the United States program had ex-

panded so swiftly that the carriers of the United States Navy outnumbered the Japanese two to one.

The New Georgia campaign had demonstrated to Halsey and
his staff the difficulty and costliness of rooting out the enemy
from powerful defensive positions. This realization became the
basis of the bypassing or leapfrogging technique in the Pacific.
Jump over the enemy's strong points, blockade them, and leave
them to stagnate.

Several staff members argued that American forces might have
"hard sledding" if they attempted to invade Kolombangara, the
next island north of New Georgia and, one night over highballs at
Halsey's house, they introduced this bypass concept. Assured by
intelligence that the Japanese were consolidating their positions
on Kolombangara, the staff unanimously decided to leap over this
island and hit Vella Lavella, the next island up the line, forty
miles closer to Bougainville.

Intelligence sources, coast-watchers, plantation managers, and
members of the clergy knew that there was a potential airstrip at
Vella Lavella and a beach suitable for a PT boat base. Halsey's
ground units could expect little resistance. After studying charts,
the staff decided to invade the southeastern shore of Vella, the
best position to flank Kolombangara.

"From that time on," a staff officer recalled, "we looked for
bigger and better opportunities to embarrass the Japanese operations which involved the bypass scheme of operations as a
method which became standard operating procedure."

Although this concept was not new in the Pacific—strategists
had suggested it as early as 1940—Halsey's staff refined the doctrine and it was eventually employed extensively by MacArthur's
and Nimitz's forces in the Southwest and Central Pacific. It saved
lives, made maximum use of limited resources, and "fooled the
Japs completely."

Early in August, Halsey learned that his son, Bill, the *Saratoga*'s Aviation Supply Officer, was coming to Noumea on the
8th to secure parts. Father and son spent that evening together,

and Bill started back for his carrier the next afternoon as a passenger in one of three torpedo planes.

The young Halsey had hardly left when an attack of flu put the admiral to bed. He was very sick and it was not until the next day, 10 August, that Operations Officer, Captain H. Raymond Thurber, reported that three torpedo planes were missing. Halsey asked, "My boy?"

"Yes, sir."

Thurber described the searches that were being made, then asked Halsey if he could suggest any additional measures.

The admiral replied, "My son is the same as every other son in the combat zone. Look for him just as you'd look for anybody else."

On 11 August Halsey issued his final orders for Vella Lavella. He organized his forces much as he had for the landings at New Georgia. The Northern Force (Task Force Thirty-One) was to seize Vella Lavella, construct an airfield, and establish a small naval base. General Griswold's New Georgia Occupation Force would simultaneously move into position on small Arundel Island (between Kolombangara and New Georgia) and bombard Vila airfield on bypassed Kolombangara. New Georgia-based planes would protect the invasion, while Task Force Thirty-Three would provide air support by hitting the Shortlands-Bougainville airfields.

There was no word of the missing planes. Usually Halsey shared his problems with his staff, but this time it was personal, and he kept to himself. "I didn't give up hope," Halsey said later, "but I knew that hope was a double-edged sword. When families of missing men begged me to hold out hope of their return, I always refused. I considered it too cruel. I would tell them frankly, 'Only a miracle can bring him home.' "

On 13 August, a search plane reported rubber rafts ashore on Eromanga, an island between New Caledonia and Efate. The next day Navy crews rescued all ten men. "Halsey nearly cried," remembered one officer, "when word came that Bill was safe."

On 15 August 4,600 American troops assaulted Vella Lavella. Halsey informed Nimitz, "We landed successfully. . . . There were many bombing attacks and we suffered a few personal casualties, but we made them pay heavily in planes. We should soon be fairly well organized at that point and from now on the wisdom of our move will be determined. . . . Our part of the present phase is almost finished. It is merely a matter of mopping up and holding what we have. . . . The next move forward is going to be tough. My land forces are thin. . . . I am, as always, in favor of throwing everything we have at the Japs, wherever we can find them.''

There was never any ground combat on Vella Lavella because the 250 Japanese on the island were more intent on escaping than fighting. The real struggle for Vella Lavella took place in the air and on the sea. Enemy bombers and fighter planes attacked shipping and ground installations during daylight hours, and seaplanes harassed the Americans at night. Combat air patrols attempted to ward them off.

Construction battalions had already started work on the airfield on Vella Lavella, surveying and clearing a strip 4,000 feet long by 200 feet wide. They built a control tower, operations shack, and fuel tanks. The first plane landed on 24 September and within two months after the invasion the field accommodated 100 aircraft. The decision to leapfrog Kolombangara yielded this air base in return for a low casualty figure.

In mid-August Washington informed Halsey that Mrs. Eleanor Roosevelt, wife of the President, was touring the South Pacific and would arrive in Noumea. Halsey's reaction was not enthusiastic. ''Among an area commander's worst problems,'' he said, ''are politicians, admirals and generals, 'special' correspondents, and 'do-gooders' who present themselves in assurance that their visit is a 'morale factor,' and are entitled to 'see it from the inside.' Mrs. Roosevelt I classed as a do-gooder, and I dreaded her arrival.'' Halsey resented wearing a necktie to play the gracious host. ''I had no time for such folderol, yet I'd have to take time.''

When Mrs. Roosevelt stepped off the plane, wearing a Red Cross uniform, Halsey greeted her and asked what she intended to do in Noumea.

''What do you think I should do?''

''Mrs. Roosevelt, I've been married for thirty-odd years, and if those years have taught me one lesson, it is never to try to make up a woman's mind for her."

Halsey suggested that she stay in New Caledonia for several days, then fly to Australia, and, on her return to Noumea, spend several more days before she flew back to the States. She handed the admiral a letter from the President, asking permission for her to tour Guadalcanal. Halsey said curtly, "Guadalcanal is no place for you, Ma'am!"

"I'm perfectly willing to take my chances," she said. "I'll be entirely responsible for anything that happens to me."

"I'm not worried about the responsibility, and I'm not worried about the chances you'd take. What worries me is . . . [that] I need every fighter plane I can put my hands on. If you fly to Guadalcanal, I'll have to provide a fighter escort for you, and I haven't got one to spare."

Halsey billeted Mrs. Roosevelt in Wicky-Wacky Lodge. That first evening Halsey hosted a small cocktail party and dinner for her, and early the next morning she started inspecting Noumea hospitals, reviewing troops, speaking to a service club luncheon, and attending a reception.

The New Georgia campaign was finished by the time Mrs. Roosevelt returned from Australia and Halsey consented— "though with misgivings"—to her visiting Guadalcanal.

"When I saw her off," said Halsey, "I told her that it was impossible for me to express my appreciation of what she had done, and was doing, for my men. I was ashamed of my original surliness. She alone had accomplished more good than any other person, or any group of civilians, who had passed through my area."

Halsey's misgivings about her Guadalcanal trip were nearly warranted. The night before her plane arrived, the Japanese sent their first bombing attack against the island in two months, and sent another the night after her departure. Once she had cleared the South Pacific area, Halsey sighed in relief.

Intelligence warned Noumea that on the night of 6/7 October Japanese surface units would attempt to rescue any soldiers remaining on Vella or to evacuate Kolombangara. Three American destroyers stood northward and engaged two Japanese destroyers in the night battle of Vella Lavella. One American destroyer, the *Chevalier,* was torpedoed and, running out of control, smashed into the *O'Bannon.* A torpedo hit the *Selfridge.* Seemingly in a state of temporary shock, the Japanese force, instead of shelling the American ships, retired to the northward. Halsey reported, "Our occupation of . . . Vella is now complete. The central Solomons campaign has ended, and has justified American strategy by bypassing Kolombangara."

Rabaul, the last remaining threat to the American-Australian-New Zealand lifeline, now haunted the staff's thinking. No operation in the Solomons, no matter how successful, could be considered complete as long as Rabaul remained strong. Resurgent Japanese troops could possibly move from Rabaul and reconquer Guadalcanal or eastern New Guinea. It was paramount that the fortress be seized or neutralized before the Allies could move toward the Philippines or operate successfully in the South Pacific. Thus the invasion of Bougainville in the northern Solomons became, in effect, the campaign to contain Rabaul. To reduce Rabaul, American air power had to destroy its facilities and cut its supply line through the seizure and the protection of airfields on Bougainville, from where bombers and fighters could blanket the Japanese fortress.

Japanese troops on Bougainville, the largest of the Solomon Islands, numbered 35,000. The island was close to Rabaul and other subsidiary bases and lay within easy reach of the enemy fleet at Truk. The invasion of Bougainville was a calculated risk.

In July 1943 the staff had decided that marines would attack Buin, Kahili, and Tomolei Harbor on southern Bougainville and the nearby islands in Bougainville Strait—the Shortlands, Faisi, and Ballale. Intelligence, however, indicated that the Japanese defenses in those sectors had been reinforced. With the bypass of Kolombangara fresh in their minds, they decided to leapfrog again and secure a beachhead where the enemy was weak.

Halsey agreed and suggested the shift in plans to MacArthur. The objectives of the Bougainville operation, he said, were to deny the use of airfields and anchorages to the enemy and to secure airfields and anchorages for the Americans, as a step toward the seizure of Rabaul. Halsey argued that terrain, strategic position, and troop dispositions indicated that southern Bougainville was important to the enemy; the invasion would have to be a major one. He advised that the Allies could save men and valuable time by avoiding the Bougainville mainland all together, suggesting the capture of the Shortlands and Ballale. In Brisbane, MacArthur approved the operation.

By September, Halsey and the staff proposed still another change in the Bougainville operation. Vella Lavella had shown the validity of hitting weak points, in preference to a thrust against fixed positions. Intelligence reported that airfield sites on the Shortlands were not good and that an invasion of the Shortlands, which the enemy had strengthened, would involve heavy casualties. Poor beaches would hamper the unloading of heavy construction equipment and howitzers for the bombardment of Kahili on the mainland.

Studying ways to neutralize the Shortlands without capturing them, the staff proposed that Halsey step up the air effort from New Georgia. They suggested the capture of Treasury Island and Choiseul Bay as airfield and PT boat base sites from which to neutralize southern Bougainville and the Shortlands.

Submarines, planes, and PT boats sent reconnaissance teams ashore at several points on Bougainville. These units reported that Cape Torokina in Empress Augusta Bay, halfway up the southwestern coast, was the best possibility.

Therefore the staff suggested that Halsey and MacArthur should decide quickly whether to mount an offensive from Choiseul to Kieta on the east coast of Bougainville or from Treasury Island to Empress Augusta Bay on the west.

When Admiral Robert B. (''Mick'') Carney, Halsey's Chief of Staff, and Colonel William E. Riley, USMC, War Plans Officer, discussed these operations with MacArthur in Brisbane on 10 September, the general wanted the Allied advance in the South and Southwest Pacific speeded up. He agreed with the leapfrog concept but argued that the staff's plan would make it impossible for Halsey's planes to strike Rabaul effectively before 1 March 1944. He insisted bombers and fighters be within range of Rabaul in time to cover his landings at Cape Gloucester on the western tip of New Britain Island sometime in late December.

To give MacArthur air assistance for his Cape Gloucester operation, Halsey had to invade the Bougainville mainland by 1 November. MacArthur directed that between 20 and 25 October South Pacific troops should land at Treasury Island and at Choiseul and on 1 November capture Empress Augusta Bay on the west coast of Bougainville.

When asked if he preferred an attack on the east coast or the west coast of Bougainville, MacArthur replied, "No, that is entirely as Halsey decides. To me it makes no difference."

Submarines patrolled the east coast and Empress Augusta Bay to gain information. Intelligence officers talked with missionaries, traders, planters, and coasters. The submarine *Gato,* scouting the east coast of Bougainville, reported that the beaches were unfit for landings. A Marine unit debarked from the submarine *Guardfish* ten miles northwest of Cape Torokina in Empress Augusta Bay. They scraped up soil samples which, when tested, showed that Cape Torokina was usable for an air base.

In Noumea the staff estimated that 1,000 Japanese soldiers were in the area of Empress Augusta Bay. The high mountains surrounding the area almost isolated it from the reinforced enemy garrisons in southern Bougainville. The staff guessed that if American troops captured Cape Torokina it would take the Japanese four months to mount a counterattack. On the debit side, the treacherous surf at Empress Aususta Bay, which had no safe anchorages, would make an invasion difficult. Only sixty-five miles separated Cape Torokina from the enemy airfields on Bougainville and it was within fighter range of Rabaul.

At a staff conference in Noumea, Halsey, estimating the risk, announced, "It's Torokina. Now get on your horses." D-Day was set for 1 November.

Prior to this date, New Zealand troops would occupy Treasury Island, midway between Cape Torokina and the American airstrip on Vella Lavella. South Pacific forces needed lightly defended Treasury, both as a protection for their flank and as a location for an airfield.

Americans would land on Choiseul which, like Treasury, lies about thirty miles from Bougainville. General Roy Geiger, commanding the Marines in the South Pacific area, reported that these two minor operations would be "a series of short right jabs to throw the enemy off balance and to control the real power for our left hook to his belly at Empress Augusta Bay." The staff expected such advances to deceive the enemy into rushing reinforcements to Choiseul, which the Allies intended to abandon.

An elaborate deception was staged at the Shortland Islands at the southern tip of Bougainville. Halsey's combat patrols deliberately left evidence of their visits, and every day photographic reconnaissance planes made low level runs across the islands. As a result the enemy moved troops and artillery over from Bougainville, firmly believing that this would be the target of the American invasion.

A few Japanese fighter planes opposed the Treasury Island landing (27 October), but the New Zealanders secured the island without heavy casualties. That same night Marines smashed into Choiseul and began their twelve-day raid.

D-Day for Cape Torokina in Empress Augusta Bay, 1 November, dawned bright and clear. General Quarters on all ships clanged at 0500. Troops lined the rails, and saw a beautiful sunrise outlining Bougainville's forbidding mountain range. After cruisers, destroyers, and planes from Munda softened up the beaches, minesweepers led transports to their anchorages. At 0726 the first boatloads of Marines waded ashore. Half the Japanese garrison of 300 were killed. The remainder escaped inland. Beach and terrain conditions were the worst that Americans had ever encountered. Running into a strong wind and rough surf, eighty-six landing craft broached and stranded, ruining cargo and overburdening the boat pool. Many beaches were rimmed by swamps and were so narrow that they became snarled with vital gear, vehicles and machinery. By 1100, however, the Marines had cleared Cape Torokina.

Admiral A. Stanton ("Tip") Merrill's Task Force Thirty-Nine (four cruisers and eight destroyers) steamed northward and met a Japanese surface unit—four heavy cruisers and six destroyers—running down from Rabaul. Just after midnight on 2 November the warships opened up and in the vicious Battle of Empress Augusta Bay, which lasted three hours, Task Force Thirty-Nine sank one cruiser and one destroyer. Except for a crippled destroyer, hit by a Japanese torpedo, the American ships received only light damage.

On 4 November American scout planes reported an enemy armada of eight cruisers, four destroyers, and a fleet train steaming toward Rabaul from Truk. At Noumea Halsey and his staff calculated that the enemy would refuel at Rabaul, then move toward Empress Augusta Bay and shell the Marines' precarious beachhead. If successful, "they would wipe us out." "This was the most desperate emergency," said Halsey, "that confronted me in my entire term" as Commander of the South Pacific Forces. "The entire Bougainville operation—perhaps the success of the South Pacific War—hung upon its being stopped."

Halsey had only two naval elements, Merrill's task force, exhausted from its action of 2 November, and Admiral Frederick C. ("Ted") Sherman's Task Force Thirty-Eight (two carriers, two cruisers, and ten destroyers). Up to now, Halsey had employed his carriers against land bases only in a cautious fashion.

The majority of the staff, including Mick Carney, wanted to send the carriers in and strike Rabaul from the air, hopefully crippling the warships. Halsey violently objected. The risks were too high, the odds too great. Aircraft would be "cut to pieces," the carriers "stricken." But after a heated discussion, Halsey relented and signed the order. "We could not let the men at Torokina be wiped out," said Halsey, "while we stood by and wrung our hands." This was one of the rare occasions when Halsey objected to a staff decision.

After Halsey signed the order, Carney recalled, "Everyone of us knew what was going through the admiral's mind. It showed in his face, which suddenly looked 150 years old."

Halsey ordered South Pacific land-based air support from New Georgia to cover the carriers, *Saratoga* and *Princeton,* during their daylight approach and retirement, enabling Sherman to send off all his aircraft against Rabaul instead of keeping some of them overhead for protection.

The *Princeton* and *Saratoga* reached their launching positions in the Solomon Sea fifty-seven miles southwest of Cape Torokina and 230 miles southeast of Rabaul at 0900, 5 November. Ninety-seven planes sped off the carriers—twenty-three torpedo bombers, twenty-two dive bombers, and fifty-two fighters. Escaping from severe ack-ack fire from the guns at Rabaul, they sneaked through the enemy's fighter screen, shot down twenty-five enemy planes, and bombed and damaged five cruisers and two destroyers anchored in Simpson Harbor. After the attack, the Japanese decided to pull their heavy cruisers back to Truk, and the threat to Empress Augusta Bay was ended.

"It was the first time," said Halsey, "that carriers ever had attacked a strong air base. They damaged practically every Jap cruiser and . . . destroyer, but . . . [our] carriers were not attacked." The entire operation opened "the taps to a funeral dirge for . . . Rabaul."

Halsey shot off a dispatch to his carriers, "May the Jap cripples be hermetically buried in Davy Jones' locker."

Carney agreed. "The hasty retreat of the Jap fleet convinced us that the days of Rabaul as a naval base were ended."

"We were biting our nails," Carney wrote Halsey after the war, "wondering how the troops were going to make out on the Bougainville landing, and it was not so many days after that you gave the green light on the desperate scheme to launch the carrier attack on Rabaul as the only alternative to possible obliteration of our beachhead troops and their covering forces."

One officer close to Halsey recalled: "The major turning point in the South Pacific campaign [was] . . . the carrier strike on Rabaul. . . . By this bold strike the Bougainville operation was . . . secured and as a result Rabaul became eventually no longer a major threat to our forces."

In summing up the effects of the Bougainville operation, the Japanese admiral who commanded Rabaul reported, "When considered with other actions of this campaign it appeared to me to be the climax of your advance up the Solomon Islands. After the battle you were able to establish bases on Bougainville which permitted you to maintain constant air assaults on Rabaul, which prevented us from providing support and air cover to our bases on New Guinea and New Britain."

The press cheered the victory. "The knocking out in one mighty air blow of the Jap plane strength at Rabaul has not only placed the entire position in the south and southwest Pacific in jeopardy," wrote a New York *Times* correspondent, "but has made possible an air blockade. . . . U.S. bombers can make Hirohito's staff pay a high price in ships to try to reinforce the Japs at Rabaul."

An additional carrier task group (*Bunker Hill, Essex,* and *Independence*), commanded by Admiral Alfred E. Montgomery, arrived in the South Pacific to bolster Halsey's fighting force. On 11 November planes from Montgomery's group and Task Force Thirty-Eight bombed Rabaul, sinking a destroyer, damaging another ship, and splashing twenty-four planes. A series of furious though unsuccessful air attacks on Montgomery's carriers inflicted only minor damage.

Halsey's landing force at Bougainville had been rendered secure by the carriers operating offensively against a major Japanese air base, and, without the benefit of escorting battleships and cruisers, they had survived a heavy air attack by knocking out enemy land-based planes. The Japanese losses at Rabaul destroyed the possibility of their successfully defending the Gilberts or the Marshalls in the Central Pacific. The carrier raids together with repeated strikes by Army Air Force bombers convinced the Japanese that Rabaul was unsafe for shipping, although their Navy was yet unwilling to give it up as an airfield. Yet with Bougainville in American control, Rabaul would soon be within reach of Halsey's land-based fighters.

On 13 November Admiral Mineichi Koga recalled the survivors of his carrier planes that had been sent to Rabaul several weeks before. Of the 173 planes dispatched from his carriers, Koga had lost half his fighters and all of his attack planes in the numerous air actions above Rabaul. His carriers became little more than floating targets until fresh air crews could be trained. With his carriers out of action, his battleships were helplessly exposed. The Japanese fleet at Truk was powerless while air defenses for the Gilberts and Marshalls no longer existed.

After the Rabaul strikes, Halsey flew northward to Bougainville. Dressed in khaki shorts and shirt and wearing a pith helmet,

Halsey held a press conference shortly after his arrival. He told correspondents, "Our program here is ahead of schedule. This, however, was perhaps the toughest beach landing of the entire Solomons campaign, but the job was well done and progress is now heartening." Halsey heaped praise on the Army Air Force in the Solomons for "knocking out every Jap airfield on Bougainville and keeping them knocked out."

Asked whether he thought the enemy might put up another last ditch stand on Bougainville, he replied, "The situation isn't the same here as during the invasion of Guadalcanal. We've got the stuff now. The Japs haven't."

During his stay on Bougainville, "where living was still primitive," Halsey visited the Empress Augusta camp, fortifications, battle areas, hospitals, and cemeteries.

On his return to Noumea, Halsey informed Nimitz, "The Bougainville job is progressing well. . . . I am deeply impressed by the enthusiasm and spirit that actuates the entire outfit in spite of terrain and beach difficulties which inherently make it the toughest job we have tackled."

"I don't have to tell you what a tough decision it was to send the *Saratoga* air group in the face of Rabaul's defenses," Halsey continued, "but the situation was extremely grave and the entire success of a South Pacific campaign was endangered by the reinforcements the Japs had thrown into Rabaul. We all owe the *Saratoga* group a debt of gratitude. . . . They did a great job and completely upset the surface ratio for the moment. I only wish it might have been possible, while the Japs were hanging on the ropes, to have smashed their cripples at Truk."

To a friend, Halsey wrote, "We are pretty well consolidated in Empress Augusta Bay and will have a field in full operation in a few days. The Seabees and Army engineers have done an outstanding and wonderful job there. The Japtards have been in a complete tailspin ever since we landed. We have killed many of them (God how they stink in the jungle) and lost very few men doing so. I see in a speech Tojo stated, 'the brave Japanese are dying like flowers in the front lines.' They don't smell like flowers after they are dead!"

Planes from airfields on New Georgia, Vella Lavella, and later from Treasury and Bougainville, stepped up raids on Rabaul to immobilize it completely. The war in the South Pacific was changing dramatically in pattern and scope. Less than two years before, the Japanese had swept down from their homeland and mandated islands and conquered millions of square miles of territory that they felt destined to exploit. Forced to fight defensively, the Allies eventually stopped the enemy and pushed them back from Guadalcanal, back from Vella Lavella, back from New Georgia, and Bougainville.

In December MacArthur's Southwest Pacific forces successfully crossed the Vitiaz Straits from the Huon Peninsula in New Guinea to New Britain Island. They captured Cape Gloucester, the northwestern tip commanding Dampier Strait, and Arawe Harbor on the south coast.

The Joint Chiefs of Staff's directive which launched the campaign against Rabaul had approved of operations following the seizure of Cape Gloucester and Arawe. MacArthur's original plans included the seizure of Kavieng on northern New Ireland and of Manus in the Admiralties in the Bismarck Archipelago. Kavieng was to become a minor fleet anchorage, a PT boat base, and a major air base with six airfields. Manus would serve as an air base while Seeadler Harbor would be made into a major fleet base complete with drydocks and repair installations.

At Noumea Halsey's staff began planning the next offensive. "After a rather bad show we had in New Georgia," Halsey recalled, "it had been the intention of my staff and me to use every endeavor to spare lives in gaining territory that must be taken. We knew Rabaul would be a 'hard nut to crack' and after we had it we would not have anything worthwhile."

Since Navy and Army planes had reduced Rabaul, the Joint Chiefs decided to bypass the island. Several members of Halsey's staff argued for the invasion of lightly defended Emirau in the Saint Matthias Islands, ninety miles north of Rabaul. By occupying Emirau and constructing airfields, the Allies would make Rabaul "absolutely impotent."

Arriving at this decision, Halsey and his staff flew to Brisbane and attempted to sell MacArthur on Emirau. The air successes against Rabaul had not convinced the general that its current effectiveness was removed. He was profoundly concerned about leaving so many undefeated Japanese behind when he advanced toward the Philippines.

MacArthur argued for the seizure of the enemy stronghold at Kavieng. Halsey's staff believed such an operation would be "a bloodbath." Like Rabaul, Kavieng could be neutralized if air forces were based on Emirau. When the conference ended, Halsey returned to Noumea convinced that MacArthur had approved of the Emirau operation.

The Gilberts and Marshalls campaigns were the first full scale amphibious operations in the Pacific. More than 200 ships carrying 108,000 soldiers, sailors, and marines under the command of Admirals Raymond Spruance and Kelly Turner and Major General H. M. ("Howling Mad") Smith, USMC, converged on two coral atolls of the Gilbert group in mid-November 1943. Makin, where the enemy had no great strength, was taken methodically by a regiment of the 27th Infantry Division, but Tarawa, a small, heavily defended position behind a long coral-reef apron, was difficult to invade. The lives of almost a thousand marines and sailors were required to dispose of 4,000 no-surrender Japanese on an islet not three miles long. But Tarawa provided another airfield. The Gilberts became bases from which planes helped neutralize the seven Japanese air bases in the Marshalls. These islands were sealed off by the carrier forces of Rear Admiral Marc Mitscher.

Soon after the Gilberts campaign ended in early December, the combined Allied planners decided that an air and sea blockade of Japan would be the ultimate objective of all operations in the Pacific. Both MacArthur's Southwest and Nimitz's Central Pacific forces would continue separately toward the major objective—the area of Formosa-Luzon-China. The enemy fleet had to be destroyed at an early date. The objective, Formosa-Luzon-China, once secured, Allied naval forces could blockade the Japanese home islands from the vital raw materials transported by sea from the East Indies through this region. The exact invasion point, be it northern Luzon, the island of Formosa, or the Chinese coast, would be determined later. The blockade was to include mining, air, and submarine attacks on Japanese shipping and ports.

Assured that Halsey's South Pacific Force had neutralized Rabaul, planners turned their attention to Truk, "the Gibraltar of the Pacific," which would have to be captured. But before Truk could be invaded, American troops first had to seize the Marshall Islands.

In early December 1943 a new Pacific time schedule dictated the invasion of the Marshalls during January 1944; from there land-based planes could pound Truk. One month later Nimitz would support MacArthur in advancing to Hollandia on the northern coast of New Guinea. Then in the summer of 1944, Nimitz's Central Pacific Force would strike Truk, and in October they would invade Guam and other Marianas islands. Once the airfields in the Marianas were operable, the superfortresses (B-29s) would attack Japan itself.

[VIII]

"A Piece of String,
a Can of Beans
and a Rusty Nail"

IN DECEMBER 1943, Halsey received orders to proceed to Pearl Harbor to confer with Nimitz. From there he was to fly to Los Angeles to attend a convention of industrialists, then to Washington.

Halsey and several staff members arrived at Pearl Harbor on 26 December. The admiral spent four days with Nimitz, discussing South Pacific policy.

Going on to San Francisco Halsey met his wife, Fan, who had flown out from Wilmington, Delaware, to greet him and son Bill, whose ship happened to be in port. It was the admiral's first meeting with Fan in sixteen months and his first with Bill since he had been downed in the Pacific.

While Halsey was in San Francisco, Admirals King and Nimitz arrived for one of their periodic conferences. Halsey attended the meetings, which involved extensive discussions of the choice of objectives in the coming Central Pacific campaign.

To control the seas and secure a route from Hawaii westward, King and Nimitz advocated continuing the leapfrogging of enemy bases which were unnecessary to Allied strategy. As at previous conferences, King emphasized that the key to the entire western Pacific was the Marianas Islands and that all current operations

110

were aimed at a drive through the Pacific to the Chinese coast to exploit its geographic and strategic position in the final push against Japan.

When King asked Halsey when he was going to take Rabaul or Kavieng, Halsey's reply was "Why take either one?" Asked what he had to suggest in lieu of it, Halsey said emphatically, *"Emirau."* He knew full well that King had no idea of "what and where Emirau was." Halsey pointed it out on the chart, showing him that the island commanded the northern approaches to Rabaul. He then stressed the importance of seizing Green Island, 120 miles away, which controlled the eastern accesses to Rabaul; and Manus in the Admiralties, north of New Britain. These operations would complete the American objectives in the South Pacific.

After the conference in San Francisco, Halsey flew to Los Angeles. At a brief news conference he told reporters, "The only good Jap is a Jap who's been dead six months. When we get to Tokyo, where we're bound to get eventually, we'll have a little celebration where Tokyo was."

Asked why the Japanese fleet had failed to fight in recent months, Halsey explained that it was difficult for any American to assess the Oriental mind.

"It's one of two things," he said. "Either they are saving their fleet until we approach the shores of the Japanese Empire, or they think they can wear us down by attrition tactics. The Japs are good. I hate to say it, but they are very good. But they are not supermen and they no longer want to die for their emperor—the son of whatever he is. Sometimes when our men are close enough to hear and our shells explode among them, they scream their heads off."

Although Halsey admitted that Japanese planes had improved slightly, he said there had been a decided deterioration in their pilots. "They're not as willing to come and fight. They've got kids in their air force."

Halsey flew to Washington, where Secretary Knox awarded him a Gold Star in lieu of a second Distinguished Service medal.

Halsey planned to attend a conference at Pearl Harbor with Nimitz and MacArthur's Chief of Staff, General Richard K.

Sutherland. Unfortunately, his plane was grounded in Fort Worth, Texas, and later in San Francisco because of bad weather. By the time he reached Pearl Harbor, the meeting had adjourned. But Mick Carney, who had represented the South Pacific forces, briefed him.

MacArthur wanted the South Pacific forces to seize Kavieng, not Emirau, for use as an air base. Halsey's plan was shelved for the present. The acquisition of Seeadler Harbor at Manus, they all agreed, was paramount as a fleet base for the drive to the Philippines. After talking about operations in the Bismarck Archipelago, they discussed a wide range of topics—the Marianas, Truk, the comparative merits of the Central and Southwest Pacific approaches to the Philippines, naval support for the forthcoming campaigns.

Prior to Halsey's departure for the South Pacific, stirring news reached Hawaii. On 31 January 1944 the massive amphibious forces commanded by Admirals Harry Hill and Kelly Turner stormed ashore at Kwajalein in the Marshalls. Kwajalein fell with such ease that the original time schedule was scrapped and a new one prepared. The victory revealed substantial enemy weaknesses in the vicinity of the Gilberts and Marshalls. A follow-up landing at Eniwetok, the westernmost of the Marshalls, could be launched immediately.

On 17 February troops stormed ashore on Eniwetok. The enemy resisted to the last man. The Japanese Navy dared not challenge as its air arm had been weakened in its effort to defend Rabaul. On 20 February Japanese ships and aircraft were chased out of Truk with heavy losses by a round-the-clock carrier raid. With the Marshalls secured and Truk battered, the Marianas were now wide open to attack and invasion.

The rapid clearing of Kwajalein and Eniwetok and the neutralization of Truk accelerated the pace in the Central Pacific. Nimitz informed King that a major amphibious landing could be made in June either on Truk or in the Marianas, depending on the analysis of photographs taken by carrier planes.

Halsey and Carney reached Noumea early in February and started work on plans to assault Kavieng. As Nimitz could not furnish more carrier support to the South Pacific forces for several months, the staff had already proposed seizing Green Island, thirty-seven miles northwest of Bougainville and within fighter range of Kavieng. At a conference in Port Moresby, New Guinea, attended by MacArthur and his staff, Carney suggested that Southwest Pacific troops capture Manus while Halsey's forces occupied lightly defended Green Island. Not only would this atoll provide an air base site, it would extend the range of PT boat patrols as far as New Ireland. Although MacArthur had decided for the time being against the occupation of Manus, he told Carney to go ahead with the invasion of Green Island.

In mid-February New Zealand and American troops went ashore at Green Island, destroying the Japanese garrison. By March 16,448 men and 43,088 tons of supplies had landed at the atoll. A PT boat base was established and a 5,000-foot fighter field was ready by 4 March.

After South Pacific troops occupied Green Island, MacArthur developed his plans for moving into the Admiralties. He directed the South and Southwest Pacific forces to secure control of the Bismarck Archipelago and to isolate Rabaul by capturing Manus, the largest island in the Admiralties, and Kavieng about 1 April. The Admiralties, which lie 200 miles northeast of New Guinea and 260 miles west of Kavieng, were well-situated to help in isolating Rabaul and in supporting the advance to the Philippines as they had two airfields and a splendid harbor.

Southwest Pacific soldiers, advancing the time schedule, went ashore in the Admiralties on 29 February. Although fighting on the islands continued for some time, troops secured Seeadler Harbor by mid-March, and construction battalions went to work rebuilding airfields and the naval base.

MacArthur, Nimitz, and the Joint Chiefs of Staff had intended that Seeadler Harbor be used by all Allied fleets. However, Nimitz urged King to give Halsey the responsibility, under CINCPAC, for developing and controlling the harbor. The Joint Chiefs rejected the idea but not before MacArthur became so angry that he directed work at Manus "restricted to facilities for ships under his direct command—the Seventh Fleet and British units."

Halsey received an urgent request in early March to fly to Brisbane. MacArthur was irate. He accused Halsey, Nimitz, King, and the entire United States Navy of conspiring to strip away his authority. MacArthur wanted Manus for his own Seventh Fleet. The issue was critical to future Pacific strategy. Nimitz would base the carriers there for the Navy's proposed invasion of Formosa or the Chinese mainland, bypassing the Philippines; MacArthur would base the Seventh Fleet there for his intended liberation of the Philippines.

MacArthur harangued Halsey for fifteen minutes. He had no intention of submitting to Navy inefficiency and, until the jurisdiction of Manus was settled, work would be restricted to facilities for ships under his own direct command.

When the blistering stopped, he asked, "Am I not right, Bill?"

Kinkaid, Carney, and Halsey answered with one voice, "No, sir!"

MacArthur, now smiling, replied. "Well, if so many fine gentlemen disagree with me, we'd better examine the proposition once more. Bill, what's your opinion?"

"General," Halsey said, "I disagree with you entirely. Not only that, but I'm going one step further and tell you that if you stick to this order of yours, you'll be hampering the war effort!"

Halsey reiterated that the command of Manus was no concern of his, but what did matter was the quick construction of a naval base. "An enlisted cavalryman could boss it for all I cared," Halsey remarked later, "as long as it was ready to handle the fleet when we moved up New Guinea and on toward the Philippines."

The conference lasted an hour and although Halsey believed that his plans had prevailed, that was not the case. "It seemed that during the night," Halsey wrote, "he had become mad all over again, and again was dead set on restricting the work [on Manus]."

MacArthur called Halsey into his office the next morning. They argued again. After an hour, they reached the same conclusion as on the afternoon before. Work on Manus would proceed.

Just as Halsey was ready to depart for Noumea, the general called him back to the office. They squabbled a third time.

Halsey accused MacArthur of putting selfish motives above national aims, of not wanting Nimitz to control Manus as he, Mac-Arthur, had arrived there first. The general retorted, "My God! You can't mean that? We can't have anything like that." Mac-Arthur finally backed down, agreeing to cancel his order.

Despite the argument, Halsey flew out of Brisbane still with a high regard for the general. "He is a damn good soldier," Halsey wrote a friend, "and he is doing a damn good job. If he wants to strut his stuff—let him strut. It does no harm and works off excess energy. He is my strategic boss, and while he has not interfered I have found my relations with him most pleasant." And after this Brisbane meeting, the relationship between Halsey and MacArthur continued to be congenial and their staffs worked well together.

The difference between Nimitz and MacArthur regarding Pacific strategy was finally resolved in March 1944 when Nimitz and Admiral Forrest Sherman went to Washington for conferences with President Roosevelt and the Joint Chiefs of Staff. King relied on Sherman to discuss the problems, although the controversy became tense when MacArthur's staff members presented the Army's side. After two days of conferences, the situation was clarified. The Joint Chiefs of Staff compromised. Aerial photographs had indicated the feasibility of invading the Marianas, while carrier strikes had made the landings on Truk unnecessary. The Joint Chiefs of Staff, therefore, told the Navy to continue neutralizing Truk and on 15 June to invade Saipan in the Marianas. Nimitz was also directed to plan an assault on Formosa in February 1945. The Army would secure New Guinea, cancel the proposed Kavieng assault, then move into the southern Philippines, especially Mindanao, late in 1944, and was to plan for landings on Luzon in February 1945.

Soon after Halsey had returned to Noumea after his meeting with MacArthur in Brisbane, the Joint Chiefs of Staff, influenced by Halsey's arguments, sent a dispatch to MacArthur, directing that the invasion of Emirau be substituted for the invasion of Kavieng. Quickly, Halsey's staff shelved Kavieng plans and revived those for the seizure of Emirau. Once on the island construction battalions were to establish an air base from which to blockade the Bismarck Archipelago and neutralize Truk. Air strikes to isolate Rabaul and Kavieng were to continue.

On 14 March Halsey directed the marines to land and occupy Emirau "at the earliest practicable date," no later than 20 March. Staffs gathered and drew up operational papers. Halsey approved them.

On 20 March, as four old battleships bombarded Kavieng, marines landed and easily occupied Emirau. There were no Japanese. Although convoys had steamed more than 800 miles through waters recently commanded by the enemy, no plane took off from Rabaul, Kavieng, or Truk to intercept them, and not a destroyer or submarine appeared. Peacefully, the Emirau invasion was completed and with it the long and difficult series of operations against Rabaul which had started with landings at Guadalcanal two years before. The Allies now controlled the sea and air in the entire region of the Japanese Southeast Area.

The months-long campaign against Rabaul was of enormous importance. It enabled MacArthur's forces to break through the Bismarcks' barrier of enemy air and sea power and move toward the Philippines. Bypassing numerous islands, Americans immobilized 125,000 enemy troops. The campaign against Rabaul also made the Japanese withdraw their carriers from the Pacific.

"I have just witnessed the completion of the South Pacific Campaign," said Halsey, "from the early desperate days at Guadalcanal to the easy seizure of Emirau Island, just seventy-five miles from the once-mighty Japanese base at Kavieng. We learned a lot of lessons as we marched up the Solomons, lessons which are saving countless lives of our men and materially shortening the road to Tokyo."

"In contrast to the Guadalcanal days," he continued, "the seizure of Emirau . . . was made without the loss of a man, and without contacting a single enemy plane, warship or soldier. This extraordinary difference can be measured almost entirely in terms of the war materiel available in each case. Even the Japanese stubbornness is no match for the steamrolling fighting power that we were able to throw at them at the end of the campaign.''

Emirau ''was a pushover'' because of the overwhelming superiority of American forces and equipment. ''Other powerful Japanese bastions of strength lie before us, and there is still before us the final goal of a crushed and surrendering Japan,'' he said. ''The men and materiel we have lost in the first Pacific victories are only a fraction of the cost in blood and treasure we must pay to achieve total victory. That cost in blood can be lessened—will be lessened—if we have overwhelming materiel power.''

Amphibious operations had worked smoothly and efficiently in the South Pacific. After the war, Halsey was asked a number of questions relating to tactics. Asked whether the relationships between ground, naval, and air components were governed by the principle of unity of command or the principle of mutual cooperation, Halsey replied, ''The Unity of Command principle is sound. Two or more co-equal commanders in the combat zone, working under the principle of 'mutual cooperation' begets confusion. I consider 'mutual cooperation' in the combat zone unsound as a military principle.''

What provisions were made for the transfer of command of ground forces from the senior naval commander to the senior ground commander? ''When the Ground Force Commander had his headquarters established ashore, and he was in all respects prepared to assume command . . . command would be shifted from the amphibious commander . . . at a prearranged time, mutually agreed upon between the senior naval commander and the senior ground commander.''

To what extent, if any, did naval commanders retain control over ground forces after the troops had landed? ''As commander, South Pacific Forces, I always retained control of all my forces, ashore, afloat, and in the air. This control was exercised through subordinate commanders. . . . I always monitored all operations at all times. There were undoubtedly at times attempted interference, but these incidents were trivial.''

Was the organization of command in the amphibious operations satisfactory? ''By a system of trial and error, the organization of command . . . became more and more satisfactory. The pattern then established for air control was a pattern for air control in amphibious operations . . . [for] the remainder of the war. No operation is entirely satisfactory to the overall commander. Each operation brought out new lessons, and by constantly studying these lessons . . . improvements were inaugurated."

"Our movements up the Solomon Islands," Halsey concluded, "were for the purpose of establishing airfields, where we could establish our land-based air—we had few carriers and sometimes none. These fields were established to neutralize and contain the Japanese air in this locality."

April passed quietly. Halsey enthusiastically received the news of MacArthur's invasion of Hollandia in central New Guinea, the first direct move in the Southwest Pacific forces' advance toward the Philippines. In May Halsey flew to San Francisco for a conference with Admirals King and Nimitz. The war in the South Pacific had ended. Halsey had fought himself out of a job. He would continue as Commander, Third Fleet, but, in June, would be relieved as Commander, South Pacific Area. This reorganization divided the entire Pacific Fleet into two teams: Spruance's Fifth Fleet and Halsey's Third Fleet. One group could plan, train, and be resupplied, while the other fought, reducing the time between operations.

On the second day of the meetings King and Nimitz penciled in June 1944 for the Marianas invasion. Washington had already firmed up the timetable—Palau, 15 September, for Nimitz; the southern Philippines, late 1944, for MacArthur.

The Palaus, Halsey said, should be leapfrogged, but King and Nimitz disagreed emphatically.

No sooner had the San Francisco meeting ended, than the Joint Chiefs of Staff issued a directive, asking Nimitz and MacArthur if the Philippines and Formosa could be bypassed in favor of a direct assault on Kyushu, southern Japan.

Nimitz and staff members flew to Brisbane to coordinate the campaigns in the Central and Southwest Pacific. "Everything . . . was harmonious," Nimitz wrote King, "until the last day of our conference when I called attention to the last part of the

J.C.S. directive which required him and me to prepare alternate plans for moving faster and along shorter routes toward the Luzon-Formosa-China triangle if deteriorating Japanese strength permitted."

MacArthur exploded and argued against bypassing the Philippines, "his sacred obligations there—the redemption of 17 million people—blood on his soul—deserted by the American people—etc., etc.—and then a criticism of 'those gentlemen in Washington, who, far from the scene, and having never heard the whistle of the pellets, etc., endeavor to set the strategy of the Pacific War.' "

Nimitz staunchly defended "those gentlemen in Washington," and told MacArthur that the Joint Chiefs were people like them, people who, with more information, were "doing their best and were succeeding admirably."

Both, however, replied negatively to the Joint Chiefs of Staff directive. Intermediate air and fleet bases were required in the Palaus and the southern Philippines. The direct invasion of Japan seemed too hazardous logistically.

Before he was relieved, Halsey flew from Noumea to New Zealand, where he learned that the King of England had appointed him an Honorary Knight Commander of the Order of the British Empire, and from there north to Espiritu Santo and on up the line to Emirau, stopping at each base to say goodbye to friends. Back in Noumea there were dispatches from MacArthur and Nimitz, congratulating him on his achievements in the South Pacific.

Halsey himself sent a dispatch to all ships and South Pacific bases. "Proudly I send this parting Well Done to my victorious services. . . . You have met, measured, and mowed down the best the enemy had on land and sea and in the air. You have sent hundreds of Tojo's ships, thousands of his planes, tens of thousands of his slippery minions whence they can never again attack our flag nor the flags of our Allies. . . . And now, carry on the smashing South Pacific tradition under your new commanders, and may we join up again along the road to Tokyo."

In a letter to General MacArthur Halsey said: "You and I have had tough sledding with the enemy, and we have had other complex problems nearly as difficult as our strategic problems; and I have the feeling that in every instance we have licked our difficulties. My own personal dealings with you have been so completely satisfactory that I will always feel a personal regard and warmth over and above my professional admiration."

"I also know, and take great pleasure in telling you," he continued, "that the members of my staff continually express their satisfaction over the way that business can be done by the South Pacific and Southwest Pacific. I must confess to a feeling of envy as I watch the battle tempo building up in your area; but the envy is tempered by an enthusiastic appreciation of the bold and masterly manner in which you are capitalizing on enemy weakness and keeping the little devils off balance. I sincerely hope and firmly believe, that I will have further opportunity to join forces with you against our vicious and hated enemy. In the meantime, I shall watch with interest and pride, your progress toward your goal."

On 15 June, Halsey turned over his command in the South Pacific to Vice Admiral John Henry Newton. During his last conference before leaving Noumea, "everyone felt the tenseness." The admiral faced sixty officers who had helped him turn the Japanese drive southward into defeat. For a long minute he looked at them and then, according to one lieutenant, "made an unforgettable talk." Words came hard, and "you could see he felt the sadness . . . as much as anyone but there was a wonderful, rough eloquence in almost everything he said."

He spoke of the dark days at Guadalcanal, the successful sweep up the Solomons, and final victory. He concluded with the brief remark, "If there is ever a design for a shoulder patch for all those who served in the South Pacific, I would recommend that they show on this patch three things—a piece of string, a can of beans and a rusty nail."

The morning Halsey left the entire town turned out. He drove up to the dock, stepped out of his car, chatted briefly with friends, and then shoved off in his barge. Admiral Newton turned to the bandleader and said, "Good God sakes, play something cheerful."

On that same day, 15 June, American forces waded ashore at

Saipan against tenacious opposition. The presence of Spruance's Fifth Fleet off the Marianas deterred Japanese troop convoys from arriving after the initial assault. But Saipan's proximity to southern Japan caused the enemy to oppose this landing with their naval power.

Moving into the Philippine Sea, Vice Admiral Ozawa commanded nine carriers, five battleships, and seven heavy cruisers. Spruance's fleet (seven heavy carriers, eight light carriers, seven battleships, three heavy and six light cruisers) moved out to meet him. Spruance took risks boldly when they seemed commensurate with the damage he might inflict, yet he never forgot that his main duty was to protect the Americans at Saipan. The battle of the Philippine Sea, 19 June 1944, proved that American carrier planes and pilots were vastly superior to the enemy's. As a result of the "great turkey shoot," the Japanese lost over 345 planes, at the cost of only seventeen American aircraft. The enemy lost three carriers, two of them to United States submarines.

Meanwhile, on the European front, the Allies had already stormed the beaches of Normandy on 6 June to begin the invasion of the continent of Europe.

When Halsey and his staff arrived at Pearl Harbor, they immediately occupied offices in the new JICPOA (Joint Intelligence Center Pacific Ocean Areas) building and quarters at 31 Makalapa. During those days at Pearl Halsey met with Nimitz and his staff on a daily basis at CINCPAC's convenient little office on the Pearl Harbor waterfront. Most of the floor space in the office was used up by canvas chairs around the walls for these morning conferences. It reflected the informality with which Nimitz liked to conduct his affairs. His desk, untidy, was littered by souvenir ashtrays, fancy paper cutters, and miscellaneous containers.

Over his desk he had three questions tacked up which he expected his subordinates to be prepared to answer about any problem.

1. Is the proposed operation likely to succeed?
2. What might be the consequences of failure?
3. Is it in the realm of practicability of materiel and supplies?

When planning major offensives the senior officers involved

talked with Nimitz and his staff, together with any other officers whose ideas Nimitz wanted to hear. He made the final decisions sometimes in the face of contrary advice, but first he listened to all the evidence carefully. The war in the Pacific was too complicated for any one officer to do all the thinking.

"He wielded authority with a sure hand," writes E. B. Potter, Nimitz's biographer, "but without austerity or arrogance. His perfect integrity was untinged with harshness. He demanded the best from those who served under him but never failed to give credit where credit was due. He was courteous and considerate without leaving any doubt who was running the show."

On 18 June Nimitz handed Halsey a copy of a dispatch from the Joint Chiefs of Staff, addressed to Nimitz and MacArthur, requesting views and recommendations on bypassing certain selected objectives and proceeding at an earlier date to Formosa or Japan. Halsey felt that the immediate objectives in the western Carolines should be bypassed and that operations against the Philippines should be accelerated.

At JICPOA the Third Fleet staff was organizing and formulating plans for the occupation of the western Carolines. On 5 July Halsey received Nimitz's staff study of the proposed operation. By establishing forces in the western Carolines, Americans would command the southern half of the crescent-shaped chain of islands that runs from Tokyo to the southern Philippines and would isolate the central and eastern Carolines, including Truk. Nimitz's western Caroline plan called for the occupation of Angaur and Peleliu of the Palaus, the westernmost of the Caroline group; Yap Island, 280 miles northeast; and Ulithi Atoll.

As Halsey and several of his staff studied the plan, they suggested modifications. Ulithi had a fine anchorage for the fleet, but they saw no need for occupying the other islands. Strategically, Yap had little value. Although enemy-held Palau imperiled MacArthur's advance from New Guinea toward the Philippines and offered an anchorage and sites for airfields, Halsey believed an operation against it would prove to be another "bloodbath like Tarawa."

Nimitz overruled their objections as the Palaus were needed as staging areas for the Philippines. The Third Fleet's mission was

ABOVE Halsey (facing camera nearest net) plays deck tennis with staff on board the *New Jersey*. (Navy Department, National Archives)

BELOW Halsey on the bridge of the *New Jersey* en route to the Philippines. (Navy Department, National Archives)

Halsey eating Thanksgiving dinner with crew on board the *New Jersey*, 1944.
(Navy Department, National Archives)

124

ABOVE Halsey greeted by Admiral Thomas C. Kinkaid as he arrives at the latter's headquarters in Australia. (Navy Department, National Archives)

RIGHT February 1945, somewhere in the Pacific. (U.S. Navy photo)

ABOVE Halsey discussing strategy with Admiral McCain in the stateroom of Halsey's flagship, February 1945. (U.S. Navy photo)

BELOW Halsey and Admiral Raymond A. Spruance on board the *New Mexico* at Okinawa, April 1945. (Navy Department, National Archives)

Halsey looking out at other units in his command, June 1945. (U.S. Navy photo)

Fleet Admiral William F. Halsey, Jr.,
February 1946. (U.S. Navy photo)

An artist's conception of Fleet Admiral
Halsey. (U.S. Navy photo)

to support the landings in the Palaus and to weaken Japanese air power over or near the Philippines before MacArthur's troops went ashore. Of great significance later in the war, the order also emphasized "that in case of opportunity for the destruction of a major portion of the enemy fleet offers or can be created, such destruction will become the primary task."

At a conference on 13 July, Admiral King, who had flown in from San Francisco, urged bypassing the Philippines completely and seizing Formosa, which Halsey viewed as more worthless than the Palaus. Admiral Spruance argued for establishing a base at Nimrod Sound, south of Shanghai. Other admirals suggested landings on the Shantung Peninsula in China or in Korea.

One afternoon Mick Carney had a chance to talk privately with King. "Are you satisfied with your job as Chief of Staff?" asked King.

"Yes," said Carney, "but I don't like the idea of sitting out the war in a staff position."

"When Bill Halsey quits fighting, I'll see what I can do," King replied.

On the 14th Halsey left Pearl Harbor and flew to Washington for conferences at the Navy Department. Mick Carney and the staff remained behind to continue studies on the western Caroline operation.

[IX]

"The Pacific War Is Picking Up"

ON AN INSPECTION TOUR of the Pacific that he planned for the summer, President Roosevelt decided to summon General MacArthur to Pearl Harbor to discuss with him and Nimitz the strategy for the next step against Japan, Formosa, or the Philippines. Neither General Marshall nor Admiral King * were invited as their ideas were already known to the President.

Roosevelt and his entourage arrived in Pearl Harbor on board the heavy cruiser *Baltimore* in late July. The strategy sessions took place between the President, the general, and the admiral at the residence of the late Chris R. Holmes on Kalaukau Avenue, Waikiki.

Stressing political and emotional factors, MacArthur favored the return to the Philippines. "Was the United States," he asked, "willing to accept responsibility for breaking a solemn promise to . . . [the] Filipinos that the Americans would return?"

Both plans, the occupation of Formosa or the Philippines, posed problems. Nimitz's primary consideration was to cut Japanese lines of communication southward. He was inclined to believe, though not convinced, that capturing Formosa was the way to do it. The invasion of Formosa would involve a hard, bloody

---

* King still favored a direct assault on Formosa without reference to the Philippines. Formosa dominated the sea lanes between Japan and the East Indies and King had no interest in fighting the Japanese on land in their home islands—a blockade by sea and air power was sufficient to win.

struggle as the enemy had already reinforced the island with planes and troops. Yet the invasion of the Philippines would demand troops, planes, and ships on a far greater scale. The only merit in MacArthur's plan, according to the Navy, was political—the United States had a definite stake in aiding those Filipinos who had been fighting the Japanese.

For three days the meetings went on, both Army and Navy arguing the merits of their positions. The President was swayed by MacArthur's appeal to America's moral commitments to the Filipinos. To bypass and seal off these friendly people and the American prisoners of war in the islands would expose them to frightful privations and mistreatment at the hands of their captors. When the President departed from Pearl Harbor, no final decision had been reached. That lay with the Joint Chiefs of Staff.

They eventually decided that after a landing at Leyte in the central Philippines, Luzon in the northern archipelago would be an easier operation than Formosa or the Chinese mainland. The invasion of Formosa, therefore, would depend on developments in the Philippines. They set the date, 20 December, for the invasion of Leyte with possible landings on Luzon or Formosa in late February 1945. They also finalized the rest of the Pacific timetable: Morotai in the Halmaheras, and Palu, 15 September; Mindanao in the southern Philippines, 15 November.

Halsey's flagship, the battleship *New Jersey,* escorted by three destroyers, sortied from Pearl Harbor on 24 August and set a course westward. "My grandiose title 'Commander Third Fleet,' " said Halsey, "may seem top-heavy for three destroyers and one battleship. The explanation is, of course, that the Third Fleet was almost identical with the powerful Fifth Fleet, which comprised well over 500 warships." When Spruance commanded them, they were designated the Fifth Fleet; when Halsey commanded them, they were the Third. "Instead of the stagecoach system of keeping the drivers and changing the horses," explained Halsey, "we changed drivers and kept the horses. It was hard on the horses, but was effective. Moreover, it consistently misled the Japs into an exaggerated conception of our seagoing strength."

Such a fleet organization together with new logistic devices had the effect of keeping every fighting ship of the Pacific Fleet at sea and speeding up the momentum of the war.

By 1944 the fast carrier task force had changed dramatically from the small, impromptu carrier task forces of 1942. It now was a mighty fleet, although it remained a task force within a fleet—that fleet embracing the invasion forces themselves and their supporting ships. The fast carrier task force was, in reality, a first rate surface fleet, but organized about and patterned from the carriers rather than battleships and cruisers. The carriers remained the primary offensive weapon, while the other ships played distinctly defensive roles.

The fast carrier task force of 1944 and early 1945 was a huge force of varying size and strength. It had perhaps fifteen carriers, six to eight battleships, eight to ten or a dozen cruisers, and possibly seventy-five destroyers. Moving between the carrier task force and its base were the oilers, ammunition ships, supply ships, and their screen of destroyers.

From their anchorages in the central and western Pacific, the far-ranging and hard-hitting force could maneuver on any course and keep to the sea as long as necessary, drawing fuel, ammunition, relief personnel, and provisions from its own ships. It could hit any target in the western Pacific, from Saigon to Tokyo.

Usually, the carrier task force was deployed in three to five task groups, for so vast a fleet could not move well as a single tactical element. Each task group, commanded by a rear admiral, was composed of several carriers and battleships, a few cruisers, and a protecting screen of destroyers. Each such task group was integrated as a fighting unit, capable of independent missions.

Most importantly, the task force served as a strategic screen for the more vulnerable troop transports and landing craft of the amphibious forces or for the marines and soldiers once they had landed.

After leaving the Hawaiian Islands behind, Halsey wrote Nimitz, "I do not have to assure you that it is a grand and glorious feeling to be at sea again; I and my staff have been drilling ourselves daily . . . using strategic and tactical battle problems, and we are all hoping that we will be fully prepared to take the maximum advantage of any opportunities the Japs leave lying around."

While Halsey's flagship steamed westward, the guts of the Third Fleet, Admiral Marc A. ("Pete") Mitscher's fast carriers, Task Force Thirty-Eight, pounded Iwo Jima in the Volcanoes, moved south, and "tore into the Palaus" on 6, 7, and 8 September, then hit weakly defended Mindanao, the southernmost of the Philippine Islands. This was encouraging news. "I am delighted," Halsey said. "Our strikes . . . dealt a crippling blow to the enemy, from which he will have great difficulty in recovering and they brought to light the fact that he is operating on a shoe-string in those areas. If we have luck with the weather, and can get at the juicy Luzon targets . . . the enemy's air and shipping operations in the Philippines should be completely disrupted."

The *New Jersey* and the escorts dropped anchor in the harbor at Manus Island. On 4 September Admiral Kinkaid, commanding MacArthur's Seventh Fleet, and his aides came on board the battleship and met with Halsey and his staff to coordinate facilities and plans. Close cooperation between these commands for the coming months were discussed extensively with agreeable solutions reached on all important subjects.

On 5 September the *New Jersey* departed from Manus to rendezvous with Mitscher's fast carriers. Halsey and his staff met daily to analyze the forthcoming campaign and to complete an "Estimate of the Situation." From intelligence sources, they knew that fuel was being stored in Manila for the replenishment of naval forces operating well south of the Empire. If they intended to sortie, the staff believed, the only American objectives they could hit and damage were the Marianas or the Third Fleet.

Viewed from the enemy standpoint, the best plan would be "to get poised as far forward as is safe and wait to catch us when and where we are vulnerable to shuttle attack [from ship to island] and with enemy shore-based air handy."

With Formosa and Luzon as potential landing points for shuttling planes, "the locus of the Japanese fleet's launching positions could be estimated with fair accuracy." For example, while the Third Fleet bombed Luzon, the staff explained, the Japanese could attack it from a point 600 miles northeast of Polillo (an island just east of Luzon) and the Americans would be hamstrung to strike back. "We could be caught the same way while running in on Formosa if the Japs had good early intelligence. The Japs could conceivably raid the Marianas at any time, but can engage our Fleet only when we project ourselves into enemy waters and within scope of his logistic capabilities. If we succeed in hitting Manila hard, the enemy's logistic bases must be nearer to the Empire.

"We are committed to offensive operations, and to create an opportunity to bring the Jap Fleet to grips; therefore, we need only consider our vulnerability while on the offensive and make suitable deployment to guard against surprise and being caught in an unfavorable or impotent position, and further to convert any apparent enemy positional advantage into an ambush or liability."

With this in mind, the staff decided that the Third Fleet need only provide 1) adequate search of critical areas, 2) diversionary striking power which could disrupt any serious threat to the main forces and, possibly, slow down the enemy until he could be "brought to bay." Specifically, in the case of Task Force Thirty-Eight, operations in the Luzon-Formosa-Okinawa area should provide 1) sure search of areas from which the enemy could launch shuttle-attacks, 2) long-range search to enable the task force to make an early start to intercept the enemy fleet. "Detailed strategic and tactical dispositions cannot be specified to cover all contingencies," the staff concluded, "but the foregoing basic principles should be incorporated in all future plans including the impending Luzon strike."

On 11 September the *New Jersey* joined up with Task Force Thirty-Eight. At 0745 the destroyer *Hunt* transferred Halsey and his staff from the *New Jersey* to the carrier *Lexington* to confer with Admiral Mitscher about the forthcoming campaign. They planned carrier strikes on the central Philippines instead of on Mindanao, where there was a scarcity of good targets. Halsey and Mitscher seriously discussed bombing and strafing the Manila area and other Luzon targets as soon as the results of the central Philippine attacks could be analyzed. The carriers fueled and prepared for an early high-speed run to the central Philippines and a dawn strike.

On the following day, the 12th, aided by a smooth sea and under cover of threatening weather, the fast carrier groups slipped into sight of Samar and launched a devastating strike on Leyte, Cebu, and Negros. Caught completely off guard, the Japanese had their airfields crowded with planes which became "sitting ducks to the fighters that suddenly swept in." Some enemy aircraft were pulled into hangars by crewmen. Others, manned by aviators, took off only to be shot down by machine guns or rockets. Still other planes were blown up or heavily damaged.

"The Yankee flyers," reported Mick Carney, "had a field day as they trip-hammered the Nip installations, burned the neatly lined up Jap planes, and proceeded to raise havoc with Japanese shipping." The Americans shot down 173 enemy aircraft, destroyed 305 on the ground, and sank fifty-nine ships, and probably destroyed another fifty-eight.

Carrier strikes on the 13th were duplicates of the first day. When the last plane returned to its carrier, enemy losses were totaled. The results were "staggering," and the lack of enemy resistance was "amazing and fantastic."

On the 14th, for the third successive day, carrier planes smashed enemy installations "far and wide." Ships sunk included two tankers, thirty-two cargo ships, two destroyer escorts, two motor torpedo boats, and twenty-two smaller craft; ships heavily damaged included four tankers, thirty-nine cargo ships, one destroyer escort, two patrol craft, two tugs, and ten smaller vessels.

Japanese commanders in the Philippines warned their troops about imminent invasion, and an air of tense expectancy settled over the military complexes. The effect of Halsey's raid had severely weakened Japanese air power.

On board the *New Jersey* Halsey called a staff meeting after an American pilot, who had spent a day and a night on Leyte in friendly guerilla hands before being rescued, reported the limited number of Japanese troops on the island. Plane reports indicated that "Leyte was wide open," "a hollow shell with weak defenses and skimpy facilities."

"In my opinion," Halsey said, "this is the vulnerable belly of the Imperial dragon."

"We saw how poorly prepared the Japs were," he wrote later, and it seemed a shame to waste time in taking outlying places "that wouldn't do us any good. . . . The Japs were fine if they had a preconceived plan and could carry it out without interruption. If interrupted, you had him going around in circles."

The time was "ripe" not only to strike Manila, but, perhaps, to mount a much larger offensive. The stepping-stone campaign up the Philippines, starting at Mindanao, should be scrapped and the invasion of Leyte itself should be commenced months ahead of schedule. Nimitz should cancel the Palau and Yap operations and MacArthur should drive straight into the central Philippines.

Halsey and his staff wondered whether they dare recommend to MacArthur that he shift his planned Mindanao invasion to Leyte. They scanned combat reports, intelligence information, and the availability of Nimitz's and MacArthur's forces. After exhaustive discussions, Halsey decided that Leyte, not Mindanao, was the best course of action. The Third Fleet could provide the necessary air support that would have come from Mindanao to cover the Leyte invasion, and the three Army divisions penciled in for Yap could be employed to strengthen MacArthur's amphibious forces.

Ironically, Halsey's brilliant strategic recommendation was based on a partly false premise. The enemy's air power was not as weak as he assumed; they were being held back, in readiness for the major amphibious landings that Tokyo expected.

On 13 September Halsey sent an urgent dispatch to Nimitz recommending that he abolish the landings at Palau and Yap and that MacArthur invade Leyte immediately.

Nimitz replied that Phase One of the western Caroline operation (Palau) was to be carried out as planned, but he would reconsider the Yap invasion and would ask Admiral King and MacArthur about Leyte.

Nimitz forwarded Halsey's suggestion to Quebec, Canada, where Roosevelt and Prime Minister Churchill were meeting with the Combined Joint Chiefs of Staff. The American Joint Chiefs immediately radioed to discover MacArthur's opinion. The general, however, was at that moment on board a cruiser in the invasion force headed for Morotai, maintaining complete radio silence. His Chief of Staff, General Richard K. Sutherland, therefore faced an awesome decision. He knew from his intelligence reports that enemy strength in the Philippines was far greater than Halsey had estimated and realized that a direct assault on Leyte would violate MacArthur's doctrine of always providing land-based air cover for amphibious landings. Yet Sutherland well understood how effective carrier air power could be in covering an invasion. He also liked the idea of an additional three divisions diverted from Yap and, above all, he knew the significance of advancing the Pacific timetable. He radioed the Joint Chiefs, over MacArthur's name, that he agreed with the proposed scheme.

The American Chiefs were dining with their Canadian counterparts at Château Frontenac when Sutherland's dispatch arrived. "Having the utmost confidence in General MacArthur, Admiral Nimitz, and Admiral Halsey," recalled General Marshall, "it was not a difficult decision to make. Within ninety minutes after the signal had been received in Quebec, General MacArthur and Admiral Nimitz had received their instructions to execute the Leyte operation on 20 October." The Joint Chiefs ordered MacArthur and Nimitz to cancel the Yap and Mindanao operations. "If MacArthur had used Mindanao as a stepping-stone," said Halsey, "he would not have reached Leyte until December 20." Six days later MacArthur told the Joint Chiefs that their decision about Leyte would make it possible for his forces to land on Luzon on 20 December, two months ahead of the earliest date they then contemplated.

On 15 September, as scheduled, units of the First Marine Division landed on the beaches of Peleliu, an island in the southern Palaus. One of Halsey's carrier groups rendered air support, first neutralizing the airfields on Yap, and then repeatedly striking Palau targets, protecting the amphibious forces.

On the same date, MacArthur's troops landed on Morotai Island, off Halmahera in New Guinea, against light opposition.

This move was a prelude to the Americans' return to the Philippines. "The Pacific War," said Halsey, "is picking up."

The Peleliu operation stalled suddenly because the Japanese had converted a wooded, rocky ridge, forming the north-south backbone of Peleliu, into a natural fortress, composed of a series of mutually supporting cave positions and organized in depth with many automatic weapons. After a quick visit to the island, Halsey wrote Nimitz, "It is a question of slow progress in digging the rats out. Poison gas is indicated as an economical weapon."

The marines moved forward, slowly but steadily, and on 30 September Halsey's task force commander announced that the southern Palaus had been secured, although there still remained some mopping up operations of isolated enemy pockets both on Peleliu and Angaur.

Halsey had been correct in his assessment of the Palau campaign. Those islands should have been bypassed when the decision was made to strike Leyte. The most valuable contribution of the bloody Palau victory was to prepare Marines for what they would experience in future Pacific amphibious operations. "I am a stubborn animal," said Halsey, "and I certainly think I was right about that and I believe the cost in lives very greatly outweighed the advantage we accrued from the seizure of Peleliu and Angaur."

The advantages of the bloodless occupation of Ulithi Island was beyond question for it provided the Pacific Fleet with an anchorage and a logistical base of major importance. Every subsequent operation of the Central Pacific forces was in part, at least, launched from there.

William J. Kitchell, Halsey's flag lieutenant, had a chance to write the admiral's wife. "The boss is fine and from what you know from the newspapers you can imagine that he is thoroughly enjoying his new job. Our mail deliveries are naturally somewhat interrupted and delayed but do keep writing. The boss looks forward so much to each mail delivery and is so disappointed if there is no word from home. . . ."

When the Joint Chiefs decided to drive on to the Philippines instead of invading Formosa, the Leyte and Luzon campaigns became vital to the survival of the Japanese Empire. With a foothold at Leyte, the Americans could strike with planes, warships, and amphibious troops from west to north, to the Chinese mainland and the East Indies, cutting off Japan's lines of communication to her raw materials.

The Philippines were part of the inner line of the Japanese defense. The islands would have to be defended at all costs by the fleet based at Singapore and in Japan, by thousands of soldiers in the archipelago, and by land-based aircraft flying to the threatened area from Japan and China. An American victory in the Philippines would not only free the Filipinos and shorten the war, but it would guarantee Japan's defeat.

Since the Philippines fell within the sphere of the Southwest Pacific command, MacArthur's troops and fleet, the Seventh, under Admiral Kinkaid, had the responsibility for liberating the archipelago. Supporting MacArthur's troops was Halsey's Third Fleet, but none of Nimitz's amphibious forces were to participate in the Leyte landings.

While MacArthur's invasion troops assembled at Manus and Hollandia for the Leyte assault, Halsey launched air strikes to neutralize the island. From bases in the South and Central Pacific, planes struck Japanese-held islands in the Marshalls and Carolines. From China, B-29s of the Twentieth Bomber Command and medium bombers of General Claire L. Chennault's Fourteenth Air Force pummeled Formosa and the China coast. General Kenney's Far Eastern Air Force from bases on New Guinea, Biak, and Morotai zeroed in on the southern flank of Leyte, hitting repeatedly at Japanese airfields on Mindanao and the East Indies.

On 21 September Task Force Thirty-Eight (with Halsey on the *New Jersey*) slipped silently and undetected in the rain to within forty miles of the eastern coast of Luzon and prepared to launch the first air attack of the war against Manila.

Once briefed on the targets, the pilots manned their planes; the carriers maneuvered into a favorable position; the first fighters took off for Clark and Nichols fields. The weather cleared over the targets and the Japanese, "caught with their flaps down," failed to launch a plane until after ten minutes of irreplaceable damage.

Throughout the day flyers bombed and strafed enemy shipping and airfields. "The Japanese reaction was confusion, inability to match the skill of the American pilots or planes, and a lack of accurate AA fire," wrote Carney. When the last fighter settled on the deck of its carrier shortly after sunset, "the Americans had left airfield installations in shambles," had shot 110 planes down, had riddled and burned ninety-five more on the ground, had sunk eleven large ships. American losses numbered fifteen planes.

After a quiet night off Luzon, Task Force Thirty-Eight launched the first strike at 0615 and, again, planes shot up enemy airfields and shipping. By noon Mitscher decided that the remaining air and shipping targets were not sufficient to warrant further strikes in the face of heavy weather building up. The carriers retired to the southeast to refuel. The Third Fleet's war diary entry for 22 September ended with the paragraph, "The fleet now had complete control of the air over the entire Philippines. Jap Philippine air has been liquidated. Shipping remaining from the first day was sunk or seriously damaged."

The demonstrated weakness of enemy air power following the heavy losses inflicted during the past three weeks caused Halsey and his staff to start preliminary planning for attacks against Okinawa, Formosa, and the Japanese home islands.

After carrier planes bombed and strafed a concentration of enemy shipping at Coron Bay in the central Philippines, Task Force Thirty-Eight withdrew to refuel and rearm. To acknowledge the accomplishments of his ships and planes, the following message, prepared by Carney, was sent in Halsey's name to all hands in Task Force Thirty-Eight: THE RECENT EXCEPTIONAL PERFORMANCE YIELDED GRATIFYING GATE RECEIPTS AND ALTHOUGH THE CAPACITY AUDIENCE HISSED VERY LOUDLY, LITTLE WAS THROWN AT THE PLAYERS X AS LONG AS THE AUDIENCE HAS A SPOT TO HISS IN, WE WILL STAY ON THE ROAD. Halsey flew to Hollandia in his Flag Coronado where he met with MacArthur to work out the final details for the impending invasion of Leyte. He went on to Palau to inspect the results of the recent assault, then flew to Ulithi, where Task Force Thirty-Eight lay anchored. Immediately Halsey and the Dirty Tricks Department worked out plans to attack the Ryukyus, Formosa, and Luzon with an alternate strike on Kyushu. They also discussed possible strikes on the Tokyo-Empire area.

On 7 October, after the ships had been replenished, Task Force Thirty-Eight rendezvoused at sea and, two days later, started a high speed run for dawn strikes on Okinawa. Due to covering weather and course changes to avoid enemy search planes, the approach was undetected. The carriers launched the first strikes at 0547, 10 October. Enemy planes were caught on the ground and, when the raid ended, the Americans had hit aircraft, airfields, shipping, and the installations of Nansei Shoto, destroying ninety-three planes and sinking forty ships and forty-one small craft. "The objectives of disrupting enemy air reinforcements of Formosa and future air reinforcements of the Philippines," wrote a staffer in the war diary, "appeared to be well carried out."

During the next few days, carrier planes in an awesome display of air strength struck Luzon and Okinawa again. Starting on 12 October planes from Task Force Thirty-Eight's carriers hit Formosa for three days in an attempt to remove the island's potential as a staging area.

The first American objective at Formosa was the enemy's fighter defenses. When aircraft roared over Formosa, they found the sky full of Japanese fighters, warned of the raid by radar. When the dogfights and bombings ended, the Japanese realized that they had lost a third of their aircraft and had suffered great damage to ground facilities.

A second American strike splashed still more Japanese planes, so that the third raid of the day found the sky empty of Japanese. Although Americans lost forty-three planes, Halsey's pilots had assured themselves air control over Formosa and secured the northern flank of the Leyte operation. Equally important, they had decimated the hastily organized Japanese naval flying groups, which had been thrown into the Formosa battle.

On the next day, the 13th, Halsey's aircraft blew up hangars, fuel dumps, shops, and parked aircraft, inflicting heavy damage. Accomplishing his mission, Halsey started to retire with Task Force Thirty-Eight. He and the staff were amazed at the slowness with which the enemy reacted to the American strikes. It appeared that the Japanese personnel, logistical, and transportation capabilities, even in the Empire, "are such that several days are required to get organized to meet a threat in any unexpected quarter."

"We watched this situation develop off Formosa," Halsey wrote Nimitz, "and it is interesting that the enemy was not able to develop well-integrated strikes on as large a scale as was frequently encountered in the South Pacific."

On the evening of the 13th, Japanese torpedo planes swooped down and made a damaging hit on the heavy cruiser *Canberra*. When she refused to sink, Halsey ordered her towed. To cover this move, he delayed his withdrawal and the next morning launched an attack on Formosa and northern Luzon. In the evening, as the task force steamed eastward, a torpedo hit the light cruiser *Houston*. She too was towed.

To the Japanese, it seemed that they had won a stunning victory. Aviators returned from attacks on American surface units and reported fantastic successes. They excitedly announced sinking or setting aflame carriers, battleships, cruisers, and destroyers, completely shattering Task Force Thirty-Eight, which was running wildly for cover. Such estimates resulted from wishful thinking, and from the inexperience of the pilots, many fighting for the first time.

Radio Tokyo announced the phony triumph to the world. All of Halsey's carriers had been sunk together with several battleships, many cruisers and destroyers. The Third Fleet had been wiped out as a fighting force. The caretaker of the Tokyo Zoo announced, "If we're lucky enough to capture Halsey alive I want him to live among the monkeys we keep in the Zoo. I'll see to it that special reservation be made for him in our Monkey Island . . . where hundreds of monkeys live at large."

One Tokyo newspaper reported: "Imperial Headquarters announcements declare these victories mean only a prelude to bigger victories in the future. We know that we have only begun to roll back the tide and we are confident that we will prepare the way for decisive operations and decisive victories. . . ."

On board the *New Jersey*, Halsey and the Dirty Tricks Department were jubilant at the enemy's gullibility and dispatched a reassuring message to Nimitz at Pearl Harbor, which CINCPAC promptly released to the press: ADMIRAL NIMITZ HAS RE- CEIVED FROM ADMIRAL HALSEY THE COMFORTING ASSURANCE THAT HE IS NOW RETIRING TOWARD THE ENEMY FOLLOWING THE SALVAGE OF ALL THE THIRD FLEET SHIPS RECENTLY REPORTED SUNK BY RADIO TOKYO.

The Dirty Tricks Department evaluated the situation and de- cided to attack once more the Japanese airfields in Luzon. They ordered two task groups of carriers, 38.1 and 38.4, to move south and bomb Luzon and two small carriers to remain behind with the crippled cruisers for defensive air cover. In view of the apparent enemy belief in the extreme claims of Radio Tokyo as to the damage inflicted on the Third Fleet, the staff planned to station two carrier groups, 38.2 and 38.3, in a position east of the dam- aged cruisers, as a trap, to intercept and take advantage of any Japanese surface movements toward the cripples.

On 14 October, late in the afternoon, Admiral Soemu Toyoda, Commander in Chief of the Combined Fleet, ordered all available air power to strike the "damaged" Third Fleet and directed the Second Striking Force (cruisers and destroyers) to move out from the Inland Sea "to mop up the remaining enemy."

When search planes reported only a few damaged warships, which they mistook for a carrier and two battleships, Admiral Toyoda (unaware of Halsey's trap) was sure of victory and or- dered the air and surface units to pursue immediately.

"Needless to say," a Japanese admiral recalled, "all this pur- suit business ended in a fiasco." While the Second Striking Force moved south at flank speed, Japanese patrol planes searched in vain for the remainder of Task Force Thirty-Eight.

American radio monitors had picked up Toyoda's order to the Second Striking Force, decoded it, and rushed it to Halsey. Quickly, he alerted MacArthur that he was canceling his support of the Leyte landing, scheduled for 20 October, in order to smash what he believed was a major element of the enemy fleet.

On 15 October Task Groups 38.2 and 38.3 were operating east of Formosa, lying in wait for the Second Striking Force to move into range, while Task Groups 38.1 and 38.4 launched their strikes on Luzon. Japanese planes from there struck back and, although their losses were heavy, pilots returned and reported great success.

Admiral Toyoda, however, was suspicious of the flyers' analysis. When his searches of the 16th reported large numbers of American carriers steaming in the Philippine Sea, he became gravely concerned. He ordered the bulk of his naval air units on Okinawa, Formosa, and Luzon to search out and destroy the carriers. But most of these aircraft failed to spot their targets, and many of those that did were knocked down before they could release their bombs.

On Formosa Toyoda was now convinced that a huge American fleet still existed, and that the Second Striking Force was heading directly into battle against superior odds. Toyoda ordered the force to change course and to steam to the Ryukyus for fuel. "It was evident," Halsey wrote, "that the enemy had received a sighting report of Task Groups THIRTY-EIGHT POINT TWO and THIRTY-EIGHT POINT THREE and had retired just before the trap could be sprung."

For the Japanese the Formosa air battle was costly. Plane losses weakened their land-based air arm on Formosa and in the Philippines and ruined all chances that their carrier groups could be organized before MacArthur's landing at Leyte. While a few hundred aircraft still remained operational, the idea of mounting huge land-based air attacks at the American amphibious forces now seemed impossible.

At Pearl Harbor Nimitz flashed a dispatch to Halsey. FOLLOWING FROM SECNAV: "MY CONGRATULATIONS TO YOU ON THE RECENT NEWS FROM THE PACIFIC AND WILL YOU PLEASE JOIN . . . [ME] IN YOUR MESSAGES TO HALSEY AND MITSCHER X THE SEA AND AIR POWER OF THE THIRD FLEET IS MAKING HISTORY AND ALL HANDS IN THE LONG LINE OF SUPPORT THROUGHOUT THE NAVY ARE GRATEFUL FOR THE OPPORTUNITY OF WORKING FOR SUCH A TEAM." IN ITS RECENT BRILLIANT OFFENSIVE THE THIRD FLEET HAS BEEN A SOURCE OF PRIDE TO US ALL AND HAS INFLICTED ON OUR ENEMY DESTRUCTION AND DISAS-

TER WHICH HE WILL LONG REMEMBER X "WELL DONE."

The only weakness, but a major one, in the American plan for the Leyte invasion was the absence of a unified command, a handicap which was to plague the entire campaign. The task of transporting, landing, and covering MacArthur's amphibious force, the Sixth Army, was the direct responsibility of Admiral Kinkaid's Seventh Fleet. This armada was divided into three elements: Task Force Seventy-Seven, under Kinkaid's direct command, and Task Forces Seventy-Eight and Seventy-Nine, the Northern and Southern Attack Forces under Rear Admiral Daniel E. Barbey ("Uncle Dan, the Amphibious Man") and Vice Admiral Theodore S. Wilkinson. Task Force Seventy-Seven, which included the bombardment, escort carrier, and other close support elements, would directly support the landing. The array of transports and warships in Kinkaid's fleet was awesome. The combat group contained six battleships, five of them of Pearl Harbor vintage, eighteen escort carriers with 500 planes, eight cruisers, thirty destroyers, and twelve destroyer escorts.

Throughout World War II Tom Kinkaid had been cast in the shade by the publicity given to Halsey and MacArthur. Characteristically he had refused to compete for attention. Yet Kinkaid had been in all the touch-and-go battles of the first year—Midway, Coral Sea, Santa Cruz, and Guadalcanal. In 1943 Kinkaid had been given one of his toughest assignments in the Navy—the command of the Seventh Fleet, known in the Pacific as "MacArthur's Navy." Kinkaid started with a scratch force and slowly built it up to a massive body of slow, unglamorous craft which transported troops to jungle-fringed beaches. Kinkaid had to smooth over many differences between MacArthur and the Navy. With monumental tact he succeeded, and the MacArthur-Kinkaid team had gained ground rapidly, to New Britain and Manus, Hollandia and Morotai. The climax of the team's drive northward was the long awaited return to the Philippines.

To support the Seventh Fleet and the Sixth Army, the Southwest Pacific forces could count on Halsey's Third Fleet, under Nimitz's command and operating by agreement with MacArthur.

The Third Fleet was, essentially, Mitscher's fast carriers, Task Force Thirty-Eight, over which Halsey exercised direct tactical command. It included nine large carriers and eight light carriers with 1,000 planes, together with six new battleships, fifteen cruisers, and fifty-eight destroyers. These ships were organized into four strong task groups of equal strength, commanded by Vice Admiral John S. ("Slew") McCain and Rear Admirals Gerald F. ("Jerry") Bogan, Frederick C. ("Ted") Sherman, and Ralph E. Davison.

After attacking targets in the Philippines, Formosa and the Ryukyus in the week preceding the Leyte assault, Halsey's mission was to support the landings themselves by striking the central Philippines immediately before and during the landing operations. Halsey was also responsible for destroying any enemy naval and air elements that might threaten the beachheads.

His operational order, which was written by him and approved by Nimitz, emphasized that if the chance to knock out a "major portion" of the enemy fleet was "offered or could be created," then this would become the Third Fleet's "primary task."

During the early October operations, Nimitz wrote Halsey, "You are always free to make local decisions in connection with handling of the forces under your command. Often it will be necessary for you to take action not previously contemplated because of local situations which may develop quickly and in the light of information which has come to you and which may not yet be available to me. My only requirement in such cases is that I be informed as fully and as early as the situation permits."

The Philippine campaign was a new challenge to Bill Halsey for neither he nor any of his staff had participated in the great carrier duels of the Pacific War—Coral Sea, Midway, the Philippine Sea. But Halsey intended to knock out Japanese carriers at the first opportunity.

Placing the destruction of the enemy fleet on a higher priority than that of protecting the landings represented a drastic change from the doctrine that the Pacific Fleet had followed all during the war. Up to October 1944 the primary task of the fleet supporting the invasion had been to protect and assist the amphibious forces. In June 1944 American surface units covering the Saipan invasion had refused to pursue a damaged Japanese naval force, remaining behind to carry out its primary mission of supporting the landing. For permitting the enemy to flee, Admiral Spruance had been chastized by some. However, had he chased the enemy he would have left the Saipan beachhead unprotected, dangerously exposing the Marines to attack. If this had happened and the invasion halted, Spruance would have received more than criticism.

Halsey was keenly aware of this. Yet he was not going to ignore a chance to fight the "Japtards." He would support the landing, preferably by destroying the enemy fleet, not by directly protecting the beachheads. Since MacArthur had absolutely no authority over him, he could maneuver his fleet as he chose. MacArthur commanded all the forces, except Halsey, who was responsible only to Nimitz. Halsey was free to assist MacArthur when and if he pleased.

This was clear during the Formosa strikes. Halsey had temporarily canceled his support of MacArthur's armada, then already nearing the beaches of Leyte, in order to set a trap for the Second Striking Force. This action left Admiral Kinkaid, who commanded the invasion force while it was still at sea, without extra support. Halsey was back on station in ample time to cover the actual invasion. But as these actions made clear, Halsey was free to employ the Third Fleet, hopefully to lure out and fight the Japanese forces.

To complicate the command structure, there was no overall commander to issue instructions to Nimitz and MacArthur. They were equals in the Pacific, taking orders only from the Joint Chiefs of Staff and, therefore, Nimitz had no direct communications link with MacArthur and Kinkaid, a system which invited confusion.

"If the two fleets had been under the same command, with a single system of operational control and intelligence," Halsey said later, "the Battle for Leyte Gulf might have been fought differently and with better coordination."

[X]

"We Go North"

IN THE EARLY MORNING HOURS of 20 October, combat ships, troopships, command ships, and landing ships moved into Leyte Gulf. Battleships of the Seventh Fleet volleyed tons of shells into the tropical shrubbery every few seconds. Cruisers and destroyers ranged beside them, peppering the shore. Now and then the naval fire stopped, and planes from Task Force Thirty-Eight and the Seventh Fleet flew overhead, bombing towns, installations, trenches, pillboxes, and supply dumps. Japanese air offered only token resistance.

All the while transports kept disgorging attack boats which fanned out in neat ranks and headed toward shore in a shower of spray. Compared to most invasions in the Pacific, the landings on Leyte were easy. Troops expanded the beachheads more than a mile inland and seized Tacloban airfield.

A few hours after the initial assault, General MacArthur waded ashore accompanied by the President of the Philippines. Walking up to a microphone, MacArthur broadcast his speech of liberation for all Filipinos to hear.

At dawn the next day, Halsey's planes struck the Bicol-Visayan area to neutralize enemy air activity in the central Philippines. From the 10th of October (the Okinawa strikes) to this raid, Halsey calculated that his aircraft had sunk 141 ships, damaged 249 others, and shot down or destroyed on the ground 1,225 planes. His loss was ninety-five aircraft, but a large number of pilots and crewmen were saved through extensive air-sea rescue forces, lifeguard submarines, and Filipino guerillas.

On 22 October submarine and aircraft reports indicated in-

148

creased enemy naval activity. Halsey and the staff estimated the situation and anticipated a Japanese "surface reaction" to the Leyte landings. The fleet was ordered to refuel and be ready to move.

Admiral Soemu Toyoda at Japanese Naval Headquarters had already issued the Sho-1 execute order for the Combined Fleet, a plan, which if carried out, would keep open Japan's lifeline to the East Indies. To execute Sho-1, the Japanese sent almost all their carrier aircraft to land bases. In a three-pronged attack against Leyte Gulf, the Japanese Northern Force (Admiral Jisaburo Ozawa) would act as a decoy, attempting to lure Halsey's Third Fleet northward from the American beachhead. This unit was composed of six carriers (which together had only 116 planes), screened by cruisers and destroyers.

The Center Force (Admiral Takeo Kurita), built around the two largest and most powerful super battleships in the world, *Yamato* and *Musashi,* also included the old battleships *Nagato, Kongo,* and *Haruna;* ten heavy cruisers; two light cruisers; and nineteen destroyers. These ships would steam through San Bernardino Strait, dividing Samar and Luzon, and descend upon Leyte Gulf. The Southern Force of old battleships (Admiral Shoji Nishimura) would maneuver through Surigao Strait to the south of Leyte and complete a pincer movement on the amphibious and fire support ships at Leyte Gulf and destroy them.

At 0016 on the 23rd in Palawan Passage the submarines *Dace* and *Darter* found the Center Force, eleven heavy ships and six destroyers. The *Darter* got a message off to Admiral Ralph W. Christie, Commander Submarines Southwest Pacific. He relayed the message to Halsey. Until the *Darter*'s report, the whereabouts of the Center Force since it departed Lingga Roads, off Singapore, had been a mystery to Naval Intelligence.

At 0632 the *Darter*'s torpedoes smashed into the flagship *Atago* and sank her. Admiral Kurita transferred hurriedly to another ship. Two more torpedoes crippled the cruiser *Takao.* To the eastward the skipper of the *Dace* observed the results through his periscope, yelling out, "It looks like the Fourth of July out there! One is burning! The Japs are milling and firing all over the place! What a show! What a show!"

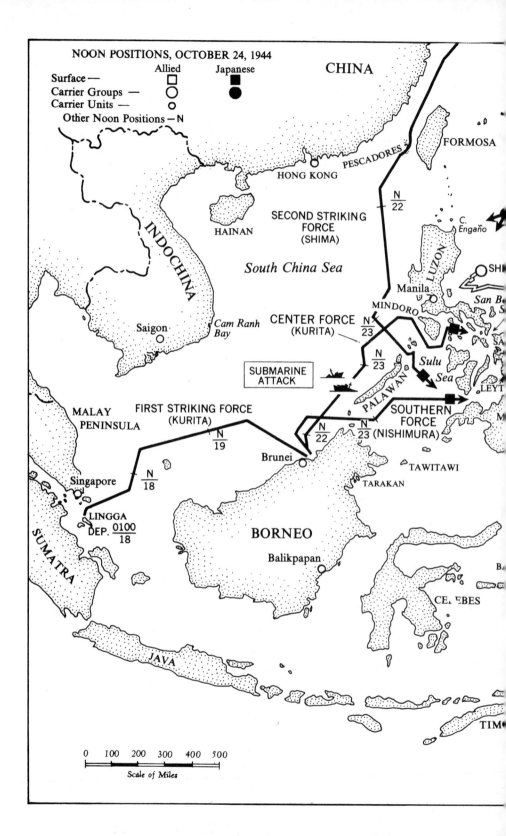

NOON POSITIONS, OCTOBER 24, 1944

	Allied	Japanese
Surface —	□	■
Carrier Groups —	○	●
Carrier Units —	○	●
Other Noon Positions — N		

CHINA

FORMOSA

PESCADORES

HONG KONG

N
22

C.
Engaño

SECOND STRIKING
FORCE
(SHIMA)

HAINAN

South China Sea

LUZON

SH

Manila

MINDORO

San B
S

Saigon

Cam Ranh
Bay

CENTER FORCE
(KURITA)

N
23

N
23

SA

Sulu

Sea

LEYT

PALAWAN

SOUTHERN
FORCE
(NISHIMURA)

M

MALAY
PENINSULA

FIRST STRIKING FORCE
(KURITA)

N
19

SUBMARINE
ATTACK

N
22

N
23

Brunei

TAWITAWI

Singapore

N
18

TARAKAN

LINGGA
DEP. 0100
18

BORNEO

Balikpapan

B

CELEBES

SUMATRA

JAVA

TIM

0   100   200   300   400   500

Scale of Miles

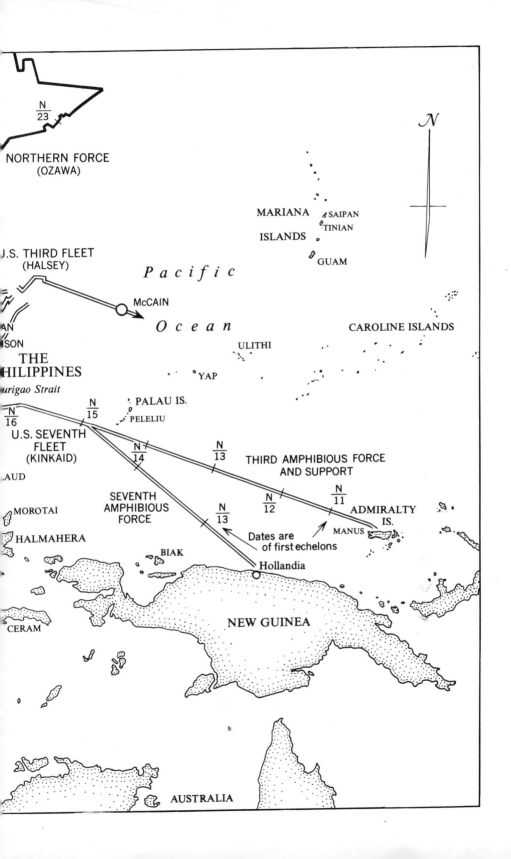

N/23

NORTHERN FORCE
(OZAWA)

MARIANA ISLANDS
SAIPAN
TINIAN
GUAM

Pacific

U.S. THIRD FLEET
(HALSEY)

McCAIN

Ocean

CAROLINE ISLANDS

ULITHI

AN
SON

THE
PHILIPPINES

YAP

urigao Strait

PALAU IS.
PELELIU

N/16   N/15

U.S. SEVENTH
FLEET
(KINKAID)

N/14   N/13

THIRD AMPHIBIOUS FORCE
AND SUPPORT

AUD

MOROTAI

SEVENTH
AMPHIBIOUS
FORCE

N/13   N/12   N/11

ADMIRALTY
IS.

MANUS

HALMAHERA

BIAK

Dates are
of first echelons

Hollandia

CERAM

NEW GUINEA

AUSTRALIA

The *Dace*'s torpedoes literally blew the heavy cruiser *Maya* to pieces. She sank in four minutes.

At that moment one of Halsey's carrier groups, Admiral Mc-Cain's, was cruising eastward toward Ulithi for rest and replenishment. The other three carrier groups of Task Force Thirty-Eight were moving westward toward the Philippines, preparing for further raids in support of MacArthur's forces. Even without McCain's surface units, Task Force Thirty-Eight still packed a considerable wallop, for each of the remaining groups included two new battleships, three or four carriers, two to four cruisers, and about fifteen destroyers.

As the result of the *Darter*'s contact report, Halsey ordered Task Force Thirty-Eight to close the Philippines at top speed and send up search planes the next morning to cover the western sea approaches for the entire length of the Philippine archipelago, a distance of 1,000 miles.

Halsey's three groups arrived on their stations. Admiral Sherman's carriers were off Polillo, an island to the east of Luzon. Bogan's units with Halsey's flagship, *New Jersey*, were 140 miles southeast of San Bernardino Strait; Davison's group was another 120 miles farther southeast near Leyte Gulf.

Halsey's carriers launched search planes at dawn, 24 October. At 0810 one of Bogan's pilots from the *Intrepid* sighted four Japanese battleships, eight cruisers, and thirteen destroyers (the Center Force) off the southern tip of Mindoro, course 050, speed twelve knots. Leaving the enemy's Southern Force, which was to enter Surigao Strait, to the Seventh Fleet, Halsey ordered Davison and Sherman to close at top speed on Bogan, near San Bernardino Strait, and to concentrate their full air power upon stopping the Center Force. At the same time he directed McCain's group to change course, refuel at sea, and be available for whatever might develop.

The Center Force was steaming for San Bernardino Strait. But this area was mined and the safe courses were unknown to Halsey. Moving his ships through these hazardous waters for a surface engagement was foolhardy. Task Force Thirty-Eight, however, was well positioned to launch air strikes.

Halsey estimated that two major elements of the Japanese fleet, the Southern and Center forces, were steaming toward a predetermined geographical and time locus and that the earliest concentration would be on the 25th, although he did not know the exact objective. He also calculated that an operation of such magnitude would include an enemy carrier force which, logically, could be expected to approach from the north, launching strikes from a point beyond the range of American carrier planes.

"We had," said Halsey, "been fighting the Japs for a long time and we thought we knew most of their tricks. . . . One of the principal things we had thought about and studied was how the Japs would use their carriers. The Japs had shuttle bombed us before, and we expected them to do it again, landing their planes [from carriers] in the Philippines."

The first strike of twenty-one fighters, twelve dive bombers, and twelve torpedo bombers, launched by the *Cabot* and *Intrepid* at 0910, hit the Center Force through heavy AA fire.

At 1031 an enemy plane from Luzon sighted and reported the position of Halsey's northern group. Immediately, Japanese aircraft sped off from Luzon airfields. "In the savage air battle," said a correspondent, "there was an unending stream of action—scenes of enemy aircraft turning and spinning crazily in dive-bombing attacks; of long, heartbreaking scenes of enemy units; of shell-torn American aircraft returning to our flight decks while other relays resumed the savage onslaught against the enemy."

During the battle not a single enemy plane got close enough to Sherman's ships to attack. Yet when the air had apparently been swept of enemy planes, a lone bomber loomed out of the clouds and struck the light carrier *Princeton*. Instantly she was ablaze. On a nearby destroyer one seaman reported, "I saw the first smoke curl up from the *Princeton*. We looked on helplessly as explosion after explosion tore into the ship, one sending a cloud of smoke billowing a thousand feet into the sky."

Halsey launched a second strike against the Center Force at 1045, which attacked at 1245. He launched a third at 1350, which attacked at 1550.

In the battle of Sibuyan Sea American planes hit the Japanese units as they moved toward San Bernardino Strait, virtually without air cover. They damaged the battleships *Yamato* and *Na-*

gato and the heavy cruiser *Myoko*. The new super battlewagon, *Musashi*, the pride of the Combined Fleet, was struck repeatedly by torpedoes and, eventually, capsized, carrying down 1,100 men.

Frantically, Kurita radioed Manila for land-based air cover, either to defend his force or to strike the American carriers. His requests were turned down. Luzon-based planes had concentrated on Sherman's group and had failed. The Japanese had nothing left with which to try again.

After the last Yankee attack, by far the heaviest, the Center Force retreated westward toward Mindoro.

Reports from American pilots exaggerated the damage inflicted on the Center Force and led Halsey and his staff to believe that the enemy had desisted from its plan of passing through San Bernardino Strait to attack Leyte. "The pilots' reports," said Halsey later, "proved to be dangerously optimistic, but we had little reason to discredit them at the time." The Center Force still had four battleships, six heavy cruisers, two light cruisers, and eleven destroyers in commission. Yet Admiral Kurita had lost more than twenty-five percent of his original element.

That afternoon the *Princeton* was still belching balls of fire and black smoke. At 1523 flames finally reached the ammunition stowage. There was a shattering explosion. All hands still on board were killed or wounded. At 1630 the last man abandoned ship, her skipper, Captain William H. Buracker. Admiral Mitscher ordered the cruiser *Reno* to sink the *Princeton*.

By now Halsey was convinced that the enemy were committed to a supreme effort, but the final proof was still lacking. There was no naval carrier strength involved in known Japanese forces converging on the Philippines. "It did not seem probable," said Halsey, "that the Japanese would commit such a large portion of their naval strength without providing some measure of naval air support."

All day long Halsey's Air Operations Officer, Doug Moulton, kept pouring over charts in flag plot, asking "Where the hell *are* all those Jap carriers!" At 1730 and again at 1925, American pilots, ranging far to the north, "caught a good look" and reported two heavy carriers, one light carrier, three heavy cruisers, and three destroyers steaming on a course 270, speed fifteen knots, 190 miles off Cape Engano, the northeastern tip of Luzon in the Philippine Sea. Nearby, steaming on nearly the same course, were four battleships, five cruisers, and six destroyers. This, indeed, was the Northern Force.

Moments later night search planes made a contact report that the Center Force had changed course and was steering for San Bernardino Strait. "We now had," said Halsey, "all the pieces of the puzzle." The movements of the Center Force in the Sibuyan Sea and the Southern Force in the Sulu Sea indicated a pincer assault of surface forces on the Leyte beachhead.

Halsey and his staff rehashed the situation. The Northern Force, the carriers, was the most powerful and effective unit at the moment. It had not been attacked or damaged by air, submarines, or surface units and its destruction would erase the Japanese carrier threat in the Pacific.

The Center Force had already been badly mauled, having been subjected to day-long strikes. "All attacks," Carney noted in the war diary, "had been launched at effective range and apparently had been pressed more aggressively and had caught the enemy in restricted waters. In addition, the force had been previously subjected to submarine attacks."

The Southern Force, estimated at two battleships, one cruiser, and old destroyers, was, the staff believed, on a "transport mission." Kinkaid could easily handle this element. They also calculated that the Center Force, even if it did return, could not arrive at Leyte Gulf during the darkness and could not effectively coordinate its efforts with the Southern Force.

The staff considered three options: 1) remain in a static defensive position in the vicinity of San Bernardino Strait and wait to determine whether or not the Center Force would sortie through; 2) divide the carrier forces, or 3) proceed with all groups northward and strike the enemy's Northern Force.

Halsey and the staff rejected the first two alternatives. There was no need for guarding San Bernardino Strait. If the Center Force did steam through, it could at best, Halsey believed, "merely hit and run." Surely Kinkaid could deal effectively with both the Southern and Center forces. The staff also refused to divide Task Force Thirty-Eight because any weakening of the assault on the Northern Force would reduce the odds of striking a crippling blow at the enemy's carrier strength. To sink the Northern Force, Task Force Thirty-Eight had to seize the initiative, Center Force or no Center Force.

"It's not my job," Halsey said, "to protect the Seventh Fleet. My job is offensive, to strike with the Third Fleet."

Kinkaid believed that it was Halsey's responsibility to support MacArthur's forces directly. He thought that the Seventh Fleet's task was to land troops and keep them ashore. The ships were armed accordingly with a very low percentage of armor-piercing projectiles. His escort carriers had anti-personnel bombs instead of torpedoes and heavy bombs. "We were not," he said, "prepared to fight a naval action."

Kinkaid's belief that Halsey planned to guard San Bernardino Strait was reaffirmed when he intercepted a message from the admiral to his subordinates. Halsey recognized that there was an outside chance that the Center Force might try to steam through San Bernardino Strait. Therefore, he adopted a battle plan and told the skippers of four battleships and several cruisers and destroyers from Task Force Thirty-Eight that their ships would be formed into Task Force Thirty-Four and would engage "decisively at long ranges." "This dispatch," said Halsey, "I intended merely as a warning to the ships concerned that if a surface engagement offered, I would detach them from Task Force Thirty-Eight, form them into Task Force Thirty-Four, and send them ahead as a battle line. It was definitely not an executive dispatch, but a battle plan."

Kinkaid and Nimitz at Pearl Harbor interpreted the words "will be formed" as an order, not a plan of battle. They believed that Task Force Thirty-Four was indeed being organized and Kinkaid thought that Halsey had concocted a scheme to protect San Bernardino Strait, which "was perfect in concept and perfect in composition of the forces assigned." Captain Wilson, Halsey's Operations Officer, commented on communications between major commanders in the area: "High command channels were cluttered with long and unimportant routine reports. Our message to the Fleet to prepare to form Task Force Thirty-Four was misunderstood by both Admirals Nimitz and Kinkaid."

"To make certain that none of my subordinate commanders misconstrued it," said Halsey, "I told them later by voice radio: IF THE ENEMY SORTIES, TASK FORCE THIRTY-FOUR WILL BE FORMED WHEN DIRECTED BY ME."

This message was received by nearby vessels but not by Kinkaid or even Mitscher. Like Kinkaid, Mitscher believed that Task Force Thirty-Four had been formed and was protecting San Bernardino. Mitscher's staff made a battle plan: to station Task Force Thirty-Four off San Bernardino with one carrier group nearby to give it air cover at dawn, and to send two other battleships north for a night gunnery action against the northern Japanese force, with the other two carrier groups hitting the latter at daybreak. In this way both the central and northern enemy forces would be met by superior American power.

Mitscher's staff pleaded with him to send their battle plan to Halsey. Mitscher refused on the ground that it was not for him to make gratuitous suggestions to superiors. Besides, he said, it would be unfair to Halsey's staff when they were at their busiest.

On board the *New Jersey,* Halsey put his finger down on the plot of the Northern Force and said, "We go north and put those Jap carriers down for keeps." The staff unanimously agreed that Task Force Thirty-Eight should make a high speed run northward and attack the enemy, basing their decision largely upon their pilots' exaggerated reports of the damage inflicted on the Center Force. With the information on hand, the staff's reasoning was sound. The Center Force had three operational battleships; the Northern Force, two battleships that had been converted to carriers (*Ise* and *Hyuga*), one fleet carrier, and three light carriers. For Halsey there was no way of knowing whether Ozawa's flattops were loaded with aircraft, and he could not assume that they were hoaxes. It was more important for Task Force Thirty-Eight to destroy six carriers than it was three battleships.

Halsey radioed an urgent message to Kinkaid, information Nimitz, King, and all task group commanders of the Third and Seventh Fleets: CENTRAL FORCE HEAVILY DAMAGED

ACCORDING TO STRIKE REPORTS X AM PROCEEDING
NORTH WITH THREE GROUPS TO ATTACK CARRIER
FORCES AT DAWN.

This message meant that Halsey was ordering Task Force
Thirty-Eight, including the battleships and cruisers of the yet un-
formed Task Force Thirty-Four, to steam northward. Kinkaid,
however, thought that Task Force Thirty-Four was already organized and that Halsey was running northward with the three carrier units and leaving Task Force Thirty-Four behind to guard San
Bernardino Strait. "It was inconceivable," said Kinkaid later,
"that Halsey could have scrapped a perfect plan" and left the
strait unprotected.

Halsey was taking a risk and he realized it, but most of his successes had been founded upon calculated risks. "Here was a bold
fighter," said Wilson, "willing to take chances if there was a fair
promise of success."

Halsey, in a dispatch to Nimitz and MacArthur, later explained
his reaction. "Searches by my carrier planes revealed the presence of the Northern carrier force on the afternoon of 24 October,
which completed the picture of all enemy naval forces. As it
seemed childish to me to guard . . . San Bernardino Strait, I
concentrated TF 38 during the night and steamed north to attack
the Northern Force at dawn. I believed that the Center Force had
been so heavily damaged in the Sibuyan Sea that it could no
longer be considered a serious menace to the Seventh Fleet."

Again, he remarked, "It preserved my Fleet's integrity, it left
the initiative with me, and it promised the greatest possibility of
surprise. Even if the Central Force meanwhile passed through
San Bernardino and headed for Leyte, it could only hope to harry
the landing operation. It could not consolidate any advantage,
because of its reported damage. It could merely hit-and-run. I felt
Kinkaid was amply strong to handle this situation if it should develop."

"When the Japanese carriers were sighted to the north," recalled Captain Wilson, "our greatest worry was that they would
reach a position by daylight the next day to permit shuttle bombing of our forces by planes flying from Luzon fields to bomb and
then land on their carriers and vice versa. Based on information

of heavily damaged Japanese forces . . . the Admiral decided to throw the full weight of the Third Fleet against the untouched carrier force coming down from the north."

"The real reason that we decided to turn north and go after [the carriers]," recalled Carney, "was the fact that the strike reports [on the Center Force] indicated a measure of damage which turned out to be far overestimated. We figured that if they'd taken the damage as reported, and they [the American airmen] seemed to be very positive about their reports, then it was perfectly safe to move over to get [the carriers] which was the end of the Japanese Navy if we could get that one off."

Halsey and the Dirty Tricks Department assumed that by heading north they were pursuing the more powerful of the Japanese naval forces; in reality, by their action, they permitted the stronger Center Force to move unseen and unchallenged through San Bernardino Strait.

Three of Halsey's task force commanders—Admirals Mitscher, Bogan, and Willis A. ("Ching") Lee (battleship force commander)—were disturbed by the move. Admiral Mitscher on the *Lexington* in Sherman's group was disgruntled over the fact that Halsey was running the show. Halsey's order to steam north and attack strengthened his belief that he had been relieved of tactical command of Task Force Thirty-Eight. After going to bed that night and leaving everything to Halsey, he was awakened by his Chief of Staff, Commodore Arleigh A. Burke, and his Operations Officer, Commander James Flatley, who informed him that the Center Force was steaming for San Bernardino Strait. They urged him to tell Halsey to change course to the south. Mitscher asked if Halsey had this information. "Yes he does," said Burke.

"If he wants my advice," replied Mitscher, "he'll ask for it." He then went back to bed.

Bogan contemplated a protest. After reading aircraft reports that Kurita's force had resumed a course for San Bernardino Strait, he discussed the situation over TBS (Talk between Ships) with Captain E. C. Ewen of the *Independence*. Ewen confirmed the reports and mentioned the ominous news that all navigation lights in San Bernardino Strait were brightly burning, after a long blackout. Bogan immediately wrote a message to Halsey incorporating this fact, then called him personally over TBS and read it. An impatient staff officer replied, "Yes, yes, we have that information." Bogan was ready to follow up with another message, suggesting that Lee's Battle Force be formed with his carrier group in support, letting Sherman's and Davison's groups fight it out with Ozawa. But after that terse reply, he gave up.

With a mass of intelligence reports, Admiral Lee realized that the Northern Force had to be a decoy with little striking power and that the earlier retreat of the Center Force was only temporary. He sent a message to Halsey stating his views. No reply was made except for "Roger." Later Lee sent Halsey a message over TBS to the effect that Kurita's groups were heading for San Bernardino Strait. After this he said nothing.

Admiral Sherman was pleased with the decision to head north. "The situation was entirely to my liking," he said, "and I felt we had a chance to completely wipe out a major group of the enemy fleet including the precious carriers which he could ill afford to lose."

Although secure in the belief that Task Force Thirty-Four was guarding San Bernardino Strait, Admiral Kinkaid routinely ordered a northern scouting patrol of amphibious aircraft equipped for night flying. None of these PBYs sighted the Center Force. The Seventh Fleet had no night search planes on the escort carriers, but Kinkaid directed Admiral Sprague to launch patrols at dawn.

Anticipating a Japanese night passage (24/25 October) through Surigao Strait, Kinkaid ordered Rear Admiral Jesse B. ("Oley") Oldendorf, commander of the Seventh Fleet's Bombardment and Fire Support Group, to prepare to challenge the move. Allied forces heavily overmatched the Southern Force. A battle line of six battleships and a left and right flank of cruisers waited to bombard the enemy if it passed the line of PT boats and destroyers.

The Southern Force consisted of two groups, which had no tactical connection. The first arrived at 2300, the 24th, and escaped the PT boats, but headed into crippling torpedo attacks from the destroyers and into punishing blows by the battleships and cruisers. The second group ran into the PT boats, realized that the first group was in trouble, and withdrew.

In the early morning hours of 25 October, American ships and planes pursued the fleeing Japanese and inflicted more punishment. In the Battle of Surigao Strait, American forces took advantage of their awesome fire power to eliminate the opposition; only a Japanese heavy cruiser and five destroyers remained afloat at the end of the battle.

At 0412 Kinkaid radioed Halsey that he had engaged the enemy in Surigao Strait. Then he added in the message, "Is TF 34 guarding San Bernardino Strait?" Halsey never received this dispatch until 0648. He was irate at the question as he was unaware that Kinkaid had intercepted his earlier dispatch about forming Task Force Thirty-Four. Halsey promptly added, "Negative." When Kinkaid received this reply, he already knew that San Bernardino was unprotected.

Off Samar Island, north of Leyte, one of Kinkaid's task groups, consisting of sixteen escort carriers, was separated into three units (Taffy One, Taffy Two, Taffy Three), each unit composed of four to six escort carriers, three destroyers, and four escort destroyers. Taffy One, commanded by Admiral Thomas L. Sprague, was patrolling off Mindanao; Taffy Two (Admiral Felix B. Stump) was operating east of southern Samar; Taffy Three (Admiral Clifton A. F. "Ziggy" Sprague, no relation to the other commander) was twenty miles to the north.

Early on the 25th, Taffy Three met the Center Force, which had emerged undetected and unchallenged from San Bernardino Strait and was steaming toward Leyte. Taffy Three launched all its planes. Enemy salvoes found their mark. Shells ripped through the escort carriers without exploding. One carrier, however, the *Gambier Bay,* received direct hits and sank. The other two American carrier units, Taffy One and Taffy Two, sent up a concerted air attack which knocked out three Japanese cruisers. Then, facing almost certain disaster, Yankee destroyers and destroyer-escorts attacked. Although losing the *Hoel, Johnston,* and *Samuel B. Roberts,* they disabled a cruiser and, with the planes, so disarranged the enemy battle position that Admiral Kurita could no longer accurately determine the course of battle. Instead of forming a battle line, he let each ship take its own course. Suddenly, at 0911, Kurita, believing that he was fighting a powerful unit of Halsey's carrier force, terminated the battle and moved northward. He had missed a chance to inflict serious damage, and, possibly, to deliver a crushing blow at Leyte Gulf.

"I did not know," Kurita said later, "that Admiral Halsey had taken his fleet north. I moved with only the knowledge that I was able to acquire with my own eyes and did not realize how close I was to victory. I see now that it was very regrettable that I did not push on at the time."

After the Center Force's departure, American escort carriers underwent another attack, the first organized suicide, or kamikaze, attack of the war. Flying in low from southern Mindanao to keep off radar screens, the Japanese planes arrived too unexpectedly for Combat Air Patrol to react. It was up to the ships themselves to avoid being struck. Some enemy aircraft were shot down by AA fire. Others crash-dived, as intended, into the escort carriers, sinking one, the *St. Lo,* and seriously damaging the *Santee* and *Suwanee.*

The Japanese Northern Force, meanwhile, had successfully drawn Task Force Thirty-Eight away from San Bernardino Strait. Admiral Jisaburo Ozawa, in command, said later, "My chief concern was to lure your forces farther north," away from Leyte Gulf, although, "We expected complete destruction [ourselves]." Ozawa could well expect defeat, as sixty-four ships were hunting his nineteen and if the disparity of planes was great, the disparity of pilots was still greater. The loss of enemy carrier pilots over Formosa had been so severe and the training of the new aviators was so far from complete that few pilots remained with enough skill to land on flight decks.

A little after 0200 on 25 October, night search planes scouting ahead of Task Force Thirty-Eight (Mitscher was now in tactical command) made radar contact with two separate Japanese surface units of the Northern Force. Receiving this intelligence, Halsey finally formed Task Force Thirty-Four (*Iowa, New Jersey, Massachusetts, South Dakota, Washington, Alabama*), and ordered it to move out ahead of the carrier groups.

At dawn on 25 October American carriers launched 180 dive bombers, fighters, and torpedo planes. "Our next few hours were the most anxious of all," recalled Halsey. "God, what a wait it was!"

"I chewed my fingernails down to my elbows," admitted Mick Carney.

Suddenly at 0850 a flash report reached Halsey: ONE CARRIER SUNK AFTER TREMENDOUS EXPLOSION X 2 CARRIERS 1 LIGHT CRUISER BADLY HURT X OTHER CARRIER UNTOUCHED X FORCE COURSE 150 SPEED 17.

By now Halsey had received the much-delayed information from Kinkaid that the enemy had been shoved back from Surigao Strait. From this he believed that the Seventh Fleet was now free to cover Leyte Gulf. Twenty minutes later he received a call for help from Admiral Sprague and his escort carrier group. Halsey was not alarmed. "I figured," he recalled, "that sixteen little carriers had enough planes to protect themselves until Oldendorf could bring up his heavy ships."

Immediately after Sprague's dispatch, Halsey received a series of messages from Kinkaid, one in plain English, urging air strikes at Leyte Gulf and support from the fast battleships "at once."

This request annoyed Halsey as he was "rushing to intercept a force which gravely threatened not only Kinkaid and myself but the whole Pacific strategy." He radioed McCain's Task Group 38.1, moving up from the south, to go "at best possible speed" to bolster Sprague's groups and notified Kinkaid that he had done so.

Just after Halsey sent out McCain's order, he received another dispatch from Kinkaid. This detailed Kurita's attack and frantically asked that Task Force Thirty-Four run southward at "top speed" and protect Leyte. Still another message arrived, stating that Oldendorf's battleships were low on ammunition, "a new factor," said Halsey, "so astonishing that I could hardly accept it."

By now Task Force Thirty-Eight was too far to the north to give the Seventh Fleet any immediate help.

Halsey was in flag plot on the *New Jersey,* which was unwarrantedly crowded. As the brain-center to which all communications flowed, from time to time it had to accommodate messengers from the coding room as well as from the navigating bridge above and from the various staffers concerned with the conduct of the entire task force. Crouched over the plot board, officers transcribed data from Kinkaid and Sprague. Halsey tried to comprehend what was happening at Leyte Gulf.

"We were up all night," Carney said. "I don't think that there ever was an operation, certainly not as far-flung an operation, about which more information kept pouring in than . . . the preliminary facts that converged on both sides. We, all of us . . . believed if Japanese aviation could be completely eliminated, the Japanese fleet was eliminated. That night we talked about it . . . the Japanese navy was a factor in all this thinking. And if their naval aviation was eliminated, we felt that there was a chance they could never be effective."

In Washington, D.C., Admiral Joseph J. ("Jocko") Clark had arrived at Ernest King's office and found the Commander in Chief pacing up and down in a rage. To Clark he began lambasting Halsey. "He has left the strait of San Bernardino open for the Japanese to strike the transports at Leyte!" He told Clark that Oldendorf's old battlewagons were not only out of ammunition, but were pursuing the Southern Force back into Surigao Strait. Even with ammunition Oldendorf's force was no match for the super battleship *Yamato* of the Center Force, which had a good chance to wreck MacArthur's invasion plans. Just as Clark was leaving, a message arrived stating that the Center Force had just retired into the Sibuyan Sea and King's tension noticeably lessened.

At Pearl Harbor Nimitz had been monitoring all radio traffic and patiently watching the battle's progress on his operations chart. He became gravely concerned over the fate of Taffy Three and, believing that Task Force Thirty-Four was still protecting San Bernardino Strait, he could not understand what was happening in Leyte Gulf. He sent a sharp dispatch to Halsey: WHERE IS RPT [Repeat] WHERE IS TASK FORCE 34 RR THE WORLD WONDERS.

In flag plot, a communications officer removed the message from the pneumatic tube and handed it to Halsey. As he read it, his hands began to shake. His face went white. He snatched off his cap and with a thunderous oath threw it on the deck. "It is utterly impossible for me to believe that Chester Nimitz could have sent such an insult—it's like a slap in the face!" he stormed.

Carney rushed over and grabbed Halsey's arm. "Stop it! What the hell's the matter with you? Pull yourself together."

Halsey gave Carney the dispatch and turned his back. Later he admitted, "I was so mad I couldn't talk." *

"They say," recalled Carney, "that Admiral Halsey was impulsive, and he sure was impulsive when that message came."

"The orders I now gave," said Halsey, "I gave in rage, and although Ernie King later assured me that they were the right ones, I am convinced that they were not."

Halsey's flag log from the forenoon watch that day, 25 October, gave the bare bones of the story. "At 0835 c/s [change speed] to 25k to close enemy. At 0919 c/c [changed course] to 000."

At 1003 Halsey received another message from Kinkaid. His situation was "critical." Fast battleships, supported by carrier air strikes, could prevent, said Kinkaid, the enemy from destroying Taffy Three and from entering Leyte Gulf.

At 1055 after flash reports indicated that the enemy's Northern Force had been seriously damaged and partly sunk, Halsey ordered his battleships and Bogan's carriers to change course and head for Leyte Gulf.

"At that moment," Halsey wrote later, "the Northern Force, with its two remaining carriers dead in the water, was exactly forty-two miles from the muzzles of my sixteen-inch guns. . . . I turned my back on the opportunity I had dreamed of since my

---

* Halsey didn't learn the full truth about the Nimitz dispatch until weeks later. All such messages were sent in code. But to make it difficult for the enemy to decode them, they were also padded with nonsensical words. The basic message was "Where is Task Force 34?" From his headquarters at Pearl Harbor, Nimitz simply wanted to know Halsey's position. Ordinarily, the man who put the words into the code would have inserted something like "Joe DiMaggio wonders. . . ." thus making it read, "Joe DiMaggio wonders where is Task Force 34?" Halsey's decoder, on receiving the message, would have realized instantly which words were padding and cut them out before showing it to the admiral. As it was, remembered Halsey, " 'The world wonders' sounded so infernally plausible that my decoders delivered it to me."

days as a cadet. For me, one of the biggest battles of the war was off, and what has been called, 'the Battle of Bull's Run' was on.''

"Second-guessers claimed I should have guarded San Bernardino Strait,'' Halsey said later. "My *real* mistake was in turning my fleet around.'' Actually, had Halsey continued northward it would not have changed the outcome of the battle.

As Halsey's force moved southward, never to reach Leyte Gulf in time, he answered Nimitz's "The World Wonders" message. He advised CINCPAC that the battleships of Task Force Thirty-Four were with Mitscher's carriers, engaging the enemy, when the dispatch arrived. Already one enemy carrier had been sunk, two were dead in the water. The battleships, he told Nimitz, were now heading for Leyte Gulf with Bogan's carrier group to reinforce the Seventh Fleet.

Mitscher's Task Force Thirty-Eight (Sherman's and Davison's groups) continued northward and, just before noon, launched a strike of 200 planes. They crippled the carrier *Zuiho* and finally sank her. Torpedo planes finished off the carrier *Zuikaku*. Then the aircraft attacked the *Ise* and *Hyuga*. The carriers changed courses erratically, AA guns flashing, and avoided the bombs and torpedoes. The only damage the planes inflicted before returning to the carriers was a single hit in the *Ise*'s port catapult. Ozawa's force, meanwhile, swung northward and returned to the Ryukyus. The American planes' total score for the day was three carriers (*Chitose, Zuikaku, Zuiho*) and a destroyer sunk, one cruiser badly damaged.

Halsey radioed Nimitz: JAPANESE NAVY HAS BEEN BEATEN AND ROUTED BY THE THIRD AND SEVENTH FLEETS.

There was jubilation throughout official Washington. At 1730, 25 October, Stephen T. Early, President Roosevelt's press secretary, dashed into the White House press room and told correspondents, "Come quick." Rushing to the Oval Office, reporters found Roosevelt seated at his desk, smiling broadly. "Obviously,'' said one writer, "he had been interrupted in his later afternoon dictation.'' On his desk lay scattered correspondence, but directly in front of him was a single sheet of paper, inscribed by his own handwriting.

He said, beamingly, he had "a real flash," just telephoned to him by Admiral Leahy. Picking up the paper, Roosevelt read slowly and distinctly, "The President received today a report from Admiral Halsey that the Japanese Navy in the Philippine area has been defeated, seriously damaged and routed by the United States Navy in that area." For a moment there was a pause. No one said a word. Then Early explained, "There's your flash" and reporters ran from the office to their telephones.

Across America newspaper headlines blared: "Main Jap Fleet Broken. Halsey Force Inflicts Staggering Blow. Our Fleet Rules Seas to Tokyo. Japan Is Crippled."

"Japan's Navy was so decisively beaten in the two-day Battle of the Philippines," said one editor, "it figures as a major factor to be reckoned with in the immediate American war plans."

"It was one of the great naval engagements in history," wrote another, "and by far the greatest in this war. It ended in the greatest naval victory in America's own history."

At the Navy Day dinner in the Waldorf-Astoria Hotel in New York, Admiral King told 1,200 guests, "The Japanese Navy has been reduced to not more than one-half its maximum strength. The enemy is welcome to know that we shall continue to press them with every means at our command. The enemy already knows—the world knows—that when the war in Europe releases the powerful forces engaged there the greater part of them will be brought to bear against Japan. It would seem that even the sons of—Heaven—can read that handwriting in letters so tall and so clear that they are visible around the world."

The major conditions affecting the Battle of Leyte Gulf were the superiority of power of the United States Navy and the immense strength of American air cover. The individual segments of the American naval units performed courageously, but the Third and Seventh Fleets, misled by a series of misinterpretations, failed to coordinate their movements. Halsey concentrated upon and forced the Japanese Center Force to withdraw temporarily into the Sibuyan Sea. He then abandoned San Bernardino Strait and MacArthur's beachhead on the assumption that the Seventh Fleet was prepared to cover the northern approaches to Leyte Gulf.

At Leyte Major General Courtney Whitney, a top MacArthur aide, said later that if the Center Force had steamed successfully into Leyte Gulf "the American invasion would in all probability have experienced a setback of incalculable proportions. The enemy's heavy guns would have experienced little trouble in pounding the remaining transports and landing craft. Shore positions and troop installations could have been bombarded almost at will."

The Sixth Army summarized its view of the probable consequences if the U.S. Navy had lost the battle. "Had the [Japanese] plan succeeded, the effect on the Allied troops on Leyte in all likelihood would have been calamitous, for these troops would have been isolated and their situation would have been precarious indeed. If it had been victorious in the naval battle, the Japanese fleet could have leisurely and effectively carried out the destruction of shipping, aircraft, and supplies that were so vital to Allied operations on Leyte. An enemy naval victory would have had an adverse effect of incalculable proportions not only upon the Leyte operation, but upon the overall plan for the liberation of the Philippines."

To counter this criticism, Halsey said, "That Kurita's force could have leisurely and effectively carried out the destruction of shipping, aircraft, and supplies in Leyte Gulf was not in the realm of possibilities. . . . Kurita would have been limited to a hit-and-run attack in the restricted waters of Leyte Gulf. He would further have been subjected to the attack of the cruisers present in Leyte Gulf. He would have been limited to minor damage. . . .

"The statement that an enemy naval victory would have an effect of incalculable proportions not only on the Leyte operation, but upon the overall plan for the liberation of the Philippines as well, can only be premised on the thought that our naval forces would be almost totally destroyed. The prognostication of such a condition could not be reasoned on one of the facts existing during this three days' engagement."

In his final report to Nimitz, Halsey wrote, "I know now how the Flying Dutchman felt; the day-to-day uncertainty and the continual need for countermanding orders and changing plans is more wearing on the Fleet than actual combat. This is not a complaint—our great mobility and flexibility are powerful assets which must be utilized—I am only telling how your forces are faring."

"There are, however," continued Halsey, "factors which I feel that I must report to you—factors that seem to me to be in violation of every sound principle of command. I realize how these compromises come to pass, but understanding does not entail endorsement."

"In the first place," Halsey said, "having two autonomous tactical Fleet Commands supporting the same operation cannot be justified from a naval viewpoint. Cooperation can never be a substitute for command in naval action, and the further employment of the SEVENTH Fleet in conjunction with, but separate and independent from, the Pacific Fleet has all the elements of confusion if not disaster. . . . The first few days at Leyte have been confusing. Under MacArthur's system, the Air, Army, and Navy are three separate commands on the same level; under that system no one agency really runs the show."

"I feel better," Halsey concluded, "for having gotten this off my chest; if nothing can be done, just consider yourself as my Father Confessor and throw this in the waste basket. Actually, we will keep plugging and will do our best to ensure MacArthur's success, and also to ensure our readiness to execute your plans."

MacArthur never blamed his friend Halsey for abandoning the Leyte beachhead to run after the Northern Force. One evening at dinner with members of his staff the general heard Halsey's name mentioned, "accompanied by certain expressions that might be classed as highly uncomplimentary." MacArthur pounded on the table. "That's enough," he stormed. "Leave the Bull alone. He's still a fighting admiral in my book."

"I have never ascribed the unfortunate incidents of this naval battle to faulty judgment on the part of any of the commanders involved," MacArthur wrote in his *Reminiscences*. "The disaster can be placed squarely at the door of Washington. In the naval action, two key American commanders were independent of each other, one under me, and the other under Admiral Nimitz 5,000 miles away, both operating in the same waters and in the same battle."

On 29 October Halsey and Kinkaid received a message from

Admiral King: A LARGE PART OF THE ENEMY NAVY
HAS BEEN EFFECTUALLY DISPOSED OF FOREVER AND
THE REMAINDER FOR SOME TIME TO COME X ALL
OFFICERS AND MEN OF YOUR FLEETS HAVE THE
HEARTIEST ADMIRATION OF ALL HANDS X WELL
DONE.

"That's something," commented Halsey, "coming from
Ernie!"

In Washington when Admiral King analyzed all the battle reports of the Leyte Gulf action, he concluded, "Apart from all
questions of the relative importance in Halsey's mission of covering the Seventh Fleet as against creating an opportunity for the
destruction of a major portion of the enemy fleet . . . [I] was
never able to fathom why planes from the Seventh Fleet escort
carriers had not adequately scouted the area of San Bernardino
Strait from the Sibuyan Sea to the Eastward before dawn on the
morning of 25 October and thus detected Kurita's approach."

In King's view, it would have been prudent for Seventh Fleet
planes to have made such a search independently, to be certain
that the Japanese Central Force had actually turned back and was
no longer approaching the area of Leyte Gulf. Consequently King
attributed the element of surprise in the Battle of Samar not only
to Halsey's absence in the north but also to Kinkaid's failure to
use his own air squadrons for searches at the crucial moment.

At Pearl Harbor the chief of Nimitz's Analytical Section, Captain Ralph Parker, in writing the CINCPAC report of the battle,
criticized Halsey's judgment. Before signing the report, Nimitz
sent it back with the note, "Tone it down. I'll leave it with you."

After the war in many wardrooms, in many Army and Navy
Clubs and wherever veterans of Leyte Gulf held reunions, the
battle was refought. The opposing forces were no longer Americans and Japanese, but Americans on both sides. The Battle of
Leyte Gulf left one great unanswered question. Was Halsey right
in steaming off to destroy enemy aircraft carriers or did he leave
a fellow admiral in the lurch?

Until 1947 officers with strong views on the matter refused to
discuss the question publicly, believing that to do so would harm

the naval service. The issue, however, was explosively reopened in 1947 by Halsey himself when McGraw-Hill published his memoirs, *Admiral Halsey's Story.* Although Halsey claimed he had no desire to start a controversy or to cast aspersions upon Admiral Kinkaid, that is precisely the effect of his pronouncements.

Halsey insisted that his decision to move north was correct. His only error in the Battle of Leyte Gulf, he said, was in turning back to aid the Seventh Fleet against the Japanese battleships. This position was reiterated in Halsey's article, "The Battle of Leyte Gulf," published in the *United States Naval Institute Proceedings* (1952). "My decision was to strike the Northern Force," he wrote. "Given the same circumstances and the same information as I had then, I would make it again."

Admiral Kinkaid argued that, even if Halsey were correct in moving north after the Japanese carriers, he did not require the entire Third Fleet to execute it.

In Washington Admiral King was upset after reading *Admiral Halsey's Story,* especially over the remarks concerning Kinkaid and the observation "that things would have been different if the command set-up had been different."

"Your 'strictures' on Kinkaid," King wrote Halsey, "are severe even though you have a 'note' in which you say you would have done as he did in the circumstances. In fact, an inference readily to be drawn from your remarks about the command set-up is that if you had had control of the Seventh Fleet, its readiness to oppose the Japanese Central Force would have been adequate, or more nearly so. I think it well to quote part of what [one of] our contemporaries says: 'Perhaps I am all wet but I still am shocked that a chap like Bill whom we all admire and like could get so far out of character as I feel he has in this book. After spinning a yarn in the first chapters he suddenly writes what can only be considered an attempt to justify his decisions in the Leyte battle—like a man almost with a sense of guilt justifying himself to himself, as well as to his peers.' "

"Personally," continued King, "I must say that I did not like the tenor of [the Leyte Gulf] installment."

Answering King's letter, Halsey wrote: "I regret that your point of view and mine do not coincide. I feel the story of the battle of Leyte will be written for many years to come. The authors will try to analyze what went on in the minds of men. There will be many instances of what the commander had in mind at various stages of the game. In order to provide an authoritative background of information as to what was going on in my mind I have honestly tried to give a forthright and straightforward statement. Thus I tried to cover my reactions and the background reasons. I could not tell my story of the battle of Leyte without a full explanation of my relations to and communications with Kinkaid. This was my sole object in writing as I did. I regret the inference you have drawn in . . . your letter. I had and have no such inference in mind. I had and have the thought that participation in the same engagement of uncoordinated forces is unsound from a military point of view. . . ."

Not only naval officers, but historians took sides. Bernard Brodie, then an associate professor at Yale University, wrote "The Battle for Leyte Gulf" for the *Virginia Quarterly Review* (1947). "The evident conclusion [about Leyte Gulf]," Brodie said, "is that the American handling of the business was anything but 'well done.' . . . That his [Halsey's] failure [to annihilate all the Japanese forces] stemmed from no want of dash and zeal but rather from errors of comprehension argues only that intelligence ought to be valued equally with boldness and courage among the necessary attributes of a fleet commander. The essential facts remain that the Japanese admirals went into that battle with the conviction that they would be completely destroyed, and that they did everything which would reasonably be expected of them to realize their conviction. But of the nine battleships which represented the main element of the strength they put into the noose, they were permitted to extricate six, along with other important ships. And in the process of permitting them to do so, Admiral Halsey exposed to the gravest peril the landing force which it was among his first duties to protect."

Halsey was incensed. "The *Virginia Quarterly* matter," he wrote a friend, "has really gotten my goat, and I have raised some hell in the proper place."

Despite the sympathy which Professor C. Vann Woodward's *The Battle for Leyte Gulf* (1947) displayed toward Halsey, the facts which the author presented made the tally of errors against the admiral more extensive than before.

"Would you be good enough," Halsey told Commander R. H. McIlwaine, USNR, who had duty in the office of the Secretary of the Navy, "to look up the war service of one Bernard Brodie and C. Vann Woodward? You are familiar with Woodward's book. Brodie has just written a very caustic attack on me. . . . To be sure, the attack only covers my intelligence, of which I have never claimed a great amount. I would like as much detail as possible as to their service, most particularly combat service, and their qualifications as critics of Naval Affairs. It is not my present intention to use this material, but to have it in case the occasion arises. I have no intention of entering a controversy with these two gentlemen (?)."

McIlwaine wrote back. "As requested I've checked up on the two 'gentlemen' referred to and find both were Reserve desk-chair boys who fought the Battle of Washington for the duration of the war. Bernard Brodie had no combat or sea duty, only that of historian for BuOrd [Bureau of Ordnance]. In this assignment he had access of all combat reports, in the highest classification, which he used in the preparation of Battle Reports for this Bureau. . . . C. Vann Woodward . . . is a historian, also of some scholarly importance, having been commissioned in the Navy and detailed to CNO [Chief of Naval Operations], where he prepared Admiral King's Annual Reports from secret reports submitted by the Fleet. He, too, never saw sea duty or any combat, spending his entire tour of duty in Washington."

To a friend, Halsey wrote, "Have you read the book called 'Battle of Leyte Gulf' by Vann Woodward? He is apparently an armchair strategist that fought bravely throughout four years of the war in a naval officer's uniform behind a tin desk in Washington braving all the terrors and dangers of that location. I do not like the book. If you or some of your friends are so inclined I think you might be able to rip it to shreds. . . . Naturally I cannot and will not undertake such a job."

To one historian, who had been critical, Halsey wrote that although "in general the account of the battle is very good and very fair, you fall down when you try to tell people what I was thinking. I do not intend to allow grossly wrong statements about my thoughts to go into . . . [the] book. I also think you make a great mistake in criticizing my strategical acts and categorically stating that they were wrong."

Halsey was angered with a book which accused him of making "the wrong decision" in steaming north. "I consider this," said Halsey, "one of the best examples of Monday morning quarterbacking I have ever read. . . . I am afraid he has forgotten his statements about calculated risks, which I knew then and know now that I was taking. I consider that they paid off amply."

"I make the following categorical statement, and I feel that no one in the Navy will attempt to deny it," concluded Halsey. "If either Admiral Kinkaid or I had been in overall command, the battle would have been fought in an entirely different manner. I lay no claim to be able to say how it would have turned out. It was only the indoctrination we had all been subjected to that enabled the naval forces of the United States to achieve a clean cut strategical victory. That such a victory was achieved, is testified to by the fact that the Japanese Navy was never again more than a nuisance value during the remainder of the war."

Halsey was particularly incensed by Professor Samuel Eliot Morison of Harvard University. In January 1951 Morison lectured on the Battle of Leyte Gulf before members of the Naval Historical Foundation in Washington. Near the end of his talk, he used the phrase, "Halsey's blunder," for ordering the task force north. Although Halsey was not present, he heard through "the grapevine" that Morison had referred to him in "a very pointed manner."

To his friend, Rollo Wilson, Halsey wrote: "Morison surely is a splendid Monday afternoon Quarterback. It is too bad we did not have some of these wonderful tacticians to run the war for us at the time."

"I realize that long after an event," Halsey wrote Morison, "it is very difficult if not impossible to place oneself in the position of a Fleet Commander at the time of the specific occurrence. Information which has subsequently become available [the lack of air strength in the Northern Force] tend to intrude upon any determination based only on the facts and on the information which were available to the Commander at the time of his decision. To correctly evaluate any decisions made at a prior time it is necessary to consider only the information available to the person who made the decision at the time such a decision was made. . . . I still feel that my only real error was in not continuing my advance to the North and completely annihilating the Northern Force, and this I would have done had it not been for the dispatches from Kinkaid and Nimitz."

Halsey grew more irate when *Leyte,* a volume in the series *History of the United States Naval Operations in World War II,* written by Morison, was published.

Halsey told Mick Carney that he and one of his staff, Leonard J. Dow, had discussed that "son-of-a-bitch named Morison."

"From his book *Leyte,*" Halsey told Carney, "it is apparent to me that it has got to be answered in some way, or I and my staff are going down in history as dubs. . . . I want to fight Morison on every point. [Dow] says that would be allowing him too much importance. He suggests I make a polite but ridiculing answer to his book and not treat it with the prominence Morison thinks it deserves—to say something about it as being a good history 'novel' (but in no way history) because it is neither objective nor factual and should in no way be considered historical—and to cite roughly, two or three passages which show his lack of intellectual integrity and let it go at that—and, make fun of his claims as being an expert on strategy and tactics. This appeals to me very much."

To another staff member, Halsey wrote, "My idea is to get the son-of-a-bitch's cojones in a vise and set up on them. . . . [I want] to poke fun at him as a very poor historian and cite some instances to prove our point. In other words, make a laughing-stock out of him."

Fortunately, Mick Carney calmed Halsey down. He wrote, "My initial thought is that any reply you make should be completely devoid of sarcasm or any effort to discredit Morison's general reputation as an historian. My natural reaction is always the same as yours: to fight. However . . . he has done excellent work at times. . . . He is firmly in public opinion as a professional and competent historian. No blast of yours, however justifiable, will destroy that structure; it would far more likely boomerang.''

Halsey replied, ''Once again, I shall probably keep my mouth shut about this matter. . . . Again, I thank you for your always good advice when I get mad—which I do frequently.''

Even today historians are divided in their opinion of the Battle of Leyte Gulf. Professor Clark Reynolds in his *The Fast Carriers: The Forging of an Air Navy* is extremely critical of Halsey, whom he feels had been away from carriers too long in the time he was Commander, South Pacific. Halsey had failed to keep up with the development of complex carrier tactics and the capabilities of modern carriers themselves. Reynolds believes that Halsey was guilty of sloppy techniques, poor staff work, and vague dispatches. Halsey could have taken two courses of action, either one of which would have stopped Admiral Kurita from breaking through. He could have divided his forces, leaving one part to patrol San Bernardino Strait, while he steamed north, or, he could have moved north to strike Ozawa, then made it back in time to halt Kurita, but that would have involved complex coordination and timing with the Seventh Fleet. ''But such tactics,'' Reynolds concludes, ''were simply too complex for Bull Halsey.''

In his *Decision at Leyte,* Stanley L. Falk feels that Halsey made the right decision. ''The fact that Kinkaid could probably have defended Leyte Gulf by himself,'' writes Falk, ''does not in itself justify Halsey's decision to go north after Ozawa—unless it was clear that Ozawa represented a more important target than Kurita. Halsey thought so. While Kurita had four battleships in his force, Ozawa had two semibattleships and four *carriers*. There was no way of knowing whether or not these carriers were loaded with planes, but it was highly unlikely that the Japanese would risk such important units without their aircraft and incredible that they should deliberately sacrifice them as bait.'' Halsey could not afford to assume that the carriers were harmless.

[XI]

"They Scared Me Thoroughly and Repeatedly"

IN LATE OCTOBER 1944, rains turned Leyte into a marsh which minimized MacArthur's superiority. The Americans had only one operational airstrip on Leyte, Tacloban. Meanwhile, the enemy was concentrating planes on Formosa, on the home islands, and on the all-weather fields of Luzon. Several days after the Battle of Leyte Gulf, MacArthur ordered the Army Air Force to relieve the battered Seventh Fleet escort carriers of the responsibility of air support over the island. But, unfortunately, after the small carriers departed, the Air Force was hamstrung to carry out its task. It did not have sufficient planes or enough available airfields.

The Third Fleet stayed on to cover Leyte and to attack other Philippine targets, especially the Luzon airfields, which, said Halsey, "should take the pressure off MacArthur."

"At the moment," Halsey wrote Nimitz, "things are calm. . . . It is definitely a period of watchful waiting, and until I see what the enemy's further intentions are in the Philippines I am unable to make any further concrete recommendations. . . . My own personal estimate is that the Philippine operations must proceed successfully and swiftly, and if the enemy continues to stubbornly pour air replacements into Luzon it may be to the best interests of all hands for us to stay in this area and periodically pull the chain and send another consignment down the sewer."

By the end of October 1944 Halsey and the entire Third Fleet were dog tired. "This session since September," Halsey told Nimitz, "has been more strenuous and uninterrupted than anything that the fleet has heretofore experienced, and it may well serve as the index to future replacement requirements. Frankly, I have an open mind on the subject, but I feel that it is one of the more important problems facing the fleet today."

"I did not carry a physical burden, as did the crews of our ships and planes," he said, "but the burden of responsibility seemed quite as heavy. Heaviest was the tension that built up under the constant threat of air attack; the attack itself was almost a relief, because you knew things couldn't get any worse."

Sunbaked and leathery, Halsey at sixty-one was still rugged and in much better health than he had been three years earlier. His day usually began around 0500, when he went to the flag bridge to sit in his high, steel chair and watch the first planes take off. Once they were gone, he went to flag plot to check the charts.

Flag plot was the nerve center of fleet operations where a flag duty officer was always on watch, a duty which staff members rotated. The principal feature of flag plot was a chart eight feet long and three feet wide. It ran between two thick rolls of paper, one for providing fresh paper, the other to contain a continuous plot of all actions recorded on the chart. A staffer constantly kept this chart up to date. It supplied all the data the staff required and from it many decisions were made.

After visiting flag plot, Halsey would descend the ladder that led from it to the flag mess directly below on the next deck. The port side of this large space was partitioned off to serve as his of-fice-living quarters. Here, in a spacious, well furnished office, he tackled the paper work. On the bulkheads hung charts and enlargements of air reconnaissance photos. The other half of the flag mess was dominated by a huge mahogany mess table—which between meals doubled as a conference table for his staff. At breakfast, lunch, and dinner some twenty staff officers sat around it with Halsey as the genial host. At mealtime he always avoided discussing fleet problems unless they were extremely pressing.

Halsey was amiable in private conversation, "his give-and-take with his staff officers was free and easy." Slackness or shoddy work incensed him and he could roar in a voice that made him renowned as "the tough guy of the fleet." Junior officers and enlisted men recognized that the admiral was "no sun-downer." Under those bushy eyebrows the Old Man's eyes gleamed with good humor.

Halsey's chief recreation at sea was watching movies. Irritated at the low caliber of motion pictures that were being shown, he once requested Nimitz "to provide new and additional movie films for ships at sea to increase recreational facilities afloat."

After the evening movie, he sat in on the nightly meetings of his Dirty Tricks Department, held around his oval mess table, where his officers concocted strategy.

Halsey felt close to his staff and they worked extremely well together. "You see," said a member, "he's had his staff with him a long time. They form a real team—almost a family. We know each other so well that there's no question as to who does what. When we talk things over one officer says, 'I'll handle this,' another says, 'I'll do that.' Halsey has always made it a point to keep his men with him."

General Dewitt Peck, USMC, who was Halsey's war plans officer in the early days of the South Pacific war, recalled, ". . . he would send for . . . his staff and say, 'Now gentlemen, here's the proposition,' and then he would turn to me—I was usually the junior one—and say, 'Now, Peck, what would you recommend?' and so on. And he'd pace back and forth and say, 'Well, now here's what we're going to do.' I never saw him make any lightning, damn-the-torpedoes-decision at all. He was a thoughtful, intelligent, forceful leader. The impressions he gave were all wrong."

After his nightly staff conference, just before midnight, he went out on the flag bridge for a last look around, then into flag plot to see the charts and messages. In his sea cabin he had one more cup of coffee and one more cigarette before turning in. He always hoped for five hours sleep, but seldom got it.

During those days at sea Halsey often paused to write personal letters. In a long letter to a friend regarding the upcoming 1944 presidential election between President Roosevelt and Thomas E.

Dewey, he wrote, "I come from a long line of established Republicans. I have only voted once, but if I had exercised the privilege in the last four Presidential elections I would have voted for FDR without a second's hesitation."

"Whether you like it or not," he continued, "FDR has shown himself a very able world's leader. I do not believe for one instant that either Churchill or Stalin are putting anything large over on him. As you say, Stalin is the biggest man in the world today because he is a realist. I quite agree. It behooves big business and Americans, in particular, to take a realistic view of the world situation and not be blinded by purely selfish local interests. These things don't amount to a damn in the big picture."

Halsey received a letter from a Navy wife living in the Bronx, New York. "Sir, I know . . . you are wondering who the little girl is whose picture I have enclosed—I have sent it because she is the reason for my writing you. Her Daddy has never seen her. He is a Lieutenant (j.g.) on your Staff and has been in the Pacific since June 31st, 1943. . . . I have just one prayer in my heart— that he could come home this Christmas to see her."

Halsey replied, "The feelings that prompted you to write, and your desire to have your husband home for Christmas are quite understandable, and you can rest assured that all of this is strictly between you and me. I wish I could play Santa Claus and deliver your lad to you on Christmas, but I would not be doing you any kindness if I held out a hope that I do not feel confident is justified.

"The war is speeding up, and there are many young officers and men who must stick to their jobs in spite of long, hard months. However, sometime after Christmas—just when I do not know—there should be an opportunity to let your husband go home to his fine young wife and that sweet youngster. So keep your chin up."

Throughout October and November Third Fleet planes pummeled Japanese airfields and shipping in the Philippines, supporting MacArthur's forces, who now were experiencing stiff opposition ashore.

One of the more successful raids was against Luzon on 5/6

November. Aircraft shot down 105 enemy planes and destroyed 321 on the ground. They hit installations, destroyed a locomotive and five tank cars, and sank or heavily damaged seventeen transports, fifty cargo ships (large and small), ten oilers, two cruisers, fifteen destroyers, and twenty-six small craft. American losses totaled twenty-five aircraft.

The net result of Task Force Thirty-Eight's air strikes in November was to weaken further Japanese air power and to destroy so much shipping that the enemy could not effectively reinforce his positions on Leyte. His garrisons throughout the Philippines were now almost isolated.

Although overwhelmingly successful against Philippine targets, Task Force Thirty-Eight still faced a serious threat to their offensive operations, the kamikazes. On 30 October, suicide divers smashed into the carriers *Franklin* and *Belleau Wood,* and another narrowly missed the flight deck of the *Enterprise.* Casualties numbered ninety-two Americans dead, sixty-six missing, and 165 injured in addition to fifty-nine planes destroyed. Two kamikazes sneaked through Combat Air Patrol on 5 November and crash-dived on the *Lexington,* killing forty-seven officers and men and injuring 140, wrecking the carrier's secondary control, and inflicting damage to the bridge.

On 25 November, while Task Force Thirty-Eight struck Luzon, kamikaze planes again attacked the carriers. One aircraft plunged into the *Essex,* another started fires on the *Hancock,* a third crashed into the *Intrepid,* a fourth dived through the *Cabot's* forward ramp. Casualties ran high: seventy-three dead, seventy-three missing, and 118 wounded. "There were moments," said Halsey, "when I was afraid it would be our last anywhere."

"We got our tail feathers burned . . . on the 25th," said Mick Carney, "and, frankly, we had to get out in a hurry."

After the kamikaze attacks, the staff tried to analyze what Task Force Thirty-Eight had done wrong as the Japanese had known its exact whereabouts. The staff examined the radio traffic and considered the possibility of leaks within the Philippine area. "We weren't sure what had caused this alerting of the Japanese," said Carney, "whereas before we had always been able to surprise them."

By further studying the problem—"Operation Picnic Strike"—they discovered that they had permitted themselves to fall into a "crystallized pattern," which was recognized by Japanese Intelligence. "We even tested this theory by duplicating that pattern at one time with no intention of striking," continued Carney, "and were gratified to note that the Japanese retired all shipping from the Philippines and made every effort to meet the incoming strike, thereby demonstrating that the Japs recognized the pattern and thought we were coming in. You needn't say that we never again permitted ourselves to do anything twice the same way."

While the staff solved this problem, they wrestled with the task of evolving tactics and techniques to halt the threat of the kamikazes. "I would be a damn fool," Halsey wrote, "to pretend that individual *kamikazes* did not scare me for a moment. I was confident that we could devise tactics to counter it, *if* our men were rested, our complement of planes was full, and our fleet was on the offensive. The early attacks, I reemphasize, caught us with tired men and few planes."

By scrutinizing enemy tactics, Halsey and his staff discovered that suicide pilots either trailed American planes to the carriers, frustrating the IFF (a radar device for the Identification of Friend or Foe); or they made a long, fast glide from high altitudes; or they skipped across the water so that radar failed to detect them. The staff attempted to nullify the first pattern by stationing radar picket destroyers well out ahead of the main task force, and directing homing planes to approach them on specified bearings. They countered the second by sending Combat Air Patrol aircraft higher and farther, and met the third pattern by establishing patrols to fly at low altitudes. For long range defense, Combat Air Patrol blanketed enemy airfields on a twenty-four-hour basis.

Each new technique had to be studied, tested, and modified. Nor did adoption end the actions of the kamikazes. A few occasionally sneaked through American defenses and scored direct hits. But what had once loomed as a monstrous hazard was brought into perspective and reduced to the size of a normal occupational threat.

After three months of sustained naval and air combat of "unprecedented intensity and scope," the Third Fleet temporarily ceased operations in the Philippines, leaving the responsibility for Leyte's defense to the Army Air Force. Steaming through the gap of blue water in the long line of breakers on the reef, Task Force Thirty-Eight dropped anchor in Ulithi Harbor. Since the *New Jersey* had departed from Pearl Harbor in August 1944 she had gone 36,185 miles and had rarely been in port. During ninety days the Third Fleet's ships and planes had shot down 1,664 aircraft; destroyed 1,782 planes on the ground; sunk four carriers, one battleship, three heavy cruisers, two light cruisers, twenty-five destroyers, two seaplane tenders, four submarines, twenty-two small warships, twenty-three tankers, 114 merchant ships over 1,000 tons, 100 under 1,000 tons, and 131 small craft. They also had damaged eight battleships, seven heavy cruisers, eight light cruisers, forty-six destroyers, three minelayers, two submarines, twenty-nine other warships, twenty-six tankers, 263 merchant ships over 1,000 tons, 113 under 1,000 tons, and 267 small craft.

Once anchored at Ulithi, Halsey sent Nimitz a dispatch, analyzing Japanese air strength in the Philippines. He mentioned the wide dispersal of enemy planes on Luzon and Formosa, the delay in the development of airfields and land-based air strength on Leyte, the suicide tactics of the Japanese and the methods worked out to overcome this. Halsey also indicated that he needed more ships and planes if the Third Fleet were to strike major targets or to carry out vital missions. "I suppose," he told Nimitz, "that [you] will be getting more demands from the THIRD Fleet over this and that; however, please believe that the things we scream for are only wanted so that your command can kill more Japs quicker."

After two weeks of rest and replenishment, the Third Fleet was ready for sea. "Our two weeks at Ulithi," Halsey wrote Nimitz, "were like two weeks in the country, Godforsaken though the country was."

Halsey wanted to make sure that his force, task group, and unit commanders were familiar with the combat plans and understood the methods worked out to stop the kamikazes. For a final briefing he decided to host a buffet supper in the Flag Officers Recreation Area on Asor Island, the last evening before sailing. After a swim and cocktails, Halsey detailed the tactics and strategy. Dinner, prepared by Halsey's cook and served by his messboys, began at 1830. "Again," remembered Commander George F. Kosco, "there was more, but less formal, shoptalk but no ringing fight talk by the Admiral." The party broke up at 2100.

At 0700, 11 December 1944, carriers and escorting destroyers began maneuvering slowly through the channel in task groups and in formation about 500 yards apart. Once through the channel they steamed in cruising formation in groups about twenty miles apart. Again, there were training exercises for gunners and pilots, while combat air patrols flew overhead at various heights and distances.

Task Force Thirty-Eight (now commanded by Admiral McCain) again was heading for the Philippines—Leyte was almost secured—to launch strikes against Luzon, preparing for MacArthur's invasion of Mindoro scheduled for 15 December. On the 13th Halsey received the startling news that a suicide diver had hit the cruiser *Nashville,* MacArthur's flagship, resulting in heavy casualties. MacArthur and his staff had transferred the flag to a destroyer. On the same day, Halsey learned that an American submarine had damaged or sunk a heavy cruiser 120 miles southwest of Saigon, Indochina. This report reaffirmed the staff's belief that some Japanese surface units, damaged in the Battle of Leyte Gulf and sent to Singapore for temporary repairs, were now at sea en route to the home islands.

On 14 December Task Force Thirty-Eight launched a dawn sweep and strike against Luzon airfields, the first of a three-day sustained attack in support of the Mindoro amphibious landings. This operation was planned to meet the mission of "maximum hold-down and destruction of Jap air power," while at the same time, giving complete defense to the carriers against kamikaze attacks. Strike after strike were flown so that all the airfields on Luzon were under surveillance or attack throughout the daylight hours. Every known or suspected airstrip in the entire area had been indexed and definite assignments were made to particular carrier groups and by carrier groups to the individual flattops for complete coverage. Night fighters relieved the attacking planes in late afternoon.

Since the primary objective was to blanket the airfields, no wholesale destruction resulted from the raids of 14–16 December. None had been contemplated. With the exception of one enemy strike that took off before 14 December, no Luzon-based planes hit Mindoro-bound convoys; those that did attack came from the Visayans, the responsibility of the land-based Army Air Force.

Halsey and the staff had hoped, after flying the strikes of 16 December, to conduct their long-desired attack in the South China Sea, where the enemy fleet after the Battle of Leyte Gulf had been reported. King and Nimitz, however, recognized that the Army Air Force at Leyte was not yet strong enough to risk moving the Third Fleet out of its support position and withheld their consent.

[XII]

"I Had No Warning"

ON THE MORNING OF 16 DECEMBER, Commander George F. Kosco, Third Fleet aerologist, received a routine coded weather report from Ulithi saying that the wind was southwest, force four, and that they had heavy rain. Kosco also had a report that the wind from Guam was force four, wind from the southeast. To Kosco, this was "an ideal situation for a tropical storm to form." He reported his suspicions to Halsey, but since a weather front was moving past the Third Fleet at the time, Kosco put it on the weather map as "a weak low," expecting it to move off to the northeast as did most normal storms. He thought it a storm of "very small caliber." That night, the 16th, Kosco received a coded report from Pearl Harbor, which gave storm indications in the same. location, "a tropical storm, very weak." Kosco "took it under advisement" and told Halsey and Carney that he didn't think it would be anything serious.

The Pacific Fleet aerological service predicted no serious weather disturbance and could not have done so since the Third and Fifth Fleets had moved so rapidly and so close to Japanese-held islands that it had not established sufficient weather reporting stations. Fleet Weather did the best it could. Broadcasts summarizing all land stations' reports were made four times a day by Radio Kwajalein and eight times a day by Radio Manus. Patrol planes from the Marianas, Ulithi, and the Palaus reported the weather situation. These patrols were of little use to the Third Fleet since they avoided bad fronts and rarely broke radio silence to send in their reports before landing. Most of the weather

186

planes' reports were at least twelve hours old before they reached
a ship in the operating area. Weather map analyses were broadcast four times a day by Pacific Fleet Central at Pearl Harbor,
whose forecasts were radioed twice daily to the Third Fleet.

On 17 December Task Force Thirty-Eight, already committed
to strike the Philippines on 19th, 20th, and 21st, retired and
searched for a fueling rendezvous. Since the last fueling on the
15th, the fleet had often steamed at high speeds and many of the
destroyers were dangerously low on fuel.

Kosco and his staff worked over the day's first weather map.
He carried the reported storm along on the map and estimated it
would swing to the northeast, away from the task force, in the
next twenty-four hours. Reports from Ulithi still had southwest
winds and east winds at Guam. Looking over the plane dispatches from Kwajalein, the Philippines, and Saipan, which were
always delayed reaching the Third Fleet, he calculated that the
storm was about 15N, 136 or 137E. He couldn't pinpoint it exactly.

At a position (14-50N, 129-57E) in the eastern half of the Philippine Sea, the ships began fueling at 1000 on Sunday, the 17th,
but a wind, varying from twenty to thirty knots, and a moderate
cross swell made fueling extremely difficult. "The wind," said
Carney, "was across the sea and it was impossible to find a
course which would prevent yawing and surging. . . . The force
is very expert at fueling at sea and had done this in the wake of
typhoons and that expertness and experience testified to the unusual conditions that existed that day."

On board the *New Jersey,* the aerologists assumed that the bad
weather was due to another weather front moving through the
area.

At 1107 the destroyer *Spence* came alongside the *New Jersey*
to start fueling. Maneuvering on parallel courses at identical
speeds is hazardous enough under merely unfavorable conditions.
But when winds and waves are so treacherous that lines part between tossing, heaving, rolling, and sea-swept vessels, collisions
become a threat.

As Halsey and the staff sat down for luncheon in flag mess,
they saw the *Spence* rolling excessively on the starboard side and

it seemed as though she might smash into the flagship. "She was riding up ahead," said Halsey, "and she'd drop well astern and charge ahead and drop astern. Of course, during this whole time she was pitching and rolling heavily."

Kosco ran up to his weather office on the navigation bridge level to see if he could discover what the weather was doing. Quickly, he calculated that there was indeed a disturbance, not a typhoon, but "a tropical storm," the center of which was located in an area approximately 300 miles in diameter. It was coming closer to the fleet than he had originally estimated and was increasing in intensity. Figuring its position again, he made "a snap judgment" and placed it at 15N, 138E. Later, still using inadequate reports, he placed it further westward, nearer the fleet, at 135E. Both on the 16th and 17th it was impossible with the weather data at hand to calculate exactly the storm's position.

At 1127 the forward and after fueling hoses parted on the *Spence*. As swells mounted, reports came in from task group commanders. The *Healy* and *The Sullivans* were experiencing steering problems. Hoses parted on board the *Collett, Stephen Potter, L. K. Swenson, Preston, Thatcher*, and *Manatee*. On board the *Capterton*, a seaman fractured his leg as the result of seas smashing over the forecastle. Halsey "knocked off" fueling operations at 1251, ordered them resumed at 0600 the following day. There was not time to spare if Task Force Thirty-Eight was to meet its combat commitment on the 19th.

Halsey directed the fleet to steam 290° toward the next day's fueling rendezvous at 17N, 128E. He made this decision based on Kosco's assumption that the disturbance was moving on a course to clear. Actually, the storm's center at 1251 was 120 miles southeast of the task force's position, instead of 450 miles as Kosco had calculated, and heading right for it.

"No warning of the typhoon," said Halsey, "was received up to this point from any outside source. The storm followed an erratic course, different . . . and contrary to available history of December typhoons."

The weather continued to deteriorate during the afternoon. From meager reports the aerologists on the *New Jersey* estimated that the storm center was "somewhere to the east of us," but would still curve to the northeast. The Third Fleet received weather reports from Pearl Harbor and Manus, but Kosco and his staff did not think these were detailed enough for the present situation.

At 1300 Kosco returned to the flag mess. By this time the mess boys had cleared away the luncheon dishes and covered the table with a green pool cloth. Staffers spread out maps and charts and Kosco placed his morning's weather map in front of Halsey. This map indicated a weak cold front stretching northeast to southeast of Task Force Thirty-Eight's position. The commander calculated that they were now in the frontal zone. The map also indicated a storm center to the southeast of the task force, 400 miles away, moving toward it. From all reports it was only a tropical disturbance and Kosco expected that it would eventually merge with the cold front and veer off to the northeast at an accelerated rate.

Kosco went back to the weather office and, with his staff, searched vainly for the position of the storm center. Only by pinpointing its location could they calculate its behavior. They studied the clouds, the sea, and the winds for any detail, no matter how small, that would help them locate the storm center.

Captain Jasper T. Acuff, commander of the fleet's fueling and plane replenishment group, was the first to make the correct guess as to the storm's position and course. He talked over TBS with the captains of two escort carriers in his group. All three agreed that the fueling rendezvous, set for 0600 on the 18th, would be directly in the typhoon's track.

On board the *Lexington,* Jerry Bogan, Commander, Task Group 38.2, was sure that a severe storm was approaching. Later he stated that unlike the aerologists on the *New Jersey,* he had sufficient warning. His aerological officer had reported to him that morning with "a rather sketchy map," which he had drawn from the information then available, indicating that "a cyclonic storm" was forming to the northeast of the fleet. At 1500 Bogan received the Pearl Harbor weather summary noting the presence of a severe tropical storm in approximately the same area as that estimated by his aerological officer, "160 miles east of the fleet, moving in a northwesterly direction."

In contrast Admiral Ted Sherman, Commander, Task Group

38.3, like Halsey and Kosco, later testified that he had no warning of the storm's approach. His aerologist kept reporting a tropical disturbance 500 miles away, to the northeast. Sherman, noticing the increasing wind and falling barometer, placed the storm's position to the southeast and much closer than 500 miles.

Captain John Moss, Chief of Staff to Admiral Alfred E. Montgomery, Commander, Task Group 38.1, on the *Yorktown*, believed he had sufficient warning. Montgomery, Moss testified later, had all the information reported from Pearl Harbor together with the opinion of the *Yorktown*'s aerologist. "Both sources of information," said Moss, "turned out to have shown the center of the storm where it actually was. In other words the estimates were pretty accurate."

Captain M. H. Kernodle, skipper of the *San Jacinto,* had received warnings for twenty-four hours "before I got into the storm, from my aerographer, from the action of the ship, and the condition of the sea." He later testified, "I was fully aware of the storm, and it was going to be severe. In addition to that, I also heard reports from other vessels who were in desperate trouble, and I was not. I had all the warnings anyone could possibly have."

Such information was not passed on to Kosco. Lacking solid data from Pacific Fleet Weather Control, basing their judgment on flimsy reports, the *New Jersey* aerologists estimated that the storm was now to the southeast. Halsey's staff selected a new fueling rendezvous "clear of bad weather" and favorably situated for the planned attack on the 19th. "That thought of striking Luzon," said Halsey, "was uppermost in our heads."

Later in the day, using its own observations together with outside information, the staff again shifted the fueling rendezvous area to what they believed to be a better location (14N, 127-30E) as the storm was now estimated to be further south than originally anticipated. Halsey ordered the fleet to change course to 270, which actually ran parallel with the typhoon track instead of, as Kosco thought, at a wide angle from it. But as the task force on this westerly course was outrunning the typhoon by five knots, the sea moderated slightly, giving an illusion of improving conditions.

At 1424 the *New Jersey* received a report from the seaplane tender *Chandeleur* at Kossol Passage in the Palaus, stating that search planes had located a storm center at 13N, 132E, wind sixty knots. This placed the disturbance to the southeast of the fleet.

With no other confirmatory evidence, the *New Jersey*'s aerologists were confronted with the possibility that the storm, which they had estimated as well to the east of them, might possibly be much more to the south. Kosco correctly advised Halsey to keep the fleet heading west until the situation clarified itself.

Bogan radioed McCain, task force commander, that the *Lexington*'s weather assessment indicated that improving conditions existed to the southward. "I felt," said Bogan, "that any rendezvous not further south was one in which we could be overtaken by the storm." Bogan's report, however, did not contain the storm's location.

At the usual staff conference in the flag mess that evening, Kosco detailed the latest weather map with the help of every report available. Some of the data came from search planes, some from intercepted Japanese dispatches, some from reports broadcast from MacArthur's shore-based groups. None supplied a definite clue as to the storm's location. Reports from ships in the task force had convinced Kosco that they could not possibly arrive at the fueling rendezvous by 0600.

On Kosco's advice, Halsey, at 2220 set still a third rendezvous for 0700 on the 18th. This position was to the northward (15-30N, 127-40E) as the storm's position was still further south than previous reports indicated. "There was," said the Third Fleet's Operations Officer, Captain Ralph E. ("Rollo") Wilson, "a definite aerological background for every one of those [rendezvous] changes keeping in mind always that we had a definite combat commitment to make."

To seek better weather, Halsey ordered the fleet to change course to 180 at midnight, reversing course to 320 at 0200, which would head the ships toward the fueling position. This move was unfortunate as it headed many ships into the path of the advancing storm.

"I was not particularly happy over this new rendezvous

point," said Admiral Sherman. Unlike Bogan, neither he nor Montgomery made their ideas known to Halsey as they believed the admiral had better and later information.

The weather failed to improve. Halsey and his staff still believed that the center of the disturbance was much further north and east than that reported by the tender *Chandeleur* and that the track would curve to the northeast, a characteristic of December storms.

Kosco awakened a little after midnight. The task force was steaming on a southerly course, which in Kosco's opinion was the best possible. In the weather office, the midnight reports failed to turn up anything new and there was no information dealing with more than an intense tropical storm.

Reporting to Carney, they went together to Halsey's quarters where Kosco reported his findings. The safest way to clear the storm area was to continue on the same southerly course.

"What do you think of a turn to the north?" asked Halsey.

Kosco replied that a northerly course might take the fleet nearer the track of the storm.

When Halsey asked about the weather outside, Kosco said that while conditions were severe, they were not excessively so.

Putting on a robe and slippers, Halsey led the way into his office where he studied the maps and charts on the bulkhead. To continue south would take the task force close to enemy-held Samar Island. Weatherwise, he saw that a southerly course was the safest, but other factors made him decide on a northwesterly course toward the fueling rendezvous.

At 0200, when directly in the path of the typhoon, the fleet changed course to 320 to make its final run toward the rendezvous position. Thirty minutes later, an orderly awakened Kosco as he had the morning watch, 0400–0800. On checking the weather situation, he realized that "something was definitely out of order." From reports in the weather office and flag plot, he knew that Task Force Thirty-Eight was in a worse storm than he had estimated. He concluded that Halsey's ships could be running into a typhoon. "We had to get out of the way fast," said Kosco.

At 0345 he and Carney went to Halsey's quarters. Halsey was still up. Kosco said that from all indications it looked like the

storm was increasing in intensity and was due to rip into the fleet
if it continued to the northwest.

They hurried into the flag mess and, along with Captain Wilson, studied "a sort of map," which Halsey had brought along.
They had no definite information. Halsey turned to Kosco and
asked, "What do you recommend?"

The commander replied that the fleet should head south immediately. But no decision was made, and Kosco went up to relieve
the watch.

Halsey called Kosco on the phone and told him to call Admiral
McCain on TBS radio and ask where he thought the storm center
was located. McCain answered that the fleet should not attempt to
fuel.

Since McCain failed to estimate the storm's position, Kosco
called Admiral Bogan on the *Lexington* and asked for an evaluation. He reported 17N, 131E. Kosco himself had estimated the
location at 15N, 131E. Overhearing the conversation, McCain
quickly calculated the storm's center at 12-30N, 131E, moving
northeast. To Admiral Montgomery, it seemed that "the location
of the center, course and speed of the storm was not definitely
fixed in everyone's mind."

According to estimates, the storm center at 0500, the 18th, was
located approximately 14-10N, 129-55E, which bore about ninety
miles ESE from the *New Jersey*'s position.

The weather worsened. Halsey and his staff decided that fueling was out of the question for 0700, but, perhaps, it could be accomplished later in the day.

To get south of the storm track and to locate suitable weather
for carrying out fueling operations. Halsey decided at 0501 to
head in a southerly direction. Once on course 180 the wind
started backing to the west and aerologists believed that the fleet
was in a safe, navigable semicircle and advised the staff to stay
on this course. Unknowingly, the fleet was to steer into or near
the path of the typhoon.

Still committed to attack on the 19th, and believing that every
effort should be made to fuel the destroyers, McCain at 070
headed his force on course 060, hoping to fuel the ships from the
large carriers. This course change courted disaster since this ma-

neuver held the fleet in or near the path of the storm. It was an error on the part of McCain, who ordered it, and of Halsey, who permitted it. Fueling proved impossible as the task force met with rapidly increasing storm conditions.

At 0803, the 18th, the Third Fleet, including Task Group 30.8 (logistical support unit), changed course to 180. ''Shortly thereafter,'' said McCain, ''our ships commenced to get into trouble.'' The seas and winds increased in violence, especially for Task Group 30.8 (including the destroyers, *Hull, Monaghan,* and *Spence*), which was to the north and east of the main element.

The whine of the storm rose in intensity. The sea heaved. Anchors disappeared every few minutes under waves, and foam boiled down along the decks, piled against bridge-houses, and sloshed over the sides. Ships took sickening cants to starboard or port and hung there, then wallowed feebly under tons of water.

This was no ordinary tropical storm, but a typhoon. ''On the forenoon of the 18th,'' Halsey recalled several days later, ''it was very definitely apparent that we were very close to a violent disturbance of some kind which I believed was a typhoon. We were completely cornered. . . . The consideration then was the fastest way to get out of the dangerous semicircle and to get to a position where our destroyers could be fueled.''

Not until 0914 did Halsey send a warning to all ships and weather stations. ''We didn't think,'' said Kosco, ''that we were dealing with a storm as severe as a typhoon until we were within 100 miles of it.'' Halsey sent a dispatch to MacArthur saying that the Third Fleet could not dodge the storm and could not send planes to strike Luzon on the 19th.

To make the ships ride easier, McCain directed the fleet to change course to 220. But during the height of the storm, Mc-Cain issued no orders to the fleet as a whole to disregard formation keeping and take the best courses and speeds for security. In Task Group 30.8 where the principal damage occurred, vessels were maneuvering to maintain formation up to the time they were disabled.

The barometer started falling dramatically. When the wind swerved further around to the northwest, Kosco was convinced that the storm was moving westward.

Carney asked the commander if he thought the course should be changed to the southeast. Kosco agreed as the aerologists were sure now that the fleet was well to the south of the storm. At 0930 McCain ordered the course changed to the southeast, 140, and ordered Task Group 38.1 to act independently.

The rain was blinding. Seventy-foot seas hit the ships from all sides. White streaks of foam lay along the tops of the deep troughs. The *New Jersey* tossed and turned as if she were a "canoe." "Our chairs, tables, and all loose gear had to be doubled-lashed; we ourselves were buffeted from one bulkhead to another; we could not hear our own voices above the uproar." All around there was nothing to be seen but ridges and valleys of water except at moments when the *New Jersey* labored to the top of a swell. Then Halsey caught glimpses of ships everywhere, great carriers and battleships, tankers, cruisers, destroyers, all plunging through waves which broke solidly over their forecastles and smashed into streams.

"The carriers," said Carney, "were having some alarming experiences, rolling very heavily, and communications became difficult by reason of material casualties, salt water soaking and the usual events in heavy weather." The *Monterey* lost steerage way. The *Independence* lost two men overboard. The *Kwajalein* temporarily lost steering control.

Planes broke loose on the *San Jacinto*'s hangar deck. "To the uninitiated," Captain Michael H. Kernodle, skipper of the *San Jacinto,* said later, "the loud sound of crashing and tearing airplanes, and the banging and tearing of the flimsy metal of the ventilation ducts, and the avalanche of heavy weights being thrown violently from side to side, and the presence of much oily water on the deck, plus a large volume of steam escaping from the ruptured atmospheric exhausts with the enclosed hangar deck space, created a wholly frightening situation.

"However, regardless of these terrifying surroundings, men on the hangar deck were lowered from the overhead and skidded on the deck in pendulum fashion on the end of lines to this violently moving pile of rubble and succeeded in securing it and holding the damage to a minimum, when to do so appeared to them to be almost certain death or serious injury."

The destroyers *Spence*, *Monaghan*, and *Hull*, apparently caught near the storm center, capsized in the giant seas and sank with practically all hands.

"It was after the course change to 140," Lieutenant Commander James A. Marks, skipper of the *Hull*, testified later, "that her capsizing and sinking occurred. . . . Roughly about 1130 the seas became mountainous and the wind increased to hurricane proportions. At this point I wish to state that there had at no time been any storm warnings received from any source whatsoever. Considerable damage was occurring as the sea grew worse. Several depth charges were torn loose from the K guns and were lost overboard. . . .

"The smokestacks were under terrific strain because of the wind. Up until shortly before the ship turned over I was greatly concerned that either or both the stacks might be torn off the ship. . . . Several of the metal covers on the ammo ready boxes were ripped completely off the boxes by the wind. The bridge structure itself was under such great strain that I was concerned that the structure itself . . . might be torn off the ship.

"In trying to alleviate the heavy rolling of the ship I tried every possible combination of rudder and engines, with little avail. . . . By this time the ship took several rolls because of high velocity wind gusts. . . . At one time the JOOD [Junior Officer of the Deck] was catapulted from the port side of the pilot house completely through the air to the upper portion of the starboard side of the pilot house.

"Shortly after 1200 the ship withstood what I estimated to be the worst punishment any storm could offer. . . . The wind velocity increased to an unbelievable high point which I estimated at 110 knots. The force of this wind laid the ship steadily over on her starboard side and held her down in the water until the seas came flowing into the pilot house itself. The ship remained over on her side, starboard, at an angle of ninety degrees or more as the water flooded into her upper structures. I remained on the port wing of the bridge until the water flooded up to me, and I stepped off into the water."

At 1002 the entire fleet veered to course 220 to avoid a disabled escort carrier. The wind now was at sixty-two knots. The *Dewey* came hard left to avert collision. The *Rudyard Bay* lay dead in the water. The *Wisconsin* lost a catapult plane overboard. Flames flared temporarily on the *Cowpens*. On the *New Jersey* the staff failed to receive positive or negative information because of separation and difficulties in communicating. Not until late in the forenoon were the aerologists able to track the storm accurately by radar and determine its position, course, and speed. Ordered to take "the most comfortable course" by Halsey, McCain directed the fleet to steer 120 at 1156.

The typhoon center was then about thirty-seven miles due north and course 120 took the fleet away from it. But by then the ships were strewn over some 2,500 square miles of sea and it was too late for some to escape.

The typhoon reached its greatest violence between 1200 and 1400. The wind roared at sixty-six knots, then, at 1310, increased sharply to eighty-three with gusts reaching ninety-three.

In late afternoon came clearing skies. Halsey promptly sent out air and sea searches for survivors. "It was," he said, "the most exhaustive search in naval history. Every ship and plane in . . . [the group] took part. We had marked off an area large enough to include the extreme limits of drift, and destroyer divisions crisscrossed it abreast, with lookouts doubled. An occasional swimmer was picked up, and sometimes a raft load." The destroyers rescued fifty-four from the *Hull*, twenty-four from the *Spence*, and sixteen from the *Monaghan*.

In the typhoon the Third Fleet lost three destroyers. The *Monterey, Cape Esperance, Altamaha, Miami, San Jacinto, Cowpens, Alywin, Dewey,* and *Hickox* suffered severe damage. Seven hundred and ninety officers and men were lost or killed. Eight were injured. One hundred fifty-six aircraft were damaged beyond repair.

On the 19th the task force fueled and on the 20th steamed westward toward Luzon, preparing for a predawn launch on the following day. However, on the 21st, the seas became increasingly heavy, and the staff concluded that successful operations could not be conducted. Halsey ordered the Third Fleet to retire and head for Ulithi, notifying both MacArthur and Nimitz of the cancellation.

Early on the morning of the 24th the ships moved into Ulithi harbor and, at 1350, Admiral Nimitz, who had flown in from Pearl Harbor, was piped on board the *New Jersey,* greeted by Halsey and officers of the Third Fleet on the quarter-deck. That evening in Halsey's mess at the round table, guests sat down to a festive Christmas Eve dinner. A Christmas tree, complete with trimmings, which Nimitz had brought along, enhanced the evening. After dinner, Nimitz responded to Halsey's introduction, paying tribute to the admiral for his outstanding, aggressive, and successful performance of the numerous hard tasks that had been assigned to him, beginning during the dark days of the war.

Throughout Christmas day, Nimitz and Halsey and their staffs held numerous conferences. Nimitz ordered a court of inquiry to investigate the loss of the *Hull, Spence,* and *Monaghan.* On the next day, Nimitz and his staff departed for Leyte and conferences with MacArthur.

When they returned to Ulithi on the 28th, they again met with Halsey and officers of the Third Fleet and discussed future operations. Nimitz consented to Halsey's long-desired wish to enter the China Sea, but only after the Third Fleet had finished supporting MacArthur's Lingayen landings. Halsey's staff immediately set to work preparing operational plans for the Third Fleet's entry into the China Sea and for strikes on the China coast. On the 29th, Nimitz and staff flew out of Ulithi for Pearl Harbor.

The Court of Inquiry, consisting of aviator Vice Admirals John H. Hoover and George D. Murray and battleship division commander Rear Admiral Glenn B. Davis, convened on board the *Cascade,* anchored in Ulithi harbor. The testimony was lengthy, detailed, and complicated. The court called many witnesses, including Halsey, McCain, Bogan, Sherman, Kosco, and commanders and executive officers of various ships.

When questioned, Halsey strongly criticized the weather warning system in the Pacific.

Q. "Did you consider that you had timely warning or did you know that a severe storm was approaching around the 16th and 17th of December?"

A. "I did not have timely warning. I'll put it another way. I had no warning."

Q. "There has been testimony from other commanders [Bogan, Montgomery] that the local conditions indicated the approach of the storm. Was that evident to you?"

A. "The local conditions commencing on the 17th were very bad. So bad that I ordered the destroyers that were alongside tankers and heavy ships to clear. A disturbance was indicated, but whether it was a severe storm or merely a local disturbance, there was no way of determining. We still thought it was a storm that had curved away to the northward and eastward and we determined to get away from it."

Q. "What seemed to be wrong with the weather service in this case?"

A. "It was nonexistent. That's the only way I can express it. After the horse was out of the stable we established a system so that such a thing couldn't happen again. Heretofore we had always received reports. This time there was only one report of a disturbance that came in. As I recollect, the only report that was brought to my attention was a report from the *Chandeleur*. These reports are brought back by planes to the base and analyzed at the base and sent out on the normal circuits, usually twelve to twenty-four hours late. It is the first time in the four months that I've been operating in this area that I haven't had reports to enable me to track a storm. The Third Fleet was the first to report the storm."

After the court completed its inquiry into the typhoon disaster, its members put the "preponderance of responsibility" on Halsey. "Large errors made in predicting the location and path of the storm are the responsibility of Commander Third Fleet."

The court stated that "principal weight" should have been given to the report from the *Chandeleur* on the 17th since no definite information about the storm's location had been received the day before. Halsey, the court said, "was at fault in not broadcasting definite danger warnings to all vessels early on the morning of December 18 in order that preparations might be made as practicable and that inexperienced commanders might have sooner realized the seriousness of their situations."

The court also criticized the "aerological talent" assisting Halsey for being "inadequate in practical experience and service

background in view of the importance of the services to be expected and required."

In conclusion, the court placed the blame for the tragedy on
Halsey and said that the "mistakes, errors and faults" were
"errors in judgment under stress of war operations and not as
offenses." The mistakes made by subordinates "are attributed to
errors in judgment, or inexperience, or both." "The court fully
realizes that a certain degree of blame attaches to those in command in all disasters, unless they are manifestly 'Acts of God.'
The extent of blame as it applies to Commander Third Fleet or
others is impractical to assess."

The court recommended that "action be taken to impress upon
all commanders the necessity of giving full consideration to adverse weather likely to be met in the Western Pacific, especially
the . . . formation and movements of typhoons." It also urged
that the Navy station weather ships in the Philippine Sea to sup-
plement the Pacific weather centrals and that reconnaissance
planes, staffed by experienced weather observers, aid the regular
searches by covering sectors where unusual weather conditions
were suspected.

The court referred the matter of further proceedings or action
to the convening authority.

Nimitz promptly approved the findings, opinions, and recommendations of the Court of Inquiry. The evidence brought forward indicated to him that the responsibility for the storm damage
and losses suffered rested with Halsey. "However," he said,
"the convening authority is of the firm opinion that no question
of negligence is involved, but rather, that the mistakes made were
errors in judgment committed under stress of war operations and
stemming from a commendable desire to meet military commitments. No further action is comtemplated or recommended." Admiral King concurred.

At the court's suggestion Nimitz planned to station three
weather ships in the Western Pacific to cover the most likely
typhoon tracks, to send out weather reconnaissance planes, and to
increase the number of automatic weather stations. He recommended to the Bureau of Naval Personnel that a greater number

of older and more experienced aerological officers be made available to the higher commands of the Pacific Fleet.

Halsey never mentioned the Court of Inquiry to his staff except in a discussion of a series of proposals for improving the weather reporting service. To him it was "water over the dam." Even in his autobiography he made no mention of the Court of Inquiry, although he allotted generous space to the typhoon.

While technicians and other workmen labored to repair the damaged ships at Ulithi, Halsey and the Dirty Tricks Department worked out combat plans which called for strikes on Formosa, Okinawa, and Luzon to support General MacArthur's amphibious forces, who were scheduled to invade Lingayen Gulf, western Luzon, on 9 January 1945.

With the approval of King and Nimitz, Halsey also planned to extend the Third Fleet's activities to the East China Sea and the Chinese mainland, after covering MacArthur's operation.

[XIII]

"Keep the Bastards Dying"

ON 30 DECEMBER, the Third Fleet steamed out of Ulithi and headed toward the Philippine Sea. Halsey sent a message to all hands, identifying himself by his code name: THIS IS BLACKJACK HIMSELF X YOUR WORK HAS BEEN SUPERB X I EXPECT EVEN MORE X KEEP THE BASTARDS DYING.

The Third Fleet's schedule called for air strikes on Formosa, 3–4 January; fueling on the 5th; a strike on Luzon on the 7th; fueling on the 8th; and a strike on Formosa again on 9 January, which was D-Day for Lingayen Gulf. Then, hopefully, the fleet would head for the South China Sea.

On Mindoro American operations had continued under sporadic Japanese attack. But such assaults ended abruptly as the enemy shifted their energy toward the Allied forces heading for Luzon. Mindoro had three operational airfields, an invaluable asset to the Luzon invasion. While the Third Fleet hit airfields in Formosa and northern Luzon, the Army Air Force, flying from Morotai, Leyte, and Mindoro, would cover the convoys and strike the airfields in southern Luzon.

On 3/4 January Task Force Thirty-Eight's planes swept in over Formosa, downing fifty-two enemy planes, destroying fifty-eight on the ground, sinking twenty-four ships, and damaging thirty-five more. The fleet fueled on the 5th, then struck northern Luzon the next day despite foul weather.

On the 6th, as MacArthur's heavy support ships were maneuvering into Lingayen Gulf, suicide bombers started attacking, crippling eleven ships. Kamikazes smashed into the battleships *New Mexico* and *California,* cruiser *Columbia,* and three destroyers. Both the cruisers *Louisville* and *Australia* were hit severely.

The enemy air attacks on the Lingayen support force might have been even more crippling if the Third Fleet had not bombed Formosan airfields. These strikes prevented Japanese planes from ever reaching Luzon from the north.

The Third Fleet again attacked northern Luzon on the 7th rather than Formosa and, at Admiral Kinkaid's request, helped cover Lingayen Gulf. Halsey sent a special personal message to the fleet for an "extra effort" in support of "our comrades of the Southwest Pacific." Halsey's carriers, Kinkaid's escort carriers, and the Army Air Force almost put the Luzon airfields out of commission. Only a few enemy aircraft flew over Lingayen Gulf that day. The Japanese decided to evacuate what planes they had from the Philippines and, after 7 January, there were no more organized air strikes on Allied surface units.

After refueling, Third Fleet aircraft again struck Formosa on the 9th. Intelligence reported that B-29s had sighted elements of the Japanese heavy fleet at sea off Kyushu and the *Ise* and *Hyuga* in Camranh Bay on the Indochina coast. Eager to engage the enemy and sever the Japanese lifeline to their southern Empire, Halsey notified Nimitz and MacArthur of the Third Fleet's intention to enter the South China Sea and destroy enemy shipping. Reports already indicated that the amphibious forces at Lingayen Gulf had landed on schedule against weak opposition.

Upon completion of the air attacks on Formosa, Task Force Thirty-Eight proceeded toward Bashi Channel and entered the South China Sea at 2330. "I had always wanted," Halsey said later, "to raid the China Sea area ever since I took command of the fleet. This stolen empire supplied oil, rubber, rice, and other materials essential to Japan's survival, and I was certain that a slash at her shore facilities and shipping would stagger her severely."

Undetected by the enemy, the ships fueled on the 11th and

planes flew extensive searches to locate enemy surface units. At 1400 Halsey reinforced Task Group 38.2 and directed it to move out ahead of the main force toward Camranh Bay. As Task Group 38.2 began its high speed run toward the Indochina coast, Halsey sent the message, YOU KNOW WHAT TO DO X GIVE THEM HELL X GOD BLESS YOU ALL X HALSEY.

At dawn on 12 January, the entire force launched heavy air strikes ranging up and down the Indochina coast from Saigon to Quinhon, a distance of 400 miles. Aircraft found no heavy surface units inside Camranh Bay. The Japanese Navy had already departed for safer waters. Planes, however, found plenty of merchant shipping. They "severely mauled" a fifteen-ship convoy off Quinhon, sinking the major part of it—nine fully loaded oilers—as well as the light cruiser *Kashii* and a destroyer. Off Cape Padaran planes destroyed an oiler, two destroyer-escorts, and a patrol craft and, off Cape St. James, struck a seven-ship convoy and four escorts. Other planes sank two freighters, three tankers, and three destroyers. All along the coast shipping was attacked. Two cargo ships and two oilers were destroyed at Saigon and others severely damaged—four escorts, three landing craft, a minesweeper, a patrol craft, five freighters, and two oilers. Aircraft also bombed and strafed air bases, docks, and oil tanks.

Japanese opposition to this raid was meager. American aircraft shot down fifteen planes, demolished twenty float planes in Camranh Bay, and destroyed seventy-seven on the ground.

Not exaggerating, Halsey said, "This was one of the heaviest blows to Japanese shipping of any day of the war and it appeared that the Japanese supply routes from Singapore, Malaya, Burma, Borneo, and the Dutch East Indies were severed at least temporarily."

During retirement the task force passed along the northern edge of a typhoon moving toward the Indochina coast and was forced to slow to sixteen knots to prevent storm damage to the destroyers.

Apprehension over MacArthur's operations caused Admiral King in Washington to direct the Third Fleet to be in position to intercept enemy forces approaching the Lingayen Gulf area from either the north or the south. Nimitz ordered Halsey to comply.

"This was in entire accord with the Commander Third Fleet's early strategic concept," wrote Carney in the war diary, "and he was already in a position to comply."

Steaming northward in the South China Sea to strike Formosa at dawn on 15 January, the seas continued rough, the weather adverse. At 0300 McCain recommended that Halsey cancel the day's attack and the task force reverse course. Halsey and the staff reviewed the weather reports and the tactical situation. Even if the ships reversed course, they would still be within range of enemy aircraft. Halsey determined to carry out the day's operations since holding down Formosan air and bombing installations was of major strategic importance.

The first sweep was launched at 0710 and the first strike at 0730. The main strength zeroed in on Formosa, while fighters swept across the Hongkong-Canton-Amoy area. Despite the foul weather, requiring instrument flying, American aircraft heavily damaged the buildings and shops near Toshien Drydock, a large factory between Takao airfield and the harbor, the Kobi Magnesium Plant, and a railroad yard; burned a warehouse at Takao main quay and barracks and drydocks at Mako; exploded ten locomotives, destroyed thirty-four aircraft, and sank eight vessels. Twelve American planes were lost.

On the following day, Task Force Thirty-Eight launched strikes against the China coast, including Hongkong, Canton, Amoy, and the coastal areas between these points. Planes worked over the Kowloon Texaco Oil Dump, Taiko Docks and Refinery, Royal Navy Yard, Aberdun Docks, Cosmopolitan Dockyard and Assembly Plant, cement and power plants, warehouses on Stone Cutters Island, Wampoa storage facilities and railroad siding, hangars, and installations.

When the last aircraft landed on the carriers, Halsey sent his estimate to Nimitz. Enemy air strength was negligible in southeast China and Indochina, had collapsed in Luzon, and was not aggressive in Formosa. The Japanese naval threat from the south was also nonexistent due to the losses and damage inflicted by the Third Fleet. "The Empire's Naval Forces," he said, "are capable of only a hit and run attack and would face early detection, stiff resistance, and harassed retreat."

"The Japanese know," he continued, "they are licked in the PHILIPPINES and would not attempt serious reinforcement."

Halsey evaluated the Third Fleet's situation and concluded that its contribution was to attack aggressively Japanese shipping along the Formosa-Okinawa line simultaneously, smothering enemy air power.

Between 2100 and 2200 on the 20th, the entire force sneaked through Balingtang Channel between Luzon and Formosa and into the Philippine Sea.

During the eleven days, 10–20 January, Task Force Thirty-Eight had steamed 3,800 miles in the South China Sea without meeting serious opposition. When he endorsed Halsey's Action Report, Nimitz said, "the sortie into the South China Sea was well-conceived. . . . It is regretted that more important targets were not within reach of the Task Force's destructive sweep." These "more important targets" were the ships of the Japanese Navy which had withdrawn well out of range of Third Fleet airmen.

At dawn on the 21st, the task force launched fighter sweeps to neutralize air bases in Formosa, the Pescadores, and the Sakishima Gunto. Strikes were launched throughout the day with emphasis upon shipping in the morning and airfields in the afternoon. A total of 1,164 sorties was flown; 104 enemy planes were destroyed; Takao, Tainan, and Kiirun were severely bombed and strafed.

Enemy planes retaliated. A 100-pound bomb hit the carrier *Langley,* exploding in the galley, ripping a hole in the flight deck, and killing one seaman and wounding nine. Two kamikazes tore into the *Ticonderoga*. The first smashed into the flight deck, just forward of the bridge structure. The second hurtled into the forward AA director, knocking all radios and radar out of commission, damaging the signal bridge, rendering the flight deck inoperable, setting the hangar deck on fire. A fighter crashed into the *Maddox* and exploded, killing four and injuring ten. On board the *Hancock,* a bomb exploded in one of her own planes; forty-eight were killed, seventeen seriously injured, sixty-four slightly wounded.

Despite the casualties, the Third Fleet struck Okinawa the following day and made an extensive photographic coverage in anticipation of the campaign to capture that island. The carriers launched predawn searches at 0615. A total of 682 sorties were flown, of which forty-seven were photographic. Without air opposition, American aircraft destroyed twenty-eight planes on the ground.

Task Force Thirty-Eight then headed for Ulithi for a well-earned rest. Here Halsey would turn the fleet over to Admiral Spruance.

"Fleet operations in this period," reported Halsey, "had decisive strategical significance; the operations in the China Sea demonstrated how vulnerable and how weak were the Japanese defenses of that vital area—vital as a route for transport of the essentials of war production. The outer defenses of the Japanese Empire no longer include Burma and the Netherlands East Indies; these countries are now isolated outposts, and their products were no longer available to the Japanese war machine except with staggering and prohibitive losses en route."

On 25 January the Third Fleet arrived at Ulithi and at 1630 Spruance and his staff came on board the *New Jersey*. Halsey met his old friend on the quarter-deck, and they went into the flag cabin. Halsey was in high spirits, and was looking forward to returning to Pearl Harbor and the States. The two admirals talked at length about the course of the war. Elsewhere on the flagship, the staff officers conferred with their opposite numbers.

Spruance's Fifth Fleet plans had always been well-thought-out, timely, and easy to comprehend. Officers knew in advance what was expected. The same commanders, however, dreaded going to sea with Bill Halsey. Although recognized as a great combat admiral, Halsey hardly ever followed a prescribed plan of action. His tactics kept the enemy off balance, but his commanders were equally befuddled by his slapdash methods. One cruiser captain recalled, "My feeling was one of confidence when Spruance was there and one of concern when Halsey was there. . . . When you moved into Admiral Spruance's command from Admiral Halsey's . . . you moved from an area in which you never knew what you were going to do in the next five minutes or how you were going to do it, because the printed instructions were never up to date.

. . . He never did things the same way twice. . . . When you moved into Admiral Spruance's command, the printed instructions were up to date, and you did things in accordance with them.''

Mick Carney has disagreed with this assessment. While Halsey gave the appearance of quick decisions, his constant aim was to keep the enemy in the dark by avoiding fixed patterns of objectives and tactics. Such methods resulted in tactical surprise. "Halsey," said Carney, "gave the appearance of precipitous action, but he had a strange intuition. I've had instances in which I have prepared a proposal for him and that I had worked out with the appropriate people there on the staff and I'd take it up and submit it to him. Well, we'd argue about it and he would say . . . this didn't quite ring a bell with him. On two or three occasions he said to me, 'I cannot fault your reasoning on this business. . . . it's convincing but I just have the feeling it's not right. We'll do it my way.' In each of those instances, his intuition was correct.''

On the afternoon of 26 January Halsey hosted a farewell party at Commodore Oliver ("Scrappy") Kessing's club on Asor Island. At midnight Spruance assumed tactical command of the Fifth Fleet. Halsey received congratulatory messages from MacArthur and the Secretary of the Navy and a "Well Done" from Ernest King and Chester Nimitz.

Halsey sent a parting message to his men. "I am so proud of you that no words can express my feelings. This has been a hard and historic operation. At times you have been driven almost beyond endurance but only because the stakes were high. The enemy was weary as you were. And the lives of many Americans could be spared in later offensives if we did our work well now. We have driven the enemy off the sea and back to his inner defenses. Superlatively well done. HALSEY.''

The Philippine campaign had been remarkable for endurance and for the damage inflicted upon the Japanese. "During this period," wrote Carney in the war diary, "the THIRD Fleet had inflicted greater loss upon the Japanese than any Fleet of any country in history inflicted upon an enemy.'' The Japanese had lost their surface strength and naval air power in attempting to hold the Philippines. In losing the Philippines Japan lost the war, for the pipeline to Indonesia was now severed.

At 0600 Halsey, Carney, and the other officers of the staff left the *New Jersey* and departed for Pearl Harbor and the States for rehabilitation and for securing first-hand the latest information on developments. After many conferences, Halsey took leave to go hunting for turkey and quail on John Hay Whitney's 4,000-acre estate near Thomasville, Georgia. More accustomed to sixteen-inch guns than a double-barreled shotgun, Halsey proved no Nimrod. He pursued the elusive quail, in boots and a flannel shirt, looking ''like a real hunter.'' But clothes and intent were not enough, as the admiral admitted. He told friends, ''I'm learning to do this kind of hunting for the first time.''

Halsey spent March in Washington on temporary duty. When he reported to Admiral King at Navy headquarters, he found the admiral sitting behind a desk, smoking a cigarette in a holder. Halsey's first words were, ''I made a mistake in that battle [Leyte Gulf].''

King held out his hand and replied, ''You don't have to tell me any more. You've got a green light on everything you did.''

But Halsey wanted to explain. ''I still think it was a mistake to turn south when the Japs were right under my guns.''

King said, ''No. It wasn't a mistake. You couldn't have done otherwise.''

At a news conference, Halsey told reporters, ''It would be the greatest crime in the history of our country if we fail to crush the Japanese completely now that the knockout is in sight. We have gone far enough in this thing now to keep on going so we will make them impotent for all time to wage another war. It can be done, and it should be done.''

Asked if he had any more famous messages to send the Japanese, Halsey laughed and said, ''Tell them I still believe in the Chinese proverb about the origin of the Jap race.''

''For the benefit of the uninitiated,'' said a correspondent, ''he explained in a considerably expurgated version how the Chinese maintained that the Japanese were the product of mating between female apes and the worst Chinese criminals who had been banished from China by a benevolent emperor.''

On 7 March President Roosevelt called Halsey to the White House to award him a Gold Star in lieu of a third Distinguished Service Medal. The President gave Halsey a hearty handshake and, after pleasantries, read the citation: "For exceptionally meritorious service to the government of the United States in a duty of great responsibility. . . . Carrying out a sustained and relentless drive against the enemy, Admiral Halsey skillfully directed the operations which resulted in the capture of the Western Carolines and a crushing defeat on the Japanese carrier force in the battle off Cape Engano on October 25, and associate attacks on the Japanese fleet in the waters of the Philippines.

"Conducting a series of brilliant and boldly executed attacks on hostile air forces, shipping and installations in the Ryukyus, Formosa, the Philippines, South China and Indo-China, Admiral Halsey was directly responsible for the great damage inflicted on enemy aerial forces and the destruction of shipping vital to the Japanese in fighting an increasingly defensive war."

After luncheon Roosevelt took Halsey upstairs to his office and told him a number of things "so secret that I would have preferred not to know them." One was Russia's pledge to declare war on Japan; the others "are still secret."

After a stay with his family in Greenville, Delaware, Halsey visited Captain Charles W. Fox, assistant supply officer at the Philadelphia Naval Air Supply Depot. Fox had been supply officer on board the *Enterprise* when she was Halsey's flagship. To a reporter at the Depot, Halsey said, "It doesn't make much difference whether the Jap fleet comes out of its home waters. They're just plain rats, and like rats you usually have to dig them out of their holes."

With the defeat of the Japanese in the Philippines the Pacific Fleet's strategy changed. Now it had to attack enemy shipping in the East China Sea and disable communications; support amphibious forces as they captured the last island bases surrounding the home islands; and strike Japan itself by bombing and strafing factories and airfields. Nimitz shifted the Pacific Fleet's role—the fleet now concentrated upon destroying or neutralizing Japanese land-based air power and airfields.

B-29s based on Saipan had already begun bombing the Tokyo area. The results from the American point of view were less than satisfactory as the superfortresses were flying under severe handicaps. The 3,000-mile round trip required them to cut their bomb loads. Lack of fighter cover obliged them to make fuel consuming climbs to around 28,000 feet, an altitude from which precision bombing was impossible. Enemy airfields in the Bonin Islands, lying between Saipan and Japan, further cut down the effectiveness of the American bombers. The capture of an island in the Bonin or Volcano groups would increase the B-29s capabilities and would provide a base for fighter planes and medium bombers within attack range of the enemy's home islands, a way station for B-29s in need of refueling, a refuge for damaged aircraft, and a base for air-sea rescue.

To gain these advantages Washington had drawn plans for the capture of Iwo Jima and also Okinawa in the Ryukyus. To direct these operations, Nimitz—newly promoted to fleet admiral—transferred his headquarters from Pearl Harbor to Guam.

To Nimitz and King the defeat of Japan was predicated on sea and air power. During 1942, 1943, and 1944, while the attention of most Allied leaders was concentrated on Europe, the war against Japan was left largely to these two admirals.

With the approaching victory in Europe, officials who had not previously been too concerned focused greater attention on the Pacific. Upon the Army's insistence, which reflected MacArthur's views, the Joint Chiefs of Staff had prepared plans for landings on Kyushu and on the Tokyo plain. King had reservations but as unanimous decisions were necessary in the Joint Chiefs meetings, he reluctantly acquiesced, still feeling that in the end sea and air power would accomplish the defeat of Japan.

The Joint Chiefs selected 1 November as the target date for the invasion of Kyushu (Operation OLYMPIC), an operation essential to a strategy of strangulation. As King studied the project, he became impressed with the strategic location of Kyushu, which he considered the key to the success of any siege operation.

On 19 February 1945 Americans waded ashore on Iwo Jima against heavy enemy opposition. Instead of the estimated five days, the capture of Iwo Jima required nearly a month of severe fighting. The Marines declared the island secured on 6 March. Its conquest cost 6,821 American lives. Even before they had won the campaign, the assault troops saw tangible evidence of the need for the island. Less than two weeks after D-Day, a B-29 made an emergency landing on the airfield. The campaign against Japan proper started even before the captured airfields on Iwo Jima were operational. On 25 February bombers and fighters from Spruance's Fifth Fleet cooperated with 200 B-29s in a massive raid on Tokyo. The superfortresses succeeded in burning out two square miles of the enemy capital, while carrier aircraft, attacking military targets, destroyed 150 enemy planes.

The Joint Chiefs of Staff, adhering to the suggestion of Spruance, decided that they had enough troops to capture Okinawa, the center of Nansei Shoto, or the Ryukyus, a string of islands between Formosa and Kyushu, the most southerly of the Japanese home islands. Its possession would enable the Allies to control the East China Sea and prepare for a possible assault on either the China coast or Japan itself. Military planners realized that the Japanese would savagely defend Okinawa since that island was only 325 miles from southern Kyushu. To pave the way for the invasion, Spruance's forces launched massive raids on the airfields of Kyushu and on the dwindling fleet in the Inland Sea.

American amphibious forces, assembled from such distant points as Espiritu Santo, Guadalcanal, San Francisco, Seattle, Oahu, Leyte, and Saipan, arrived off Okinawa in the early morning hours of D-Day, 1 April. Supported by Spruance's ships and planes, 50,000 soldiers and marines went ashore, and advance elements seized two airfields. By noon the invaders had thrust across to the east coast. But Japanese resistance stiffened and swarms of kamikazes struck the fleet continually, taking a heavy toll of men and ships. Instead of hitting kamikaze airfields and installations, the Fifth Fleet was held at Okinawa as its planes were needed to support ground troops, advancing against the strongly intrenched Japanese.

At Guam Nimitz followed the Okinawa operation intently.

Since 17 March the Fifth Fleet had been exposed to the threat of the deadly dive kamikazes day and night. With a count so far of ninety ships sunk or badly damaged, the Okinawa campaign had proven to be the most costly naval operation of the war. Nimitz decided that a change in the fleet's leadership was necessary and timely. Spruance and Mitscher had been under constant fire since February when the Iwo Jima campaign had begun. Their combat loads had multiplied. Nimitz turned to Bill Halsey.

Halsey arrived back in Pearl Harbor in early April. Mick Carney and most of the staff were already there. All were saddened by the news of the death of President Roosevelt at Warm Springs, Georgia, on 12 April.

After a detailed study of American objectives in the Pacific and drawing blueprints for the possible invasion of Kyushu, Halsey and several staffers flew to Guam to meet with Nimitz in preparation for Halsey's relieving Spruance.

Between briefings Carney talked with General Curtis E. ("Iron Pants") LeMay, who commanded the XX Bomber Command (B-29s) on Saipan. The admiral asked if the superfortresses could help the Third Fleet by flying typhoon patrols. LeMay thought it a splendid idea and agreed to do so. "However," said Carney later, "I was informed that I was off reservation and that the agreement within the Joint Chiefs of Staff was that XX Bomber Command was not to be under CINCPAC."

Halsey did not return to Pearl Harbor directly, but flew to Okinawa for conferences with Spruance. Halsey received a thorough briefing on the situation. Here at Okinawa the news was flashed that Germany had surrendered in Europe. "Perhaps," Halsey recalled, "I should have been tremendously jubilant, but my principal feeling was eagerness—to get the men and gear that were now released from Europe." The combined forces of the Allies were indeed released for operations against Japan.

When he returned to Pearl Harbor, he told his and McCain's staffs that their major objective was to shake the fleet loose from Okinawan waters. He saw no profit in confining the ships to defensive actions against kamikazes. Halsey insisted that the fleet had to go on the offensive as soon as possible and cripple Japan by massive air strikes.

At Guam Halsey hoisted his flag in the *Missouri* (the *New Jersey* was undergoing repairs) on 18 May and, along with escorts, he headed for Okinawa. When the flagship arrived, the Third and Fifth Fleet staffs began the change of command routine. Spruance wanted to remain at Okinawa to finish the campaign, but his staff, exhausted, were happy at being relieved. Halsey officially relieved Spruance on the 28th amid one of the heaviest enemy air attacks of the campaign. One hundred and fifty Japanese planes in fifty-six separate raids sank or crippled fourteen American vessels.

Halsey went ashore to meet the Army and Marine commanders. "Halsey," said Carney, "had a very definite requirement in his own life style . . . for that personal contact. He knew them all personally. . . . My trouble with him was keeping him out of the front lines."

Unhappy as he was in a defensive role, Halsey had no alternative. He continued supporting Okinawa but urged that American air power based on the island be strengthened so that his fast carriers could be relieved of their covering duties. He instigated the transfer of Marine Air Group Fourteen from the Philippines to Okinawa. These pilots, who had been MacArthur's "flying artillery," would fill the supporting role when Task Force Thirty-Eight decided to mount its offensive.

By June the buildup of air power on Okinawa and the successes of the B-29s operating against Kyushu out of China and Saipan permitted the Third Fleet to leave Okinawan waters.

Talking with war correspondents on board the *Missouri,* Halsey "served notice of mighty blows against Japan's waning military and naval power." His intention was "to beat hell out of the Japs wherever they may be found." He challenged the remnants of the Japanese fleet "to come out for battle" and, at the same time, warned against possible attempts by certain elements in Tokyo to seek an "advantageous peace with the hope of preparing for another war." Describing Japanese industrialists as "a political nucleus of peace seekers," Halsey said, "When they see an economic empire crashing down around their ears they will try to save what they can out of the wreckage if they can get rid of the militarist. Knowing how wily, deceitful and unprincipled the

Japanese are, we can see the game they're trying to play. The only peace we should consider is absolute, unadulterated and unconditional surrender.''

After the press conference broke up, a New York *Times* reporter wrote, "An offensive mood hangs over the Third Fleet with the return of Admiral Halsey to the wars. There is a general feeling that his return will mean more trouble and more surprises for Japan just as it always has. Veterans of the fleet remember the Navy's spectacular sweep through the Philippines in late autumn that paved the way for the reconquest of those islands.

"There are at least two underlying practical factors that point to increased naval activity in the coming months. One is Halsey's own background, which constantly stresses the offensive and the element of surprise. The second factor is the time element. The time is approaching for a change of naval pace as the battle of Okinawa grinds toward a bitter conclusion.''

On 2–3 June aircraft from Task Force Thirty-Eight struck southern Kyushu.

Already the fleet had received from weather centrals warnings of tropical disturbances forming far to the south and east. These reports did not permit accurate plotting of the storms' tracks, but indicated ''in a general way'' that the storms were moving westward, then recurving north toward Okinawa.

After pouring over the weather reports, Commander George F. Kosco felt that Task Force Thirty-Eight was out of danger in the Okinawa area. When he reported to the Third Fleet staff, Halsey said that he could not discount the warnings. He issued a typhoon alert to all ships on Sunday, 3 June. Air operations for the next day against Kyushu were canceled.

[XIV]

"It Was a Sort of Sausage Shaped Image"

EXCEPT FOR THE WEATHER WARNINGS, the line of cirrus coming from the south was the only sign of an approaching disturbance. The *Missouri* received a message from CINCPAC stating that a typhoon, or a tropical storm, was approaching Okinawa and on the morning of the 4th it would be somewhere around 22N, 126E. Commander Kosco advised Carney at 0630 to cancel his scheduled flight from the carrier *Shangri La* to Okinawa as a sharp cold front would pass the island and he would be grounded. Kosco guessed that the typhoon was located at 17N, 128 E. Until the *Missouri* received further reports "we did not know definitely where the storm was located."

In flag mess, Halsey asked Kosco's opinion of the disturbance. The commander replied that CINCPAC's storm report was in error and recommended "staying in a status quo for six to eight hours until the situation cleared up." The *Missouri* aerologists were convinced that the storm was further to the southeast than CINCPAC's report indicated. "I never did discard his report," Kosco emphasized, "but in my mind there was a doubt."

Halsey and the staff considered this information. Kosco informed them that his recommendation was based on his knowledge of storms and the general situation, yet he dared not dispute CINCPAC's warnings until he had further data.

216

With nagging doubts in their minds, the only logical thing to do, Halsey believed, was "to move to the east to get clear of the storm that was well to the westward and moving on a northerly course. I decided to haul out to the eastward to get sea room to maneuver and avoid the storm." Halsey ordered the fleet to prepare for heavy weather and to proceed eastward on course 110.

"The situation in regard to weather," said a staff member, "was that nobody knew exactly where the storm center was and we were taking precautionary measures. We considered that the storm had not been definitely located."

Actually two storms had developed. The first typhoon (No. 1) had continued to the northwest and disappeared on the forenoon of the 4th at a position 200 miles southwest of the task force. Apparently many of the storm reports received by the *Missouri* referred to this typhoon.

The second typhoon (No. 2), which eventually inflicted damage on the ships, formed at a point about 550 miles south of Okinawa and moved north northeast, finally curving to the northeast. This typhoon moved with increasing speed and, by the evening of 4 June, was traveling at twenty knots on a path which would carry it astern of the easterly moving Third Fleet.

At noon Kosco calculated the storm center at 21–20N, 126E, "but I was very much in doubt as to my estimate."

At 1540, 4 June, communicators on the *Missouri* intercepted a plain language dispatch from Nimitz's Advanced Headquarters, Guam, to two hospital ships, the *Relief* and *Bountiful*. The report stated that at 0900 on the 4th a storm center was suspected at a point about 160 miles southwest of the task force, moving north northeast; a second storm center had been "more definitely placed" about 375 miles south southwest of the same group, heading north. Kosco regarded this dispatch as of little value because it reported two disturbances and "I was at the time of the definite opinion that there was only one storm. . . . Also the storm center did not agree with my historical record and it indicated the storm was moving north and I did not believe it could be moving north."

A coded message reached the *Missouri* at 2130, the 4th, stating that the first of the two storms (i.e., No. 1) was now believed to be non-existent, but that at 1500 the second storm (typhoon No. 2) was moving north from a position about 350 miles south southwest of the Third Fleet. Unfortunately, Halsey and Kosco discounted these two reports as they indicated *two* storms.

At 1700 Halsey and staff estimated the typhoon center was located about 230 miles west of the Third Fleet. Actually, the typhoon in this area, No. 1, had already dissipated itself, while the only existing storm, No. 2, was positioned 200 miles to the southward of the force.

At 2234 Halsey, on the advice of Kosco, recommended to Mc-Cain a course change to 150. McCain, however, preferred the more easterly course in order to maintain the tactical position of his task force and so it was agreed to stay on course 110.

"I am not quite sure of why we did not take a course 150 shortly before midnight as recommended," Kosco wrote later. "From all of our evidence it would have taken us to a position which was in latitude south of the typhoon, and that was what Halsey wanted. This was my recommendation even though we weren't sure at the time where the typhoon was located. We did not think it further to the north and the west than its actual position."

At the same time, Admiral Joseph J. ("Jocko") Clark, Commander Task Group 38.1, on the *Hornet,* received a report from the *Ancon,* en route from Leyte to Okinawa, stating that at 1930 it had obtained a radar weather fix on a storm center at a point 130 miles southwest of the fleet. In conjunction with CINCPAC's earlier report, this information gave "another very definite position of the storm."

"We plotted the two positions," said Clark, "and it gave a track of about 030 for that storm. It was a very illuminating dispatch to us and told us that although a storm was there, we would have passed ahead of it by morning and our present course (110) and speed would carry us well clear. We felt that the course . . . would take us well clear of the storm and we had no seas to speak of [and] the wind was moderate."

Shortly after midnight, the *Missouri* received the *Ancon* weather report. It was delayed reaching Kosco as it was not sent "urgent" or "operational priority" and, said the commander later, "we had many more messages than 38.1 because we were receiving from many more other channels and in his case it received prompt attention and in our case had to wait its turn."

To Kosco, the *Ancon* report was the first authentic information about a typhoon and was the only report of the day that was of "any value." It indicated that the Third Fleet was in a dangerous semicircle and that in all probability the typhoon would continue to curve to the east and place the task force in the violent part of the storm if it continued on the present course. "All rules and all precautionary measures," said Kosco, "indicated that we should make every effort to get into the safe semi-circle."

"Typhoon movements," wrote Halsey later, "are very unpredictable and they are very prima donish in their actions. I had no information that I or that my advisors thought of any definite value about the position of this storm. The first information I received that I considered authentic was . . . a dispatch from the *Ancon*. . . ."

If the *Missouri*'s aerological staff had considered the *Ancon* report in conjunction with the positions given by CINCPAC's dispatch for the second storm center, typhoon No. 2, it would have shown that this storm was moving northeast and that the easterly course of Task Force Thirty-Eight would have by midnight carried it clear (east) of the typhoon track.

Halsey discounted the possibility of a typhoon to the south and estimated the storm center to be west of the fleet. Finally, at 0114, Halsey recommended course 300 "until the weather improves, then west." His intention was to cross the storm track to the northwestward. McCain suggested that the fleet keep going east. "My reason for recommending this with an increase of speed was that I had a better idea of where the storm was on the assumption that the storm's course was northeast." But when Halsey said 300, "I decided after consideration that 300 was a good course in view of the reports."

At 0115 Task Force Thirty-Eight executed this course change. The effect of this was to run the fleet directly back into the path of the typhoon, since the storm was then about seventy miles southwest of the fleet, moving northeast rather than east. Both Admirals Clark and Donald B. Beary, Commander Task Group 30.8, were surprised and dismayed at the change.

"We were already well clear to eastward of the storm," Clark said later, "and if we had continued to the east, the storm would have passed well astern, but now Halsey was taking us right back into the track of the storm. Because Halsey was quite as well aware of the situation as I, there was nothing for me to do but carry out orders."

At 0150, Admiral Arthur W. ("Raddy") Radford, Commander Task Group 38.4, informed McCain that, based on his estimated position of the storm center, "a revision of the present course (300) appears best."

The weather rapidly deteriorated. The barometer fell. Waves heightened. The storm was worst in the vicinity of Task Group 30.8, which was eighteen miles south southeast of Task Group 38.1 and thirty miles south southwest of Task Group 38.4, which included the *Missouri* and *Shangri La.*

Admiral Beary, who had been directed to conform to the movements of the *Missouri,* signaled McCain, "Believe this course (300) is running us back into the storm."

"At that time," said McCain, "I did not think well of course 300 and recommended to Halsey that the fleet come to course 000."

"I discussed this with my advisors," said Halsey, "and any-where from north around to west appeared to be acceptable. The possible path of the storm by that time we suspected as traveling in a northwesterly direction. A choice between a north course and a course of 300 was more or less immaterial except that a north-erly course might keep us in the path of the storm a bit longer, but, again, that was anybody's guess."

At 0248 the task force came to the new course, 000. "After that," said McCain, "the situation was fairly clear and free of apprehension, unless and until the storm took a sudden turn to the north."

The course 000 was fine for Task Group 38.4, sixteen miles away from Task Group 38.1, but Clark and Beary needed twenty minutes to get sea room to start the maneuver. The typhoon was closing quickly from the south behind them, causing heavy swells and rain.

About 0310 Admiral Beary, whose task group was closest to the typhoon center and whose ships were "riding very heavily," recalled: "I reported to Commander Third Fleet that I was unable to hold this course and that I was coming back to 300."

Beary directed his ships to proceed independently on courses varying between 300 and 240. At 0535 Task Group 30.8 moved through the typhoon center and, during the height of the storm, Beary reported average wind velocities of seventy knots and seventy-five-foot waves.

"The ship," said Captain George Mundorff, skipper of the *Windham Bay,* "was pitching violently and the bow would alternately plunge deeply, the screws just clear of the water and racing madly, and then rise to extraordinary heights before plunging again. Finally as the bow crashed down with a particularly violent shudder the forward lookout platforms and numbers one and two forty MM gun sponsons collapsed and fell away. Although the fact was not known at the time, a projection on the collapsed flight deck pierced the forecastle and permitted water to enter the forward hold and chain locker through a hole about six inches in diameter."

"Seas were phenomenal," reported Captain Joseph I. Taylor, skipper of the *Salamaua.* "With extremely heavy spray, the sea and ceiling appeared to merge. The situation was further complicated by the fact that the *Salamaua* was surrounded by several ships and continually heard ships reporting over the TBS they had lost steering control. . . . On several occasions ships came so close that the radar lost them in the sea return. All ships turned on navigation lights but spray was so heavy visibility was nil."

Groups only a few miles apart experienced totally different weather. Task Group 38.1, which was nearer to the storm center than Task Group 38.4, had experienced increasing typhoon conditions on the northerly course. Clark's radar indicated an unusual cloud formation to the southwest. The admiral went out on the bridge and looked for himself. "It was," he said, "a sort of sausage shaped image and seemed to have a definite motion . . . and seemed to be traveling pretty fast. We studied it and decided it was a storm but made sure before saying anything about it."

Clark and his staff plotted the motion of the image on radar and found its course, north northeast, an intersecting one with that of Task Group 38.1. "We were positive we had a storm," a storm into which the Third Fleet was running "right for the center."

At 0401 Clark hurriedly signaled McCain, "My radar shows center storm bearing 245 moving 030." Clark received no reply. His radar indicated that the ships were sixteen miles to the edge of the storm's inner ring. At 0420 he signaled McCain again, "I can get clear of the storm quickly by heading 120. Please advise." This course would have taken the group clear.

McCain replied, "We have nothing on our scope to indicate storm center."

Clark shot back, "We very definitely have. We have had one for one and a half hours."

Clark intercepted a message in which McCain asked Halsey's advice. Halsey's answer was "Posit," which means, "Keep your relative position with respect to the guide."

"I weighed the considerations," said Clark, "as to whether I should leave the formation at that time and it was very clear in my mind that Commander Task Force Thirty-Eight desired me to continue with him." Task Group 38.1 continued on the northerly course.

McCain realized that Clark's ships were already in the storm area. "But still," he said, "we were on a course with the wind and sea abaft the beam and were heading, in my opinion, to the navigable semi-circle along the shortest route. I really could not see anything to be gained by changing to the southeast at this time."

By 0500 the winds were beginning to build around Task Group 38.1. Clark decided that a northwesterly course would take his ships across the typhoon's path more quickly than the course due north. With the approval of McCain, he turned his group around to 330 at 0507 and, on this course, it crossed the storm's path at 0510, at a point forty miles ahead (northeast) of the approaching storm center. However, the carriers *Belleau Wood* and *San Jacinto* began rolling heavily. "At 0516," said Clark, "I decided that I better get to the west of the storm as quickly as possible and get the seas away from the sterns of the CVLs."

Clark turned his group first westward, then southward and signaled McCain, "We are maneuvering to find best course. Should be out soon. The wind is now ninety knots."

As a result of the course changes, Clark's ships recrossed the typhoon center, experiencing mountainous seas and wind velocities. The *Pittsburgh* reported her bow broken off and floating on her port side. The *Hornet,* Clark's flagship, and *Bennington* suffered severe bow damage. Nearly every ship in the task group suffered some damage as a result of passing through the typhoon's center. Clark sent a dispatch to his group, "Maneuver independently to get the best course. The heaviest part of the storm is west of you." Ahead of and to the northward of Clark's ships, Task Group 38.4, McCain's and Halsey's, was never in trouble, passing the typhoon's track ahead of the center, with comparatively moderate wind. At 0400 Halsey and Carney decided that "it possibly was not a typhoon after all."

By 1000, the 5th, the Third Fleet had cleared the storm. Reports came into the *Missouri.* The carriers *Hornet* and *Bennington,* the escort carriers *Windham Bay* and *Salamaua,* the cruisers *Pittsburgh, Baltimore,* and *Duluth* suffered major damage. Twenty-six other ships reported minor damage. The storm destroyed or damaged 146 aircraft. Six officers and men were lost or killed, and four were seriously injured. Halsey's only consolation was that no ships sank.

"The typhoon, Halsey's second," Clark said later, "had inflicted serious damage to many ships and was almost equivalent of a defeat in battle."

Halsey sent an irate message to Guam, attention Fleet Admiral Nimitz. He was angry. The early warning messages had been garbled. The *Ancon*'s urgent warning message had been critically delayed by coding regulations. Estimated storm conditions had been at a confusing variance.

At Guam Nimitz ordered a Court of Inquiry to investigate.

Clark and his staff set to work preparing a chronological record of the events of the typhoon, track charts, and photographs of the radar images showing the path of the storm. Transferred by breeches buoy to the destroyer *McKee,* Clark was taken to pay a call on McCain on the *Shangri La.* "His personal loyalty to Halsey,'' said Clark, ''made him non-committal when I said that if he had released me I could have avoided the eye of the storm.'' But McCain did say, when Clark was leaving, ''I am sorry you had to get *your* ships damaged.'' This remark ''nettled'' Clark because, he reflected, only the day before, when these ships were dropping bombs on Kyushu, ''they were *his* ships. He certainly took credit for their performance in his press releases, but when they got damaged, they were no longer *his* ships, they became *my* ships.''

Clark next paid his respects to Halsey on the *Missouri*. ''There was very little conversation,'' Clark remembered. ''He knew and I knew who was to blame for my ships turning back into the typhoon.'' Shortly before noon, Clark returned to his flagship, the *Hornet*.

Despite the typhoon's damage, Task Force Thirty-Eight fueled and planes conducted support missions over Okinawa on the 6th and 7th. The Third Fleet launched a long-range fighter sweep of 200 planes against Kanoya airfields on southern Kyushu. Aircraft saturated dispersal areas, installations, and anti-aircraft defenses. Two days later they struck Okino Daito Jima with napalm, rockets, and bombs.

The Okinawa campaign was now over. On the night of the 10th, the Third Fleet turned south toward the new fleet base at Leyte for repairs. After evaluating the strikes against Kyushu, Halsey sent Nimitz a dispatch. THE GLORIOUS DAYS OF CARRIERS SPEARHEADING THE PACIFIC OFFENSIVE ENDED WHEN THE SPEAR ENTERED THE HEART OF THE EMPIRE. TARGETS ARE SCARCE. IT NOW REQUIRES CAREFUL PLANNING AND SMART EXECUTION TO SELECT, FIND, AND DESTROY TARGETS THAT MERIT THE HUGE EFFORT AND COST OF CARRIER STRIKES. . . . THE B-29S CONTINUE TO REDUCE THE NUMBER OF AVAILABLE, VITAL STRATEGIC TARGETS. THE JAPANESE AIR FORCE WILL CONSERVE ITS STRENGTH TO REPEL A MAJOR INVASION. IT WILL NORMALLY AVOID AERIAL COMBAT WITH CARRIERS.

On 17 December the Court of Inquiry convened on board the battleship *New Mexico* in San Pedro Harbor, Leyte. The court included two of the men who had sat at the previous investigation,

Vice Admirals Hoover and Murray, together with Vice Admiral Charles A. Lockwood. From the first day the court was tense. Taking a swipe at Nimitz, who had planned to bolster the weather gathering service, Halsey blamed the lack of information from weather centrals and slow communications for the disaster. "As the responsible commander in the combat zone," said Halsey, "I believe that I am fully entitled to have every bit of information that can be made available about storms. . . . I believe we have the facilities in this area to have given me . . . information. I did not get it.

"They send a plane out to report the presence of a storm, its force, its direction and movement. The ordinary pilot knows something about weather but not the scientific approach to it. He gets into a front—he doesn't like it and I don't blame him—we have all been in fronts, we get tossed around, and from some position in that front he reports a bearing of the storm center."

"On this false information, as a consequence," Halsey continued, "a tremendous amount of erroneous information comes out. I believe I am correct in the statement . . . that we got a report of one plane and he was 500 miles in error. It must be a trained aerological team that is doing this work. The amount of damage we sustained in the typhoon last December and the amount of damage we sustained in this typhoon in June is pretty nearly as bad as anything the enemy has ever inflicted on us."

"Had I any knowledge beforehand of the track of this typhoon such as I now possess," said Halsey, "it would have been the easiest matter in the world to have employed it away ahead of the storm. I was without such knowledge, from my own point of view, the point of view of my staff, of any specific knowledge of this storm, until I got the report from the ANCON. This report was delivered to me four and a half hours after the time of its file."

Admiral Clark had a stake in the proceeding as several of his ships suffered heavy damage and he could be held responsible. His legal counsel, Lieutenant Herman Rosenblatt, USNR, a lawyer in civilian life, questioned Halsey in detail, putting the blame squarely on his shoulders.

After the session with Halsey on the stand, Clark took Rosenblatt aside and cautioned him, "Herman, you can't talk to a four-star admiral like that."

He replied, "Admiral, that's the only way I know to prove your innocence. If you think that is embarrassing, just say the word and I'll pull out. But I can tell you that your throat is going to be cut from ear to ear unless I can hang the blame on the one man who is responsible. And that is Admiral Halsey."

Clark decided to let Rosenblatt handle his defense in his own way. Rosenblatt established the fact that Halsey alone had made the decision to turn to 300.

By his testimony, Admiral Clark also blamed Halsey. Clark presented all information concerning his part in the typhoon. He gave longitudes and latitudes, speeds and ship movements, and displayed his track charts. "I believe," he said, "that had we turned east anytime before the winds began to get too high we would have been better off though that would have involved going into the so-called dangerous semicircle. . . . I believe that the key to this whole situation is the turn . . . to 300."

Realizing that his interpretation of the weather reports had been poor, Halsey's counsel, Colonel Charles T. Brooks, USMC, questioned Clark and tried to trip him up on his testimony concerning his correct analysis and plot of the storm.

Before the court adjourned, the Judge Advocate, Captain Ira H. Nunn, USN, summed up the case, "It is my opinion," he said, "that the testimony that this court has heard contains sufficient material to make a prima facie case of culpable inefficiency in the performance of duty on the part of the Commander Third Fleet."

"It is also my opinion," he continued, "that the record discloses that an act or omission by the Commander Third Fleet was the proximate cause of the disaster. . . . The proximate, or legal, cause of damage to the Third Fleet on June fifth, was the turning of the Fleet to course 300. Any other inefficiencies either subsequent or previous to that moment . . . may be contributory causes, but the outstanding and proximate cause, the legal cause, of the disaster was that change in course at a time when the officer who caused that change to be made had in his possession, or in the exercise of reasonable care should have had in his possession, sufficient information which if properly and promptly evaluated would have shown the danger involved."

Long overdue for a shore billet, Clark had already hauled down his flag on 13 June and Rear Admiral Tommy Sprague had relieved him as Commander Task Group 38.1. On his way to the States, Clark stopped in Guam to pay a visit to Nimitz, who questioned him at length regarding the typhoon and expressed great displeasure with Halsey and to a lesser degree with Mc-Cain. "He minced no words," said Clark later, "in charging Halsey with gross stupidity in both typhoons, especially the latter, where Halsey had good weather information."

At San Pedro Harbor, members of the court in their written opinion criticized Nimitz's and Halsey's staffs because they "were not organized to a sufficient degree in their communications and aerological divisions to effectively and efficiently [have] handled the emergency which developed on 4 June 1945." The court was extremely critical of Halsey. It pointed out that Nimitz's advice, in his letter of 13 February on lessons of the December typhoon, had not been followed; and that there was "a remarkable similarity between the situations, actions and results" of the two encounters. The court also concluded that the maneuver which led to this result "came about . . . when Fleet course was changed from 110 to 300 . . . this course change was extremely ill-advised considering the known location of the storm center."

The court held Halsey primarily responsible for the damage and losses sustained and, to a lesser degree, Admiral McCain. Clark and Beary also incurred "blame" because "they continued on courses and at speeds which eventually led their Task Groups into dangerous weather, although their better judgment dictated a course of action which would have taken them fairly clear of the typhoon path."

The court recommended that "letters be addressed to Commander Third Fleet and Commander Task Force Thirty-Eight pointing out to them errors committed and lack of sound judgment displayed. Lessons which might have been learned from a similar encounter . . . were either disregarded or not given proper consideration."

The court also recommended that "serious consideration" be given to assigning Halsey and McCain to other duties.

Neither Nimitz nor King agreed on this recommendation. At Guam Nimitz wrote the court, "CINCPAC has considered, not only the events under inquiry, but the outstanding combat records of the officers to whom responsibility has been attached in this case. Commander Third Fleet . . . has rendered invaluable service to his country. His skill and determination have been demonstrated time and again in combat with the enemy." Nimitz decided to take no further action.

In Washington Secretary of the Navy James V. Forrestal was ready to retire Halsey on the spot. He was dissuaded on the ground that Halsey was a popular hero, and that any such action would lower fleet morale.

Admiral King, after reviewing both typhoons, concluded that "the primary responsibility for the storm damage and losses in both cases attaches to Commander Third Fleet, Admiral William F. Halsey, Jr., U.S. Navy." "The gravity of the occurrence," he wrote Forrestal, "is accentuated by the fact that the senior officers concerned were also involved in a similar, and poorly handled situation during the typhoon of December 1944. . . . Responsible officers on each occasion had sufficient information to enable them to avoid the worst part of the storm area had they reacted to the situation as it developed with the weather-wise skill to be expected of professional seamen."

"Notwithstanding the above," King concluded, "I recommend that no individual disciplinary measures be taken, for the reason stated by . . . Fleet Admiral Nimitz."

In an endorsement on the record of the earlier court of inquiry, King asked Halsey if he had anything to say in view of the second typhoon. Halsey still clung to the belief that the major blame for the disasters rested with the weather reporting service. In a letter to Forrestal concerning the two typhoons, Halsey wrote, "I have repeatedly made detailed recommendations for a typhoon warning service which would enable a task fleet commander at sea to conduct his forces to areas of comparative safety. This weather service did not exist in December 1944, nor was adequate and timely information available to me to completely avoid damage from a typhoon 4–5 June 1945; in the latter instance positive information as to the location and direction of movement of the typhoon was not available to me from any source until a matter of hours before the typhoon arrived among the fleet forces. And it must be remembered that task fleets cover great areas. . . .

"I have no wish to avoid my proper responsibility in these instances; however, I also wish to state unequivocally that in both the December 1944 and June 1945 typhoons the weather warning service did not provide the accurate and timely information necessary to enable me to take timely evasive action. For that inadequacy I cannot accept responsibility."

[XV]

"Men, the War Has Ended"

DURING HIS STAY AT LEYTE, Halsey visited Manila and was "delighted to see the harbor littered with sunken Japanese ships." He lunched with MacArthur, whom he found in exceedingly good spirits.

Repaired and replenished, the Third Fleet moved out of San Pedro Harbor at 0530 on 1 July to carry out Nimitz's Operational Plan 4–45. The Third Fleet was given the task of attacking "Japanese naval and air forces, shipping, shipyards, and coastal objectives" as well as covering and supporting Ryukyus forces. Now that organized enemy resistance on Okinawa had ceased, Halsey was free to hit Japan from within its home waters.

Halsey's Operational Plan 9-45 called for the Third Fleet to attack the enemy's home islands, destroy the remnants of naval power, and cripple Japanese industries and communications. Aircraft would strike inland, the big guns of the battleships and cruisers would bombard coastal targets; together they would literally "bring the war home to the average Japanese citizen."

Preparations for the attack on the Empire had been carefully worked out. B-29s had made a thorough reconnaissance of Hokkaido and northern Honshu. Navy B-24s had photographed the Tokyo area. Submarines had located the minefields.

After several days of training exercises at sea, Task Force Thirty-Eight commenced a high speed run at twenty-five knots to a rendezvous point for launching strikes against Tokyo. In the

230

campaign against the home islands, Navy planes were to strike during the daylight hours, Army B-29s at night.

Early on the morning of 10 July pilots assembled in the ready rooms and listened to final briefings on the missions. Meanwhile, the flattops and their escorts were moving into the wind. Over the loudspeakers came, "Pilots, man your planes." Grabbing helmets and other gear, airmen went to the flight deck, clambered into their planes, went through pre-starting routines. The bullhorn sounded, "Start engines." After their engines warmed, planes sped off in quick succession to rendezvous above their carriers, then headed toward the targets.

Aircraft flew 1,160 offensive and 124 photo sorties over the Tokyo area, dropping 454 tons of bombs, firing 1,648 rockets.

Back home in the States, New York headlines read, "Carrier Planes Swoop on Tokyo Area. 3D Fleet Strikes. 700 Planes Deal a Surprise Blow." "154 Enemy Planes Smashed in Carrier Blow. No U.S. Warship Attacked. Fighters Sweep in at Dawn in Opening of Halsey's Attack."

After refueling, the fleet struck the relatively untouched part of Japan, the Hokkaido-northern Honshu area on the 14th against token opposition. On the same day, the battleships *Massachusetts, South Dakota,* and *Indiana,* the heavy cruisers *Quincy* and *Chicago,* and nine destroyers conducted "a deliberate bombardment" of the steel plant at Kamaishi, Honshu. Flames erupted in oil storage tanks, coke ovens, and the foundry. Shortages of raw materials had reduced the output of the Kamaishi plant to less than half its capacity. Damage from this ship bombardment was extensive and production stopped altogether.

The enemy's failure to hit the task force indicated to Halsey's staff that the Japanese were hoarding their air power against an expected invasion of the home islands and they realized that the Japanese had little air strength left. "In my opinion," said Halsey, "his shortages were even reaching the point of no-return, the point where collapse of his whole war machine would become inevitable. Since three years before, in our South Pacific days, I had argued that Japan's ultimate end would be collapse."

The Third Fleet, now joined by British Task Force Thirty-Seven (Admiral Sir Bernard Rawlings), stepped up the pace.

British surface ships augmented by the battleships *North Carolina* and *Alabama* bombarded six major industrial plants at Hitachi, eighty miles northeast of Tokyo. They lobbed a total of 1,238 sixteen-inch shells on Hitachi and two cruisers expended 292 rounds of six-inch shells at electrical installations a few miles south of the city. The task forces retired for fuel, and Halsey now shifted his operations to the southwest part of Kyushu and the Inland Sea.

The air strikes of the 24th and 28th were among the heaviest of the war and the most destructive of shipping. At Kure and Kobe aircraft sank fifty-three merchant ships and badly damaged twenty-two warships, totaling 258,000 tons, including the battleships *Haruna, Hyuga,* and *Ise,* the two heavy cruisers *Tone* and *Aoba,* two destroyers, several transports, cargo ships, and oilers. Bombing and strafing, planes ripped apart the flight decks of the *Amagi* and *Katsuragi.* The Kure naval yard "ceased to exist." "It was a crippling, destructive blow at the Japanese Inland Sea defenses," said Halsey. "What is left of the Japanese Navy is helpless, but just for luck we're going to hunt them out of their holes. The Third Fleet's job is to hit the Empire hard and often. We are doing just that, and my only regret is that our ships don't have wheels, so that when we drive the Japs from the coast, we can't chase them inland."

That same day, Halsey received a letter from an old friend. "I congratulate you on the good work you are doing. Keep it up. Bomb Hell out of those yellow Bastards; you sure are making a swell job burning up the cities."

After the strikes against the Kure Naval Base, battleships and cruisers shelled Hamamatsu on the south coast of Honshu; planes hit Tokyo and Nagoya. During the night of 30 July a destroyer squadron shelled the railroad yard and an aluminum plant at Shimizu.

The forces refueled to prepare for a strike against Kyushu and Korea. Bad weather interrupted this operation and Halsey directed that the attacks begin again on 5 August. The Third Fleet was making its swing on the evening of the 4th when a message from Nimitz abruptly transferred operations to northern Honshu and Hokkaido. The Twentieth Air Force on Saipan was ready to drop the atomic bomb on Hiroshima.

During the middle of July, Nimitz had forbidden the Third Fleet to hit Hiroshima or Nagasaki. He gave no explanation. Halsey was puzzled. "I was out to destroy Japan," he said, "and not to try to protect it. So I did not know what it was all about." Finally Rear Admiral William Purnell came on board the *Missouri* on 22 July, under Nimitz's orders, and handed Halsey the first word of the bomb. Purnell said that the bomb drop was planned for 2 August on a Kyushu target.

Months before, Halsey had heard that a squadron of planes were experimenting on a "hush-hush" plan, "but I did not know what it was and I am glad I did not know it."

The bad weather that delayed Halsey's strikes also delayed the atomic bomb drop, which eventually was made on the 6th.

To Halsey, "it was a mistake ever to drop it. Why reveal a weapon like that to the world when it wasn't necessary?"

"The Japanese," continued Halsey, "were utterly defeated . . . before the atomic bomb was ever used. All the atomic bomb succeeded in doing was to leave less Japs to be fed. . . . I do know that the Japs were utterly defeated and knew it long before the first atomic bomb. . . . We knew the condition of Japan was bad, almost disastrous, but we did not know the full story of how little they had left to resist with until we got into Japan."

Admiral King held similar views. "True," he said, "the devastation already wrought by past bombing, as well as the terrible demonstration of the power of the first bombs, augured nothing less for the Japanese than total extinction, yet without sea power there would have been no possession of Saipan, Iwo Jima and Okinawa from which to launch these bombings."

Although bad weather hampered the Third Fleet's air operations on 8 August and fog blanketed Hokkaido on the 9th, heavy surface bombardment groups plastered Kamaishi. As the fog lifted, the fleet launched devastating strikes against northern Honshu airfields, destroying or damaging 392 planes. On this same day, 9 August, the second atomic bomb was dropped on Nagasaki. On the next day, heavy air strikes were again launched against northern Honshu, hitting two previously undetected air bases where planes were being assembled.

The first hint of peace came to most of the wardroom officers on the *Missouri* that night, the 10th, during the movies. The news did not come dramatically in a single electrifying announcement. The Executive Officer first heard the rumor that "the Japs have surrendered" when he was called to the phone. There was whispered information in the wardroom that something "big had broken."

In flag mess, two decks above, some of the staff were discussing a flash report from San Francisco that the Japanese were willing to surrender. Nothing official had yet been received. Nor had the rumor interrupted Halsey's movie except for a few minutes. Suddenly, a watch officer brought Mick Carney a transcription of a radio transcript. Carney read it aloud. "Through the Swiss Government, Japan stated that she is willing to accept Allied surrender."

Halsey's first comment was, "Have we got enough fuel to turn around and hit the bastards once more before they quit?"

Overnight Halsey's dispatch boards doubled in thickness. The questions and instructions poured in on such diverse subjects as military government units, whole blood, post office ships, staff cars, sanitation equipment.

Despite the flood of messages that indicated Washington's confidence in the eventual surrender of Japan, there was no suggestion that the Third Fleet slacken its attacks.

Task Forces Thirty-Seven and Thirty-Eight refueled on 11 August, but bad weather hemmed in the planes for their strike on Tokyo. Halsey notified his forces to hold their aircraft until 13 August.

Then Carney walked into Halsey's cabin with an intercept from the Army News Service: "The American Secretary of State, speaking for the Allied Powers, has accepted the surrender of Japan, provided that the Supreme Allied Commander rule Japan through the authority of the Emperor."

Halsey and the staff realized that this report was unofficial, but they were reluctant to attack an enemy whose surrender was actual though not yet ratified. But the question still haunted Halsey. Had Japan really surrendered? He and his staff discussed the situation, and the majority agreed that the honorable course was to cease fire. However, Carney felt the Third Fleet's armistice was premature. "We have never trusted the Japanese before, and this is a hell of a critical time to start." Halsey agreed, and signaled his ships, ATTACK TOKYO AREA TOMORROW UNLESS THE NIPS BEAT US TO THE PUNCH BY THROWING IN THE SPONGE.

Early on the 12th the Third Fleet started a high speed run toward the launching rendezvous. However, at 0100 the *Missouri* received a dispatch from Nimitz ordering it to cancel the strike.

Halsey passed the word at once, adding SITUATION NOT CLEAR BUT MAY DEVELOP RAPIDLY X MEANWHILE MAINTAIN STRONG DEFENSIVE CAP; and, later, I WILL ORDER IMMEDIATE ATTACK IF ENEMY SEARCHES OR SNOOPS.

A second dispatch from Nimitz canceled Halsey's first message. The Third Fleet was ordered to FOLLOW ORIGINAL SCHEDULE OF STRIKES. Within an hour on 13 August the aircraft were launching for Tokyo. Within a few hours, Americans had weakened the enemy's air power by 422 planes.

On the 14th the Third Fleet refueled again. Halsey heard nothing on the surrender. He sent a dispatch to his forces, I INTEND STRIKING SAME GENERAL TARGET AREA ON THE FIFTEENTH. The first strike was launched the next morning, 15 August, at 0415. At 0614, the second horde of planes zoomed off the flight deck. As Halsey readied a third strike, he was handed a top secret dispatch from Nimitz: SUSPEND AIR ATTACK OPERATIONS X ACKNOWLEDGE.

He immediately held the third strike back, and recalled the other planes. The admiral was breakfasting on the *Missouri* when his Air Operations officer gave him the news that Japan had ended the war. He burst out, waving the message, shouting, "Admiral, here she is!" It was a transcript of President Truman's official announcement. Halsey yelled "Yippee! Yippee!" and pounded the shoulders of everybody around him.

Halsey's first thought at the news was, "Victory!" His second was, "God be thanked, I'll never have to order another man out to die!" His next was, "I am grateful for the honor of being in command of the Third Fleet on this day."

Halsey wrote later that "I hope [history] will remember . . . that when hostilities ended, the capital of the Japanese Empire had just been bombed, strafed, and rocketed by planes of the Third Fleet, and was about to be bombed, strafed, and rocketed again. Last, I hope it will remember that seven men [on the first strike] did not return."

At 1055, 15 August, Halsey received a dispatch from Nimitz: CEASE OFFENSIVE OPERATIONS AGAINST JAPANESE FORCES X CONTINUE SEARCHES AND PATROLS X MAINTAIN DEFENSIVE AND INTERNAL SECURITY MEASURES AT HIGHEST LEVEL AND BEWARE OF TREACHERY OR LAST MINUTE ATTACKS BY ENEMY FORCES OR INDIVIDUALS.

Fifteen minutes later battle flags and Halsey's four-star flag were flying from the *Missouri*. Whistles and sirens sounded for one minute. At 1113 Halsey ordered the flag hoist to the fleet, "Well Done," run up.

Captain Harold Stassen, one of Halsey's staff, had the forenoon watch and kept the flag log. His last entry was at 1145. "So closes the watch we have been looking forward to. Unconditional surrender of Japan—with Admiral Halsey at sea in command of the greatest combined fighting fleet of all history. There is a gleam in his eye that is unmistakable!"

Nimitz sent a dispatch to Halsey. THE DAMAGING BLOWS BY THE FORCES OF YOUR COMMAND FROM 28 MAY TO 15 AUGUST WERE IMPORTANT FACTORS IN CAUSING THE ENEMY TO QUIT X NEARLY 3000 PLANES WERE DESTROYED OR DAMAGED X THE REMNANTS OF HIS NAVY WERE DUG OUT OF THEIR HIDING PLACES AND DESTROYED X LARGE NUMBERS OF HIS MERCHANT SHIPS OF ALL SIZES WERE SUNK X NO PART OF THE EMPIRE WAS SAFE FROM YOUR ATTACK X HIGHLY EFFECTIVE STRIKES AGAINST HIS INDUSTRIAL ESTABLISHMENTS SERIOUSLY WEAKENED HIS PRODUCTIVE CAPACITY X AIRCRAFT AND SURFACE SHIPS DID

MUCH TO DISRUPT HIS COMMUNICATION AND TRANS-
PORTATION FACILITIES X THEY ATTACKED HIS PORTS
HIS RAILROADS HIS HARBORS AND HIS FACTORIES
WITH GUNS AND BOMBS X IT WAS A JOB SUPERBLY
WELL DONE BY AIRMEN AND SEAMEN—FIGHTING
MEN ALL X WELL DONE.

At 1300 Halsey made his broadcast to the Third Fleet. "Men
. . . the war is ended. You, in conjunction with your brothers in
arms, of all services and all branches of all services have contributed inestimably to this final result. You have brought an implaca-
ble, treacherous, and barbaric foe to his knees in abject surrender. This is the first time in recorded history of the misbegotten
Japanese race that they as a nation have been forced to submit to
this humiliation. . . ."

"Your names," he continued, "are writ in golden letters on
the pages of history—your fame is and shall be immortal. . . .
Whether in the early days, when fighting with a very frayed shoestring, or at the finish, when fighting with the mightiest combined
fleet the world has ever seen, the results have been the same—
victory has crowned your efforts. The forces of righteousness and
decency have triumphed. Victory is not the end—rather, it is but
the beginning. We must establish a peace—a firm, a just, and an
enduring peace."

Even while Halsey was speaking, an air battle raged overhead.
The first of four attacking enemy planes was shot down. Two
more were splashed several minutes later and the last exploded in
the air when hit by accurate destroyer anti-aircraft fire at 1445.

The Third Fleet was the only fighting force at hand with sufficient strength to take Japan into custody and enforce the Allies'
will until occupation troops arrived. All available Marines on the
ships were organized into a provisional regiment, 2,000 strong.
Four naval battalions, numbering 1,600 men, completed the initial force available from the Third for the landings. Following the
pattern employed by amphibious forces in the South Pacific, an
expeditionary command, Task Force Thirty-One, was organized
with Rear Admiral Oscar C. Badger, USN, as commander. In
collaboration with Halsey, Badger prepared his operational plan
and set up his task organization with commanders and personnel

detailed from the forces afloat for this duty. Plans called for the
occupation and development of the Yokosuka Naval Base and air
station, the manning of enemy vessels with nucleus crews, the
demilitarization of Japanese installations, the rescue of POWs,
supply drops to POW camps.

Aid requested from Nimitz was provided expeditiously and by
20 August, the Fleet Landing Force components were being
transferred to transports and landing craft as these ships became
available. Assembly areas were delineated southeast of Tokyo
just outside of any effective Japanese air threat. An enormous
heterogeneous fleet gradually assembled so that at one time 250
ships of all classes were maneuvering in the area.

General Douglas MacArthur, the newly appointed Supreme
Commander of the Allied Powers in the Pacific, desired all services—Army, Navy, and Marines—to make simultaneous landings in Japan, but since the Army troops in the Philippines could
not be transported in less than ten days, he set 26 August for
D-Day. However, with typhoons forming to the southward, Mac-
Arthur postponed the landing forty-eight hours. With many of
his ships crowded and short of stores, Halsey was reluctant to
keep his force at sea in typhoon weather, so he requested and
received permission to enter Sagami Bay, at the mouth of Tokyo
Bay, on the 27th.

The Third Fleet neared the coast of Japan at dawn, 27 August.
At 0725 General Quarters sounded on the *Missouri* and other elements of the Third Fleet. Quietly the crews reported to assigned
battle stations, all helmeted and wearing blue dungaree trousers
and lighter colored shirts, life preservers strapped on.

The Japanese Navy had been ordered to send out an escort to
steer the Allied ships through the minefields and to deliver
officers empowered to arrange the surrender of the nearby Yokosuka Naval Base. When the escort, the destroyer *Hatsuzakura*,
neared the *Missouri,* Mick Carney and Halsey watched her from
the flag bridge. "She was so frail, so woebegone, so dirty," said
Halsey, "that I felt ashamed of our having needed four years to
win the war."

Carney pointed toward the destroyer, "You wanted the Jap
Navy, Admiral. Well, there it is."

At 0745 the American destroyer *Nicholas* and the *Hatsuzakura* met seventy-five yards apart. Bluejackets lowered a whaleboat from the *Nicholas* and rowed alongside the enemy destroyer. The two Japanese emissaries were then transferred in the little boat to the *Nicholas,* which got underway, leaving the *Hatsuzakura,* still flying her battle flag, under close surveillance of another American destroyer.

On board the *Nicholas* an officer asked one of the emissaries about the condition of Tokyo. He replied, "Leveled." What about Hiroshima was the next question. "Horrible."

At 0845 the *Nicholas* went alongside the *Missouri* and sailors promptly stretched a rope cable between the two ships. Ten minutes later the first Japanese was transferred to the battleship in a modified b's'n's buoy. Both Japanese officers, Captains Y. Takasaki and I. Otani, who wore the Third Order of the Sacred Treasure, were uniformed, as were the two interpreters, in olive green with white shirts and grey ties. After being searched and disarmed, they met with the Third Fleet staff (Halsey purposely did not attend). Carney presided over the meetings, assisted by Admiral Badger, commanding the land force. It took only a few minutes for the Americans to obtain the necessary hydrographic and minefield information. The Japanese were also given instructions concerning the Allied occupation of Tokyo Bay and the Naval Control Zone around Yokosuka. Once the emissaries had left the *Missouri,* Carney issued the following orders to the staff: "With reference to the Japanese, an attitude of cold, impersonal formality will be maintained at all times; they are required to obey the orders of the forces of occupation, and such obedience will be demanded and enforced; but every effort shall be bent toward the avoidance of conduct not in keeping with the prestige of our traditions. . . .

"And, finally, it must be remembered that these are the same Japanese whose treachery, cruelty, and subtlety brought about this war; we must be continually vigilant for overt treachery, and equally vigilant that we not become blinded by outward subservience and docility. They are always dangerous. . . ."

That afternoon the *Missouri* followed by the *Iowa* and the destroyers *Nicholas, O'Bannon,* and *Taylor* moved in the van of the Third Fleet and British units as they entered Sagami Bay and anchored. The nearest point to shore from the *Missouri* was less than 3,500 yards away and sailors could see the summer palace of the Emperor at Hayami and, over the port bow, towering in the clouds, snow-capped Fujiyama.

On 28 August, in final preparation for the landing of 10,000 sailors and marines at Yokosuka Naval Base, an advance force of ten ships led by Admiral Badger's flagship, *San Diego*, left Sagami Bay for the twenty-mile trip around Niura Peninsula into Tokyo Bay. All hands were alert to the possibility of mines—either Japanese or American, the latter dropped by B-29s—although minesweepers had spent hours searching for undersea explosives in the harbor. Carrier planes roared overhead as the unit steamed through the channel.

On the next day, three battleships, including the *Missouri*, two cruisers, and many destroyers anchored off Yokosuka. "When we entered . . . that morning," said Halsey, "Yokosuka was a sorry sight. It was a sort of Dorian Gray picture of what ailed all Nippon. The big cranes stood idle, shipping lay at piers half sunk; the shops were deserted and largely stripped of their machinery which had been sent underground in the faint hope that war production might somehow be continued."

Nimitz and his staff landed in Tokyo Bay from Guam early in the afternoon in two Coronado seaplanes and taxied immediately to his flagship, *South Dakota*.

Elements of the Army's Eleventh Airborne Division began landing at Atsugi Airfield, near Tokyo. MacArthur had ordered the Third Fleet not to recover POWs until the Army was ready to do so, "but circumstances forced us to jump the gun." On the night of 28 August, an American picketboat had picked up two British prisoners, who related a tale of such inhumanity that Halsey found it almost impossible to credit. The next day it was corroborated by a Swiss doctor, representing the International Red Cross. Listening to the prisoners, Halsey became convinced that it was no time to stand on protocol. He ordered a rescue group, which included the hospital ship *Benevolence*, up to Tokyo to stand by for a sudden signal.

Halsey explained the urgency of the POW situation to Nimitz.

"Go ahead," Nimitz told Halsey, "General MacArthur will understand."

The rescue force—Operation Swift Mercy—which included Captain Harold Stassen, went ashore. Planes from the fleet led the small boats up the estuaries leading to the prison camps. At the infamous Omori 8, the commandant demanded to see the Americans' credentials. "I have no authority to release these men!" he stormed.

Stassen retorted, "You have no authority, period!"

By 1910 that evening the first POWs were on board the *Benevolence* and, by midnight, 794 had been brought out of the prison camps. Within fourteen days, 19,000 Allied prisoners in the eastern two-thirds of Honshu had been liberated.

On board the *South Dakota* Nimitz held a press conference. "The surrender," he told the correspondents, "had come before any invasion had taken place, and that had been brought about primarily by seapower, spearheaded by carrier-borne aircraft." Seapower had made possible the Pacific advance and, hence, provided bases for soldiers and marines and land-based aircraft. The same seapower had made possible the use of the atomic bomb, providing bases from which planes could carry it. "Without seapower," Nimitz reiterated, "we could not have advanced at all."

H-Hour for Allied landings in the Tokyo area was set for 1000 on the 30th. Spearheaded by the marines, units occupied the forts bearing on the entrance of Tokyo Bay, others entered Yokosuka Naval Base. They met no opposition.

At 1100 a short, stocky Japanese vice admiral arrived at Yokosuka's main battleship dock and saluted Mick Carney and Admiral Badger. They returned the courtesy. Thirty marines stood at attention in two lines. Badger accepted the paper representing the surrender of the base and Carney formally accepted the capitulation in a simple ceremony lasting only ten minutes.

Headquarters of the Third Fleet and of the landing forces were quickly established there, and Halsey's flag was hoisted over the air station. Later, after inspecting the naval base for two hours, Halsey recalled, "Despite the Japs' reputation for cleanliness . . . the filth that I saw was appalling. The officers' club, which had been evacuated only a few hours before, was overrun with rats of an extraordinary size and character. They ignored our presence in some rooms but squeaked angrily when we entered others. . . . The civilians were also dirty. Worse, they were apathetic. . . . We found occasional evidence of malnutrition in urban areas, but the country folk looked well fed.''

2 September 1945 had been set for the day of the formal Japanese surrender. The *Missouri,* Halsey's flagship, was designated for the ceremony—the *Missouri* was named for President Truman's native state, and had been christened by his daughter. Halsey's staff worked ''like Hong Kong coolies'' to organize the ceremony. They rehearsed every step of it, provided for every nuance of etiquette, and smoothed away even the possibility of a ''bobble.''

Commencing at 0705 guests to witness the signing of the surrender came on board the *Missouri.* At 0830 Admiral Nimitz, the United States representative and Senior Officer Afloat in Tokyo Bay, came to the quarter-deck, followed at 0850 by General Douglas MacArthur.

Nimitz and Halsey were at the side to meet him. ''As always,'' said Halsey, ''his manner to me and my staff was heart-warming.'' MacArthur greeted them by their nicknames and remarked to Mick Carney, ''It's grand having so many of my side-kicks from the shoestring SOPAC days meeting me here at the end of the road.''

MacArthur, Nimitz, and Halsey went into a cabin. Halsey said, ''General, will you and Chester have a cup of coffee?''

''No, thanks, Bill. I'll wait till afterwards,'' MacArthur answered.

Nimitz responded, ''So will I, Bill. Thanks all the same.''

Halsey added, ''God, what a great day this is! We've fought a long, long time for it.'' Suddenly one of Halsey's staff appeared and notified the three men that the Japanese envoys had arrived.

At a table on the deck of the *Missouri* in the shadow of No. 2 turret, there were two sets of the surrender documents. MacArthur and Nimitz took their places behind the table and Halsey joined the line of naval officers. The ceremony opened with MacArthur making a short address. When he finished, he pointed to a chair at the opposite side of the table and said, ''The represen-

tatives of the Imperial Japanese Government and of the Imperial
Japanese staff will now come forward and sign.''

The Foreign Minister, Mamoru Shigemitsu, who was to sign
for Emperor Hirohito, limped toward the table, leaning on a
cane. He had lost a leg to a grenade thrown by a Korean in
Shanghai. He took off his gloves and silk hat, sat down, dropped
his cane, picked it up, and shuffled the papers.

Halsey, looking on at the scene, felt certain that he was stalling
for time, ''though God knows what he hoped to accomplish.''
''His performance made me so mad I wanted to slap him and tell
him, 'Sign, damn you! Sign!' ''

Once Shigemitsu put his signature to the documents, General
Yoshijiro Umezu, who was to sign for the Imperial General Staff,
did his job quickly.

MacArthur was next, as Supreme Commander for the Allied
Powers, then came their various representatives, led by Nimitz.
His War Plans Officer, Admiral Forrest Sherman, and Halsey
were invited to stand behind him while he signed. At that moment MacArthur put his arm around Halsey's shoulders and
whispered, ''Start 'em now.''

''Aye, aye, sir!'' Halsey replied.

Instantly, 450 planes from Task Force Thirty-Eight roared
over the *Missouri* mast high.

The surrender ceremony finished at 0925 and all Allied representatives went to Halsey's cabin. ''If ever a day demanded
champagne,'' said Halsey, ''this was it, but I could serve them
only coffee and doughnuts.'' The party soon broke up. The occupation of Japan had begun. Troops poured into the Tokyo area.

Nimitz returned to Guam the next day.

Later, at a press conference in his headquarters at the Customs
Building in Yokohama, MacArthur reminisced about the black
years in the Pacific war when the Japanese had come near invading Australia. Traces of anger broke to the surface. His voice
grew tight and hoarse at the memory of some of the first incidents
of the war. Then, he smiled and waved his hand and said, ''Well,
all that doesn't matter anymore now.'' In summing up, he called
Halsey ''the greatest fighting admiral of this or any war. When
Halsey finds a Jap, he goes after him and fights like a tiger.''

[XVI]

"I'm Too Damned Old to Fight Another War"

O N   8   S E P T E M B E R , accompanied by one squadron of the historic Seventh Cavalry, MacArthur, Halsey, and the general's staff drove from Yokohama to the United States Embassy in Tokyo. When the caravan stopped, the officers passed by American guards placed at twenty-yard intervals. MacArthur, Halsey, and the others took up positions at 1100 with their backs to a lilypond and facing the damaged Chancellery. The general stood several yards in front of the other members of his party. The band played the "General's Colors"; the drums, four ruffles; the trumpets, four flourishes; then, "The Star-Spangled Banner." The honor guard then presented arms and the flag which had flown over the United States Capitol at the time of Pearl Harbor slowly went up the flagpole.

Later, after touring Tokyo, Halsey said, "What impressed me most about the devastated areas, besides their vast extent, was the presence of iron and steel safes among the ruins; dozens and dozens of them stuck up from the ashes in every block." Remembering the broken-down transportation, torn up communications, and the filth of Japan, Halsey remarked, "I am a little ashamed to think it took so long. I wonder why it took four years?" "If MacArthur is given his way and not interfered with by well-meaning—and otherwise—bureaucrats in America and/or

244

elsewhere," he continued, "Japan will never rise above a fifth or sixth place power."

Less than two weeks later Admiral Spruance relieved Halsey, who immediately departed by air for Pearl Harbor with his staff. The admiral would always remember MacArthur's final farewell words, "When you leave the Pacific, Bill, it becomes just another damned ocean!"

Already Halsey had sent in his request for retirement from active service. "Due to the capitulation of Japan and the cessation of hostilities throughout the world," Halsey officially wrote King and Nimitz, "the Navy will soon return to peacetime functions. It is my belief that the younger officers should be given higher commands with wider responsibilities. Therefore, that upon completion of my duty as Commander THIRD Fleet . . . it is requested that I be placed on the retired list of the United States Navy in accordance with Article 1665 (1) U.S. Navy Regulations."

Both King and Nimitz approved. In Nimitz's endorsement, he said, "It will be difficult—if not impossible—to overestimate the value of Admiral Halsey's splendid services to our country." King added a "Well Done."

At Pearl Harbor early in October, Halsey held a press conference, and to a surprised group of reporters he talked of his forthcoming retirement. "I'm an old man," he told reporters. "Let the young fellows take over. . . . I've applied for retirement, but they haven't told me yet what they plan to do about it." Although nearly thirteen months below the retirement age of sixty-four, Halsey explained that he was "tired" and that his job was finished.

At Pearl Harbor Halsey formed Task Force Thirty and sortied for the West Coast on the morning of 9 October. The task groups separated and proceeded independently to their various assigned ports. Task Group 30.2, which included Halsey's flagship, *South Dakota,* headed for San Francisco. On 15 October just before entering the harbor, Halsey talked to the press on board the *South Dakota.*

"The Jap on the street knows he is defeated," said Halsey. "I traveled around the Tokyo, Yokohama, and Yokosuka district, much of the time on foot, and watched the people. They are a dejected, shabby, pitiful-looking crowd. They go up the road on odd days, and come back on even days. The ordinary Jap is a stupid animal, but even with his stupidity he knows now he is defeated.''

Halsey then declared that the biggest blunder committed by the Japanese hierarchy was to start the war. "They were not only stupid to start it, but stupid in handling their ships from beginning to end, thank God. And the psychology of the Japs toward the end, in their use of suicide planes, bombs and boats, was evidence of a desperate nation.''

The battleships *South Dakota, Alabama, Colorado, Wisconsin,* the cruiser *Vicksburg,* and destroyers and submarines passed beneath the Golden Gate as bands played "There'll Be a Hot Time in the Old Town Tonight." Tens of thousands lined the bridge and jammed vantage points along the Marin and San Francisco shores to watch the homecoming warships. Whistles and sirens shrieked; planes roared overhead. The task group maneuvered into San Francisco Bay and, while most of the ships anchored off Yerba Buena Island just south of the San Francisco-Oakland Bay Bridge, the *South Dakota* tied up at Pier 1.

On the following day as the siren atop the Ferry Building wailed at noontime and San Franciscans cheered, 1,300 officers and men of the fleet headed by Admiral Halsey paraded up Market Street amid the blare of bands. When the procession reached City Hall, Halsey and his men were welcomed and the admiral was given the Gold Key to the city. Once a band had finished playing "Anchors Aweigh," Halsey spoke to the huge throng.

The speech finished, the men were guests of the city at a buffet luncheon in Civic Auditorium; Halsey and several of his staff had luncheon with city dignitaries at the St. Francis' Green Room. That evening, comedian Bob Hope broadcast his radio show from the deck of the *South Dakota* with Halsey as his guest star. Later the admiral spoke at a dinner in the Palm Room at the Palace Hotel attended by distinguished San Franciscans.

On 17 October Halsey flew in his personal Douglas R5-D transport from San Francisco to Los Angeles. He emerged from the plane, smiling and waving, wearing a freshly pressed uniform

on which were pinned his decorations and his much treasured
Navy wings.

Halsey was met by a welcoming committee headed by Mayor
Fletcher Bowron. He was escorted to the corner of Eleventh
Street and Broadway, where the parade formed at 1100. Crowds
lined up ten deep on the sidewalks. As the parade neared its end
police forcibly ejected a man from the running board of the admiral's car. "I just wanted to shake the hand of the man who shook
the foundations from under Japan," he said later. "Bobby-sox-
ers," said an aide, "just go crazy over the admiral. We're going
to put him on a circuit with Frank Sinatra."

Once the welcoming ceremonies ended on the steps of City
Hall, Halsey was hustled to the Biltmore Hotel for a Victory
Chest luncheon, after which he went into seclusion to rest before
appearing at a banquet at the Coconut Grove, attended by 850
civic, military, and motion picture celebrities. In high good
spirits, Halsey spent most of the evening dancing with Mrs. Richard Smart, a young Honolulu socialite.

Halsey flew east the next day, the first stop on a speaking tour
of American cities. "I'm barnstorming," Halsey told the press.
"Barnstorming in the interest of the children and grandchildren
of all of us. . . . I'm too damned old to fight another war and I
don't want them to have to fight one."

There were more motorcades, bands, police sirens, civic recep-
tions, press conferences, and placards. The hero had come home.

Epilogue

IN NOVEMBER 1945, at San Pedro, California, Halsey hauled down his four-starred admiral's flag and turned over the command of his fleet to Rear Admiral Howard Kingman. "In hauling down my flag," Halsey said, "I am terminating my sea-going career of slightly over forty-five years. This is far from a pleasure. But I deem it necessary for me because of my age [63] to step aside so that younger men can take over the greatest Navy in the world." Leaving the fleet, Halsey told reporters, "is like cutting off my right arm." In Washington Admiral King described Halsey's upcoming retirement from the Navy as "the last scene, last act of one of the most brilliant performances in naval history. Admiral Halsey inspired his men to victory . . . his unswerving determination overcame all enemies from hell to high water."

A month later Washington promoted Halsey to Fleet Admiral of the United States Navy, five stars. "My only fear," he wrote a friend, "is that the extra stripe is going to interfere with my drinking arm."

Those first years after the war were marred for the Navy by the controversy over the merger of the armed forces and a single Department of Defense. Nimitz and most of the admirals fiercely opposed unification. Halsey went to Washington to testify before the Senate Military Affairs Committee. "If we can gain unified command in the field under the Joint Chiefs of Staff," Halsey testified, "why should we resort to a single department? The problems of one service are not those of the other. Each is large,

249

each is complex, each is highly specialized. That's why I believe
in the two or three department system. Under this system, the
Navy is represented at cabinet level by one who is familiar with
its problems. Our design, research, production and procurement
are highly specialized. This is true not alone of the Navy, it is
true of other governmental departments. . . . Each service must
have its own voice in making its plea for appropriations. . . .
I've seen what happens when you get a single department of
defense. As naval attaché in Germany for two years, I saw the
German Wehrmacht. I saw how a single department gradually
grew into a military force that dominated the civilian government. Is there anyone who could deny that a single 'super secretary' might easily become prejudiced to the needs of one or the
other services?''

Despite the strong objections voiced by the admirals and generals, Congress created the Department of Defense. James Forrestal, the former Navy Secretary, was appointed its first Secretary.
Despite his opposition to the formation of a single department,
Halsey wrote Forrestal: ''Congratulations on your appointment as
Secretary of Defense. To me, as to the rest of the country, the announcement was no surprise. All logic pointed toward you as the
man most qualified to bring life to this new development in our
military establishment. Navy men will miss their exclusive claim
on you, but we will take special pride in sharing your leadership
with the Army and the Air Force.''

In the years of his inactive duty status, Halsey became chairman of the University of Virginia's Development Fund. He had
had close ties with Virginia ever since he spent a year there
before entering the Naval Academy. He and his wife settled
down in Charlottesville. ''We've moved in,'' he wrote a friend,
''and are actually keeping house and thoroughly enjoying it. It is
the first time I have had a home of my own for nearly fifteen
years, and you can imagine what a joy it is.''

As a fund raiser Halsey made many public appearances,
chaired meetings, wrote letters and traveled extensively. Although he was ''a valuable asset'' to the University because of
his name, he discovered that the returns from extensive canvassing
were ''disappointing.'' The University's goal had been set at

$18,000,000, but by 1946 the Fund had realized only $540,622.

During the summer of 1946, Halsey, as an adviser to the Navy Department, made goodwill tours of South America, where he received the Order of Liberator (Venezuela); Order of Ayacucho (Peru); Grand Cross of Legion of Merit (Chile); National Order of the Southern Cross (Brazil).

Halsey had already set about writing his memoirs with the help of Lieutenant Commander J. Bryan III. "My narrative," Bryan wrote Halsey in September 1946, "has been stuck for the past week on the Battle for Leyte Gulf, which is damn near as complicated to write as it must have been to fight." McGraw-Hill's advance for *Admiral Halsey's Story* (1947) was $20,000. *Saturday Evening Post* paid $60,000 for the magazine rights.

When the first articles appeared in the *Post,* Admiral Kimmel, who never had secured the public vindication for Pearl Harbor that he sought, wrote Halsey from Bronxville, New York. "Thanks for your kind words about me in your articles. . . . I'm sure they will give the public a better understanding of my actions. I am sincerely grateful and appreciate what you have done."

Halsey let his agents handle his public appearances and radio programs. In March 1947 they wrote Halsey: "The 'Gangbusters' [radio program] deal has not come off. Personally we feel that from a long-range standpoint, it's better for you not to be linked up with this particular program. . . . As I mentioned to you, the crime programs at present are under heavy attack by educational and parent-teacher groups. If you so desire, I'll be glad to conduct a quiet campaign during the next few weeks to endeavor to uncover other radio possibilities for you."

Although nothing came of the radio programs, his agents sought out a lecture manager to handle Halsey's public appearances. "I have estimated the amount of money he could make from lectures," wrote the manager. "If there is a real danger of any war—or such danger becomes imminent—the interest would be increasingly greater, and of course fees would average higher. I'd say fees should run from $500 to $750."

There was no war in 1947 and the demand for Halsey's lectures was minimal.

Along with his duties as chairman of the Development Fund, Halsey embarked on a business career. In January 1948 he was elected director of the Carlisle (Pennsylvania) Tire and Rubber Company and, later, became a director of the International Telephone and Telegraph Corporation, chairman of the board of All-American Cable and Radio Corporation, and president of International Telecommunications Laboratories (both companies were ITT affiliates).

On 1 March 1947 the Navy placed him on the retired list. "I take this opportunity," Forrestal wrote Halsey, "to express my sincere regret on the occasion of your retirement. . . . Your heroic achievements on the seas have been conspicuously instrumental in developing the world's mightiest Navy. Your almost legendary deeds of valor in combat have achieved the most overwhelming victory in the history of naval warfare and have earned for you a place among the great military leaders of all times."

In Charlottesville Fan Halsey, who had long suffered a mental disorder, took a turn for the worse in December 1949. Halsey suddenly decided to give up the house and store the furniture. "It is," Halsey wrote a friend, "too much of a burden to keep this house going by myself. The Development Fund is being cut down and my services are no longer needed." Eventually Fan was placed in a sanitarium in Pasadena, California. With most of his business commitments centering in New York, Halsey took up business headquarters at 67 Broad Street, lived at the Hotel Ambassador, 51st Street and Park Avenue, and became a familiar figure in the nightspots of New York. One night at the Stork Club Halsey saw a clergyman at the next table. He leaned over and said, "My grandfather was a preacher. It must be quite a tough job, writing a sermon every Sunday and preaching it." Then Halsey switched the conversation to prayer and its benefits. "I guess," he sighed, "I should have prayed in the middle of a battle, but I don't seem to recall doing it. Frankly, I think I cursed."

Leonard Lyons, the New York *Post* columnist, often sat at Halsey's table, listening to the admiral reminisce about the war years. Lyons once heard him remark, "I'll bet there was nobody in the war more scared, more often and for as long as I was."

When the Korean War erupted in June 1950, the United States was caught unprepared. In the opening stages, Halsey was noncommittal. He told reporters, "I'm out of the picture entirely now. I'm not in the know, and anything I said would be improper." But as the war dragged on, Halsey spoke out.

In a speech before the American Life Convention in Chicago, Halsey said, "we were caught unprepared for the situation we found in Korea. We had occupational troops in Japan, young and inexperienced. They were well below full strength. Not too good equipment, especially in those early days, we were hopelessly outnumbered by excellently trained troops, yet we held at the crucial moment. The buildup of our forces was a magnificent accomplishment."

"If the Korean War ends shortly," Halsey continued, "it does not end the necessity for preparation to repel the real threat to our ways of life. The aggressive Russian communistic drive to control the world will continue. We have learned not to trust them. We know we cannot depend on their word, written or spoken, be it honeyed soft or vituperatively insulting. Their records for cruelty and tyranny are plain for all to read. It is not a pretty picture, but it must be faced. We must know the beast that opposes us. His God is the God of force. He respects one thing, and one thing only—force. We must prepare to oppose him with force."

On 11 April 1951, President Truman relieved General Douglas MacArthur of command in Korea because of their differing attitudes on the conduct of the war. MacArthur had wanted to win total victory in Korea by bombing China, even at the risk of involving the United States in a third World War. Truman had restricted MacArthur's military actions in Korea and continued to fight a limited war of containment, seeking a negotiated peace.

Halsey defended the general and, in a letter to a friend, wrote, "I should be delighted to talk with you about the MacArthur situation, although I believe you will need an asbestos suit. . . . Having been through somewhat of a similar situation with MacArthur during the war I know exactly what a strain he must have been under."

Halsey collapsed with pneumonia on his way to Idlewild Airport to greet the returning MacArthur. After a quick recovery at Roosevelt Hospital, Halsey went on a business trip for ITT to

Europe. He sailed on the *America* with his daughter, Margaret, and his sister, Deborah. During the next seven months, they visited London, Paris, the Scandinavian countries, Germany, and Italy. Halsey's thoughts ran back to "the good old days" when he was skipper of the destroyers *Benham* and *Shaw* and naval attaché in Germany. He returned to the United States "thoroughly tired."

During the mid-1950s Halsey looked after his business interests and enjoyed the social whirl of New York. He vacated his rooms at the Ambassador Hotel and moved into a friend's apartment at 530 Park Avenue.

In 1954 he flew to Australia as a guest of that government to commemorate the Battle of the Coral Sea. Just before leaving he wrote Admiral Felix B. Stump, Commander in Chief, Pacific Fleet, at Honolulu. "We are going to go through so many climates that I will have to come with enough wardrobe for a June bride. I believe I shall wait until my arrival in Honolulu to buy some slack pants and aloha shirts to knock about in while there."

To Vice Admiral J. L. Holloway, Jr., Chief of Naval Personnel, he wrote, "It's been quite an expense for me to get my gear in shape for this trip. As you know there's a great deal of rivalry between Australia and New Zealand. Because I was in command in the New Zealand area during the war they invited me to come there, as soon as they learned of my trip to Australia, which makes my trip quite a bit longer than I wanted to undertake."

In 1957 Halsey resigned his board chairmanships to devote full time to the campaign to preserve his former flagship, the *Enterprise*. However, he suffered a mild stroke in July while vacationing at Fishers Island, Long Island Sound, with his daughter. This left him with a slight speech impediment. Later he was in California to see how James Cagney was doing as lead in the movie, once entitled *The Admiral Halsey Story*, but later renamed *The Gallant Hours*. During his stay in California, one reporter remarked, "The admiral is looking and feeling well and we think that this trip did him a world of good."

Halsey returned to Fishers Island in the summer of 1959. On 15 August, as usual, Halsey sunbathed and waded along the beach. The next morning, Bert Frazer, the country club manager, noticed that the admiral had not come in for breakfast. He investigated and found Halsey dead from a heart attack, alone in his bedroom. News of his death spread rapidly.

From the summer White House in Gettysburg, Pennsylvania, President Dwight D. Eisenhower wrote, "His great personal contribution to the successful campaigns in the Pacific and the exploits of the forces under his command are a brilliant part of American military history. I have lost a warm personal friend. All Americans have lost one of their great natural leaders."

Former President Truman, then living in Independence, Missouri, told reporters, "He made a wonderful reputation in the Pacific. He was highly thought of by all of us."

At his home in Berkeley, California, Admiral Nimitz said, "In the death of Fleet Admiral Halsey the Navy and the country have lost one of their most distinguished naval officers. No one is more keenly aware than I of the great service he gave to our country. No one is more appreciative than I of his staunch support in those trying days of 1942 when our enemy seemed unbeatable. . . . He has left for all of us a shining example of courage and service."

On 19 August a flag-draped coffin was loaded on a plane at Floyd Bennett Field in Brooklyn as a Navy band played "Eternal Father." Halsey's friend, Rear Admiral Walden ("Pug") Ainsworth, was delegated escort commander for the trip to Washington. After the plane landed at Anacostia Naval Air Station the coffin was taken to the Washington National Cathedral, where Halsey's body lay in state. Formal funeral services were held at the Cathedral on 21 August. Burial with full military honors followed at Arlington National Cemetery.

Bibliographical Note

THIS BOOK IS BASED primarily on the manuscript sources noted in the bibliography. However, for background material and specific incidents I have relied throughout the text on two fine books about the Pacific War, Edwin P. Hoyt's *How They Won the War in the Pacific: Nimitz and His Admirals* and Clark G. Reynolds' *The Fast Carriers*. E. B. Potter's and Chester W. Nimitz' *Sea Power, A Naval History* proved excellent for summaries of campaigns. *Admiral Halsey's Story* (memoirs) is a splendid source of anecdotes. For some of the details concerning the controversial Battle of Leyte Gulf and the events leading up to it, I have leaned on Stanley L. Falk's *Decision at Leyte* and Samuel Eliot Morison's *Leyte*. This, of course, does not mean that I fully concur with their conclusions. To reconstruct the campaigns against Rabaul, John Miller's *Cartwheel* was valuable. For details of Pacific campaigns I have used Morison's other works. *Halsey's Typhoons* by Hans C. Adamson and George F. Kosco was helpful for the typhoon episodes. General Dewitt Peck's quote relating to Halsey and other incidents are in Frank M. Benis' *Halsey*.

Bibliography

MANUSCRIPTS

Naval History Center: Admiral William F. Halsey Papers; Admiral Ernest J. King Papers; Files of CINCPAC, COMSOPAC, Commander, Third Fleet. Judge Advocate General's Office, "Proceedings of a Court of Inquiry into 3rd Fleet Losses and Damages in Typhoon of 18 December 1944," "Proceedings of Court of Inquiry into Typhoon Damage to Ships of 3rd Fleet, 4 June 1945 off Okinawa."

GOVERNMENT DOCUMENTS

U. S. Strategic Bombing Survey (1945–1947); *Pearl Harbor Attack, Hearings before the Joint Committee,* 79th Cong., 1st and 2nd sess., 40 vols. (1946); *Hearings before Senate Military Affairs Committee to Provide for Department of Armed Forces,* 79th Cong., 1st sess. (1946).

NEWSPAPERS

New York *Times,* Wilmington *Journal,* San Francisco *Chronicle.*

MAGAZINES

Life, Newsweek, Saturday Evening Post, Time, U. S. News & World Report.

259

ARTICLES AND BOOKS *

Adamson, Hans C., and George F. Kosco, *Halsey's Typhoons* (1967); Barbey, Daniel E., *MacArthur's Amphibious Navy* (1969); Brodie, Bernard, "The Battle for Leyte Gulf," *Virginia Quarterly Review* (1947); Buell, Thomas B., *The Quiet Warrior: A Biography of Admiral Raymond A. Spruance* (1974); Burke, Arleigh, "Unforgettable 'Bull' Halsey," *Reader's Digest* (1973); Cannon, M. Hamlin, *Leyte: The Return to the Philippines* (U.S. Army in World War II series, 1954); Cant, Gilbert, "Bull's Run: Was Halsey Right at Leyte Gulf?", *Life* (1947); Carney, Robert B., "The Principles of Sea Power," *USNIP* (1953, 1955); Clark, J. J., with Clark Reynolds, *Carrier Admiral* (1967); Collett, John A., "The Aircraft Carrier—The Backbone of Aero-Sea Warfare," *USNIP* (1942); Dyer, George C., *The Amphibians Came to Conquer: The Story of Admiral Richmond Kelly Turner*, 2 vols. (1972); Falk, Stanley L., *Decision at Leyte* (1966); Field, James A., *The Japanese Navy at Leyte* (1947); *The Forrestal Diaries* (Walter Millis, ed., 1951); Forrestel, E. P., *Admiral Raymond A. Spruance* (1966); Benis, Frank M., *Halsey* (1974); Greenfield, Kent Roberts, ed., *Command Decisions* (1960); Halsey, William F., and J. Bryan III, *Admiral Halsey's Story* (1947); Halsey, William F., "A Plan to Control Japan," *Collier's* (1945); *Id.*, "If War Comes, We'll Win It," *American Magazine* (1954); *Id.*, "The Battle for Leyte Gulf," *USNIP* (1952); Hessler, William H., "The Carrier Task Force in World War II," *USNIP* (1945); Hoyt, Edwin P., *How They Won the War in the Pacific: Nimitz and His Admirals* (1970); Isley, Jeter A., and Philip A. Crowl, *The U.S. Marines and Amphibious War* (1951); Jones, D. Clayton, *The Years of MacArthur, 1941–1945*, vol. II (1975); Jones, George E., "Brain Center of the Pacific War," *New York Times Magazine* (1945); Walter Karig, *Battle Report. Pacific War, Middle Phase* (1947); *The End of an Empire* (1948); *Victory in the Pacific* (1949); Kimmel, Husband E., *Admiral Kimmel's Story* (1955); King, Ernest J., and Walter Muir Whitehill, *Fleet Admiral King* (1952); Lewis, Charles L., *Famous American Naval Officers* (1971); Lord, Walter, *Day of Infamy* (1957); *Id.*,

---

* *United States Naval Institute Proceedings* abbreviated as *USNIP*.

Incredible Victory (1967); MacArthur, Douglas, *Reminiscences* (1964); McCain, John Sidney, "So We Hit Them in the Belly," *Saturday Evening Post* (1945); Merrill, James M., *Target Tokyo: The Halsey-Doolittle Raid* (1964); Miller, John, Jr., *Cartwheel: The Reduction of Rabaul* (U.S. Army in World War II series, 1959); Morison, Samuel Eliot, *History of United States Naval Operations in World War II*, 15 vols. (1947–1962); Potter, E. B., "Chester William Nimitz, 1885–1966," *USNIP* (1966); *Id.*, "The Command Personality," *USNIP* (1969); *Id.*, "The Navy's War against Japan," *USNIP* (1950); *Id.* and Chester W. Nimitz, eds., *Sea Power, A Naval History* (1960); Pratt, Fletcher, "Nimitz and His Admirals," *Harper's Magazine* (1945); *Id.*, "World War II and the Changing Conception of Sea Power," *USNIP* (1946); Puleston, William D., "The Impact of Aviation on Sea Power," *USNIP* (1943); Reynolds, Clark G., *The Fast Carriers: The Forging of an Air Navy* (1968); Roupe, R. H., "Halsey's Famous Signals," *USNIP* (1951); Shaw, James, "The Rise and Ruin of Rabaul," *USNIP* (1951); Sherman, Frederick C., *Combat Command* (1950); Smith, Holland, *Coral and Brass* (1949); Smith, Robert R., *The Approach to the Philippines* (U.S. Army in World War II series, 1953); Strope, Walter E., "The Decisive Battle of the Pacific War," *USNIP* (1946); Taylor, Theodore, *The Magnificent Mitscher* (1954); Tomiji, Koyangi, "With Kurita in the Battle for Leyte Gulf," *USNIP* (1953); Vandegrift, A. A., with Robert B. Asprey, *Once a Marine: The Memoirs of General A. A. Vandegrift* (1964).

Index

Coral Sea, Battle of the, 36, 43, 48,
76, 94, 145–46, 254
Cruiser Bombardment Group
(Japanese), 60
Curtin, John, 65

Davis, Glenn B., 198
Davison, Ralph E., 146–47, 152
Department of Defense. *See* United
States Department of Defense
Destroyer Division Forty-three, 67
Doolittle, James H., 32–36
Douglas Dauntless (SBD), 20
Douglas Devastator (TBD), 20
Dow, Leonard J., 175
Duncan, Donald ("Wu"), 32

Early, Stephen T., 166
Eisenhower, Dwight D., 255
Eleventh Airborne Division, 240
Emirau Island, 107–09, 111, 112,
116
Empress August Bay, Battle of,
102–03
See also Bougainville
Eniwetok Island, 112
Espiritu Santo, 80
Ewen, E. C., 159

Faisi. *See* Bougainville
Falk, Stanley L., 176
Far Eastern Air Force, 139
Fifth Fleet, 118, 121, 131, 186,
207–08, 212–15
First Marine Division, 137
Flatley, James, 159
Fleet Landing Force, 238
Fletcher, Frank Jack, 18, 20, 21,
23, 26, 36
Formosa, 94, 108, 114, 115, 122, 129,
130–32, 134, 140–44, 147, 162,
177, 183, 201, 202–08, 210
Forrestal, James V., 228, 250, 252
Fourteenth Air Force, 139
Fraser, Peter, 80–82
Frazer, Bert, 254–55
Fubuki, 50
Furutaka, 50

Ghormley, Robert L., 32, 45, 47–52,
61

Gilbert Islands, 93, 108
Grandy, Frances ("Fan") Cooke, 7
See also Halsey, Frances G.
Green Island. *See* Marianas
Griswold, Oscar W., 91
Grumman F4F Wildcat, 20
Guadalcanal, 45–48, 50–62, 63, 64,
66, 74, 78, 82, 108, 116, 120,
145
See also Solomon Islands
Guam, 109

Halsey, Eliphalet (ancestor), 6
Halsey, Frances G. (wife), 8, 110,
252
Halsey, Margaret (daughter), 254
Halsey, William F. (father), 6
Halsey, William F., Jr.:
aircraft carrier, first experience
with, 9
and Army, 84, 106
on assassination of Yamamoto,
87–88
on atomic bomb, 233
attacks Japan, 230–32
awarded Gold Star, 111, 210
awarded Honorary Knight
Commander, OBE, 119
awarded Navy Cross, 8
awarded South American
decorations, 251
at Battle of Emirau, 116
at Battle of Leyte Gulf, 139, 155,
161–67, 170–76
at Battle of Manila, 139–45
at Battle of New Georgia, 85–92
at Battle of Rabaul, 80, 103–05
at Battle of San Bernardino Strait,
152–60
at Battle of Santa Cruz, 53–56
at Battle of Savo Island, 67
at Battle of Vella Lavella, 96
at Bougainville, 100–107
and Browning, 71
and Burke, 67–68, 70
as commander in South Pacific,
replaces Ghormley, 51, 61
as Commander South Pacific
Area, relieved as, 118